ROBINSON JEFFERS

Robinson Jeffers

Dimensions of a Poet

Edited by

Robert Brophy

Fordham University Press
New York
1995

LC 94–45792
ISBN 0–8232–1565–2
ISBN 0–8232–1566–0

Library of Congress Cataloging-in-Publication Data

Robinson Jeffers, dimensions of a poet / edited by Robert Brophy. p. cm.
Includes bibliographical references.
ISBN 0–8232–1565–2 (hardcover)—ISBN 0–8232–1566–0 (paperback)
1. Jeffers, Robinson, 1887–1962—Criticism and interpretation.
I. Brophy, Robert J.
PS3519.E27Z747 1995
811'.52—dc20 94–45792
CIP

Chapter 10 is reprinted from *The Excesses of God: Robinson Jeffers as a Religious Figure* by William Everson with the permission of the publishers, Stanford University Press. © 1988 by the Board of Trustees of the Leland Stanford Junior University.

Printed in the United States of America

CONTENTS

INTRODUCTION

The essays that follow attempt to illustrate the art and complexity of Robinson Jeffers, while at the same time presenting new insights into his reception among his contemporaries. The essays presume some familiarity with Jeffers's works but should be intelligible without close or recent contact with the poet. It is hoped the reader will be moved to renew acquaintanceship.

For many years, Jeffers was best available through the Modern Library *Roan Stallion, Tamar and Other Poems* (1935) and *The Selected Poetry* (1938). Since 1965 he has been on bookstore shelves in a Vintage paperback *Selected Poems*. That same year the Sierra Club issued *Not Man Apart*, a stunningly beautiful book of photographs of the Big Sur Coast opposite lines from Jeffers. In 1977 his poems appeared in three Norton–Liveright reissues: *The Women at Point Sur, Dear Judas and Other Poems*, and *The Double Axe*. His *Selected Letters* were edited in 1968 by Ann Ridgeway and illustrated with moving photographs by Leigh Wiener. Since 1987, Jeffers's centennial year, his poetry has been newly available in *Rock and Hawk: A Selection of Shorter Poems*, brilliantly edited by Robert Hass, and in *Robinson Jeffers: Selected Poems*, compiled by the English poet and critic Colin Falk. The standard edition for Jeffers's poems is *The Collected Poetry of Robinson Jeffers*, edited by Tim Hunt in three volumes (1988–1991), with the fourth to appear shortly.

Some of the contributors' critical points of entry may come as a challenge to the reader; Zaller, Hunt, Beers, and Rothman, in particular, have moved beyond even the current status of Jeffers criticism. Their essays are at the cutting edge. The writers take for granted the importance of the poet and the complexity of his art; in many ways they are proposing to break new ground. Soldofsky, Glaser, and Everson take up an equally daunting task—an attempt to place Jeffers in the perspective of Western civilization's Christian Humanism and American poetry's landscape-centered mysticism. Each contributor to the collection has been long and thoroughly immersed in Jeffers scholarship. Together they represent some of the most conversant, knowledgeable, and active research in the field of Jeffers studies.

The background essay which begins the series, "Robinson Jeffers: Poet of Carmel-Sur," touches the basic biographical facts of Jeffers and his career, rehearses Carmel geology and geography, and gives an oversight of the central themes and metaphysical stance of the poet. It tries to capture the earnestness and humanity of Jeffers, his daily routine, family life, religious reverence for cosmic nature, and his status not only as an American western writer but also as a cultural commentator on Western civilization's more than two-thousand–year progress toward the setting sun.

Alex Vardamis's summation of Jeffers's critical reputation, "In the Poet's Lifetime," focusing chiefly on the poet's contemporary scene, is witness to the misunderstanding that characteristically followed Jeffers's poetry. The response of the 1920s was almost entirely uncritical in its surprise and delight at the newly discovered "genius," but most of it missed Jeffers's intent, being sidetracked by the strong voice and scandalous subject matter. The criticism of the 1930s reads more like a review of the literary tastes and sociopolitical preoccupations of the time than genuine insight into the strengths and weaknesses of this new figure who was not easily categorized. Humanists like Yvor Winters attacked him for misanthropy and value-negating primitivism; religious reviewers warned of his pagan vision; Marxists and other social critics reproached him for lack of empathy and engagement. New Critics saw in him a formlessness and artistic crudity (which our contributors' articles certainly challenge). Vardamis's key work on the poet, *The Critical Reputation of Robinson Jeffers*, is especially valuable in understanding the extremely uneven reception of the poet. It gathers and records all available critical responses until 1962, excerpts key phrases from these, and summarizes the quintessential in each book, article, and review. A projected second edition should provide an overview of the directions of Jeffers criticism as it approaches the turn of the century.

Robert Zaller, in the third chapter, examines Jeffers's understanding of human history in the context of the poet's philosophy of Inhumanism.[1] His "Robinson Jeffers and the Uses of History" begins with Jeffers's own distinction between the ephemeral and the perdurable, emphasizing that, for the poet, there is in *Being* no stasis, only change. All duration is relative: stars and grass are inherently the same stuff. Human agency does not create beauty or value in the world but merely alters it, gives it a peculiar, reflective quality. The evolutionary progress of life-forms on earth and their terminus in human consciousness Jeffers terms a "fall."[2] In his view, history reflects the human mode of duration within the divine cosmic process, radically unstable and ultimately meaningless except in relation to the vast whole.

But human consciousness by its very transgression, transcendence, or endurance of the natural order paradoxically finds the creator and finds its realization in divinity. Zaller takes Jeffers's tragic protagonists as windows into the historical process. History is civilization goaded by great savior-figures into ever new culture-cycles (as Jesus in "Dear Judas" and Attila in "At the Birth of an Age").

Viewing Jeffers's concept of history as partly inspired by Hegel, Zaller sees the Hegelian process as modulated by a Nietzschean frame which subordinates history to the decidedly cyclical tidal force of the cosmos. According to Jeffers, history teaches little except its own evanescence, its own successive integration into the divine cycles of the universe. Zaller consequently sees Jeffers subordinating the "prose of history" (the particulars of cause and effect, individuals and empires) to the "poetry of history," the directionless tide of change, which is the life of the all-beautiful God.[3]

Terry Beers's "Telling the Past and Living the Present: 'Thurso's Landing' and the Epic Tradition," the fourth chapter, implicitly addresses the naïve dismissal of Jeffers by those who valued the nuances, ironies, intimate textures, and ambiguities championed by the New Critics. Beers's essay searches out the complexity of a point-of-view which is variously distributed between the authorial voice and characters in Jeffers's "Thurso's Landing," title poem for the volume which won for Jeffers the cover-story of *Time* magazine for April 4, 1932. Beers argues that the multiple viewpoints of characters and narrator are not dialogical, since they disagree not about facts but about the evaluation of events, and that the voices, significantly sharing a common figurative language, end in confluence.

Beers emphasizes the epic qualities of Thurso's world as constituting Jeffers's effort to identify the parameters of mankind's heroism in the universe. The essayist finds in this Jeffersian concern a "kinship" with poets whom he seemed to distance himself from, the so-called Modernists Eliot, Williams, and Pound—a kinship in their mutual search for affirmations and didactic voice, in their emphasizing codes of behavior which readers could respond to, and in their upholding transcendent values significant to the community.

In his "Jeffers's 'Roan Stallion' and the Narrative of Nature," Tim Hunt establishes Jeffers's relationship with (and reaction against) the Modernists, locating his difference from them in his strategy of immersion in reality through the narrative. Jeffers sees his contemporaries rightfully subverting nineteenth-century modes and practices by stylistic experiment, but not challenging the premise that imagination or the artifact could stand above and against the material world or the poem's subject matter. For Jeffers, the real was not in the mind or in the poem but in external nature, which was engaged and unfolded by the work of art.

Having set forth this Jeffers–Modernist relationship, Hunt uses the terms of his argument to explore Jeffers's approach to narrative and then to offer "Roan Stallion" to test this approach. In essence he contends that the Modernists saw art as a process of making and the poem as a reality unto itself, whereas Jeffers understood art (here, narrative art) as a process of knowing, since the poem actually breaks into our alienated consciousness, thence enabling it to discover the nature of the world and to achieve a transcendence.

Hunt's key insight is that Jeffers, true to his scientific education, viewed nature (the whole world of *Being*) as both a knowable object and as a transcendent process. The poem therefore needed not just to comprehend nature but also to enter into nature's very unfolding, becoming in itself a process. In Jeffers's narratives the characters express nature; they reveal nature's flux, and the pain of their being engages the readers in nature's process and brings us, in Hunt's words, "to the momentary and partial simultaneity of being and knowing."

This assertion (that subject, character, and reader must not just observe nature but partake in nature's process) Hunt fleshes out and demonstrates through the dilemmas of the developing consciousness within California, Jeffers's female protagonist. She is drawn to the roan stallion as toward nature's power and, through the narrator's progressive deepening of her conflicted relationship, drawn also to more profound being and consciousness. At the story's end, as Hunt proposes it, she and the narrator "each move toward their intertwined moments of crisis and vision."

From consideration of narrative voices and reader induction into nature, the sixth chapter turns then to specifics of verse patterns with David Rothman's "'Divinely Superfluous Beauty': Robinson Jeffers's Versecraft of the Sublime." Early in Jeffers's career, hostile critics argued that his versification was formless, indeed had no poetic matrix. It probably did not help when at times Jeffers or his sympathizers suggested that his poetry had the beat of waves outside his house, or echoed his notoriously slow pulse, or, as in "Continent's End," imitated the cosmic tides.

Lawrence Clark Powell had dealt with Jeffers's metric in his "Introduction to Robinson Jeffers" (Dijon 1932); more germinally Arthur Klein had studied the prosody and carried on a correspondence with Jeffers himself about it. But Klein's work found publication only in his M.A. thesis at Occidental College. He died before putting his study into final form.

It is clear that Jeffers works with accentual verse instead of strict meter (iambic, dactylic, etc.). It is also clear that although a regularity can be commonly traced, there is much that is irregular, or, as Rothman says, "arbitrary." Rothman's contention is that Jeffers's verse is neither traditional nor "free." Informed by both Milton and Whitman, it moves beyond them both, and Jeffers drew upon his technical innovations to help him express the inhuman, the sublime, and the divine. Far from being "mealy-mouthed" (Blackmur) or "hysterical" (Vendler), Jeffers was a careful and knowledgeable poet. He cared deeply about language and understood the fundamental role of craft in the creation of powerful poetry.

It would take multiple studies to examine the world of Jeffers's poetry beyond the few lyrics Rothman analyzes, but he argues that these poems can easily represent Jeffers's method in the vast majority of his work, even in the narrative and dramatic genres. There will of course be those who will question and disagree with his conclusions, but Rothman's willingness to take on the challenge is welcome.

"Robinson Jeffers and the Female Archetype," chapter seven, originated as a panel for the American Literature Association in Baltimore in fall of 1993. Robert Zaller moderated; papers were read by Mark Jarman and Mark Mitchell. Two scheduled female panelists being unable to appear, Jacqueline Brogan added her own insights from the audience. At a later date Betty Adcock and Diane Wakoski submitted written responses to the symposium.

One must puzzle over the relative immunity of Jeffers to feminist criticism for two decades. Like Hawthorne's heroines, Jeffers's are the most actuated of his dramatis personae. Almost all are movers if not instigators of plot. Some yield heroic proportions—such as Tamar, who willingly becomes a divine agent of holocaust for her Point Lobos family home. Only Tamar has power; her acts are violent, indeed apocalyptic, but Jeffers seems to suggest that, at one level at least, she is but performing saturnalian rites at the cycle end. Medea, Jeffers's other titaness, acts to counter the manipulations of her once-hero husband, Jason, who could renounce marital fidelity for Corinthian power and Greek culture's triumph of reason and mind. To some the story is a revisiting of Euripides's *The Bacchae*" recapitulated in Jeffers's "The Humanist's Tragedy"—the arrogance of Apollonian power cut down by avenging feminine forces of Dionysus.

The panel pursues Jeffers's female archetype into various arenas and on several levels. Mark Jarman investigates savior-madness in Jeffers's California and Tamar before proceeding to the unique figure of Clare Walker, the Loving Shepherdess. Mark Mitchell turns from narrative to lyric genre, examining the feminine in Jeffers's imagery of mother, matrix, binder, and nourisher.

Tim Hunt's interjection regarding Jeffers's poem "Daughter of God in Russia," an unfinished and unpublished manuscript, presents an early Jeffers positing a female who is neither aggressor nor victim but liberator—yet who is then unable, for whatever reason, to follow her creator's direction to its finish.

Jacqueline Vaught Brogan, who had presented a paper at the 1992 ALA San Diego conference on the female archetype in Jeffers's "Cawdor," takes up again her misgivings about Jeffers's women as being either passive victims or instigators of violence. Her responses are vigorously engaged by Betty Adcock in Adcock's post-panel contribution. Adcock also discusses the female which she sees at the heart of Jeffers' work, archetypal energies for good, while male forces thrust society toward separation from nature.

Diane Wakoski, for her part, takes the question of Jeffers's feminine beyond gender, seeing the poet as searching for an expression transcending the human but limited by it. She finds Jeffers's attitudes more androgynous, indeed transcendent of the human gender or species. To her, man or woman victimhood in Jeffers is the tragedy of humans doomed because of tragic flaws.

Kirk Glaser's "Desire, Death, and Domesticity in Jeffers's Pastorals of Apocalypse" addresses the poetic strategies by which Jeffers celebrates the Absolute. In Jeffers's world of values, one remembers, "Desire" is something to be purged; therefore, the poet eschews the sexual cycle and a valuing of human survival. "Death" is the only way to God, a negative process of putting aside self, human, and eventually natural values in order to reach to a transcendent god described in terms of white light and tides of fire.

"Domesticity" entails the paradox of Jeffers's wishing not only to be part of his landscape but also to establish a home within it. "Pastorals of Apocalypse," as a phrase, seems an oxymoron, pastorals being peaceful, apocalypses giving vision only through destruction. Glaser's comment that "Jeffers struggles to make his vision of God conform to a nature that destroys all it creates" seems to express well the seeming paradox.

Glaser's essay explores the paradoxes in how one can write one's way into centrality and permanence. He examines, as touchstones, seven early and late poems. "Fire on the Hills" seems an especially stark starting-point, yet it attempts a new vision of God and of reality as merciless and inhuman in value, pointing beyond pity and fear to the terrible numinous. "Post Mortem" and "Continent's End" reject the cycle of generation, giving a negative quality to female fertility and earth-mother centrality.

For Glaser, Orestes's final speech in "The Tower Beyond Tragedy" bespeaks the mystic Jeffers's oneness with nature, but moving on to a vision beyond the natural world into the ineffable, which only the masculine isolato can reach. "Return," on the other hand, illustrates Jeffers's meeting this mysticism in purely physical immersion, while "The Beauty of Things," a late poem, defines poetry's very purpose in integrating human nature with the larger nature, "breaking from the romantic paradigm of nature versus human consciousness (and culture)."

Glaser concludes that Jeffers purposefully revises romantic conceptions and injects "ideas of nature's primacy and our consciousness as an expression of nature" back into modern thought, an idea which he relates to Muir and Thoreau and which he finds central to many twentieth-century writers who concern themselves with the natural world, writers such as Gary Snyder and Mary Oliver and many of the Native American tradition.

Alan Soldofsky's "Nature and the Symbolic Order: The Dialogue Between Czeslaw Milosz and Robinson Jeffers" following to some extent in the same vein as Glaser's, comments upon a dialectic between the Polish Nobel laureate and the Carmel reclusive poet over the nature of the universe and the relative importance of human consciousness and values. Jeffers celebrates a transhuman magnificence; Milosz wishes to reassert the symbolic order engendered by two thousand years of Christian humanism.

Milosz encountered Jeffers's work when he came from Paris to Berkeley to teach in 1960. The self-transplantation from European to American landscape was dislocating, disorienting, almost like a visit to another planet. The imposing, raw physicality of the West Coast and the frailty of human life in the face of nature's force and indifference threatened to uncenter Milosz from the values by which he lived. In the new setting, the human world and the Christian faith seemed unanthropomorphized; human presence seemed minimal, irrelevant, canceled.

Jeffers had encountered this contrast of civilized vs. unhumanized earth in 1929 when he spent the better part of a year in Ireland and England with his family. In "Subjected Earth," he reflects on and apostrophizes the Old World landscape: "Soft alien twilight / Worn and weak with too much humanity . . . meek-smiling slave. . . ." He then contrasts this with his own coast: "that unhumanized world / With all its wave of good and evil to climb yet, / Its exorbitant power to match, its heartless passion to equal,/ And all its music to make" (*CP* 2: 128).[4] To Jeffers "the unhumanized world" better bespeaks God; to Milosz it refracts God's image. Milosz made pilgrimage to Carmel as it were to confront the poet's ghost, toward which he felt an unsettling affinity and revulsion. Soldofsky's study, highlighted by that imagined spectral meeting, gives the reader new insights into both poets and into their intensely divergent views of the human scene and of the God who presides over each.

This aesthetic and philosophic straining toward an understanding of God, as seen in the studies of Glaser and Soldofsky, is offered resolution in the final essay. The brilliance of William Everson's "All Flesh is Grass" lies in his cutting through the questions of Jeffers-as-philosopher (much discussed by critics) to say that the poet is not philosopher but mystic. With this formulation, practically all expectations are changed. Jeffers's perception of the world is seen as ultimately neither scientific nor reasoned but profoundly experiential. He does not believe or disbelieve in God depending on understandings or proofs; he is buffeted by the divine presence.

Once Everson has established Jeffers's center as what Rudolph Otto calls the *Mysterium Tremendum*, the *Totally Other*, a kratophany which demands awe and total obeisance, Everson's argument focuses on three frequently questioned elements of Jeffers's poetry: its preoccupation with violence, its use of the preternatural, and its prophetic disposition.

Everson begins his essay, here excerpted from *The Excesses of God: Robinson Jeffers as a Religious Figure*, with a quote from a scientist's awed description of the 1906 Vesuvius eruption, attesting the "infinite dignity in every manifestation of this stupendous releasing of energy." This "manifestation," Everson suggests, is only a liminal spark when compared with the awesomeness of the cosmic hierophany which the poet habitually experienced and which shines forth in almost every poem. Jeffers's experience of the divine was cosmic, yet reflected in each natural phenomenon. Everson piles text upon text to validate this.

He turns then to "attributions" of this kratophanic sense. Jeffers's poetry is notoriously involved with violence. In awe of the numinous and transhuman majesty, Jeffers, in Everson's view, embraces apocalypse, not because he loves violence or is nihilistic or, as some have it, fascist, but because he intuits the power and the glory, that barely speakable blasting mystery of divine energy (the "possible god" of "Roan Stallion's" hilltop theophany) which propels the cycle of life and holds as momently dispensable all the manifestations of being and beauty in the world, imminently ready to hurl them into oblivion.

Everson then examines the preternatural in Jeffers (an element which readers often wonder at, given Jeffers's hard, scientific mind)—his free use of ghosts, for instance, of visions, voices, Doppelgängers, and apparitions—in "Tamar," "Roan Stallion," "Mara," "Hungerfield," and many other poems. These phenomena Everson attributes to Jeffers's wish to evoke demonic dread of the kind that is fundamental to religious experience and that in its underlying intensity must be and is retained, "however much a higher development seems to supersede and outstrip it."

And, finally, the question of prophecy. Some thoughtful critics see a contradiction between Jeffers's voice as seer and as prophet: if from the vantage point of the Morning Star no thing is evil, pain and violence, arrogance and sadism, pollution and clear-cutting of wilderness, then why cry out for change?

But Everson sees that mysticism and prophecy are two directions to the same numinous experience:

> Jeffers does not speak from the point of view of one who annuls the self as he approaches the divine—this he keeps to himself—but he does emphatically speak from the point of view of one who comes back, of divinity's specific application to the human condition, and this he shouts to the world.

In his essay, Alan Soldofsky imagines for us the spectral meeting of two poets diametrically opposed in their concepts of God and the world. Most of us readers come to Jeffers perhaps not from such contradictories as Milosz does but from our own "well-lighted places" to deal with a poet whose only home was the universe, hardly well-lighted except for the Big Bang and cataclysmic implosion which begin and end it. In his essay Soldofsky quotes "Signpost," a quintessential Jeffers poem (*CP* 2: 418). It begins with a word which might warm our minds: "civilized." But to Jeffers the word signified something like blinded, alienated, introverted, out-of-touch, lost. Civilization was for him a condition to extricate oneself from because it made over all things in mankind's image, thereby obscuring the numinous. To achieve a saving perspective, Jeffers suggests climbing an imaginary Jacob's ladder to the hierophanic cosmic whole. To best become human we must inhumanize ourselves; to more surely find the divine we must learn a larger, more reverent, more ecstatic creaturehood.[5]

It may be difficult to agree with Jeffers but he challenges the heart and broadens the mind. In our own personal dialectic with the poet, unsettling as it may be, we might well be forced to define more carefully our own basic values and find more authentically our own center. That is perhaps the greatest gift of Robinson Jeffers's poetry.

ROBERT BROPHY

NOTES

1. In the Preface to *The Double Axe* (1948), Jeffers gives a name to his career-long philosophy of "Inhumanism": "A shifting of emphasis and significance from man to not-man; the rejection of human solipsism and recognition of the transhuman magnificence. . . . This manner of thought and feeling is neither misanthropic nor pessimist. . . . It involves no falsehoods, and is a means of maintaining sanity in slippery times; it has objective truth and human value. It offers a reasonable detachment as rule of conduct, instead of love, hate and envy. It neutralizes fanaticism and wild hopes; but it provides magnificence for the religious instinct, and satisfies our need to admire greatness and rejoice in beauty" (vii).

2. Jeffers's thought has parallels in Mark Twain, especially in Twain's ridicule of mankind's skewed "moral sense" and degradation within the animal kingdom. Jeffers's idea is most starkly expressed in the first lines of "Margrave" (*CP* 2: 160ff.).

3. Jeffers describes his god as self-torturing: accepting and indeed choosing the pain arising from the violence inherent in all being—for the sheer ecstasy found in the unending discovery of new forms of being and beauty. See the final lines of "At the Birth of An Age" (*CP* 2: 481–84).

4. "Subjected Earth" appears in a volume of verses written in Ireland

and England during 1929, entitled *Descent to the Dead*. In many of the poems, Jeffers speaks as though enriched by the imagined indifference and wide vision of one dead—lying alongside the ghostly denizens of Irish cairns and dolmens which were focal points for that year's meditations on life.

5. To Jeffers the great sin is idolatry. To give obeisance to anything but the ineffable, effulgent god, who is all things, constitutes false worship and self-blinding. Dogmas are necessarily second-hand religious experience and inevitably idolatrous ("Roan Stallion," *CP* 1: 194). See Everson's *Excesses of God* for a discussion of Jeffers's poetry as religious and mystic rather than philosophical or esthetic experience.

Works Cited

CP *The Collected Poetry of Robinson Jeffers*. Ed. Tim Hunt. 3 vols. to date. Stanford, CA: Stanford UP, 1988, 1989, 1991.

Everson, William. *The Excesses of God: Robinson Jeffers as a Religious Figure*. Stanford, CA: Stanford UP, 1988.

Jeffers, Robinson. *Dear Judas and Other Poems*. New York: Liveright, 1929, 1977.

——. *The Double Axe and Other Poems*. New York: Liveright, 1948, 1977.

——. *Not Man Apart: Lines from Robinson Jeffers: Photographs of the Big Sur Coast*. San Francisco: Sierra Club, 1965.

——. *Rock and Hawk: A Selection of Shorter Poems by Robinson Jeffers*. New York: Random, 1987.

——. *The Selected Letters of Robinson Jeffers*. Baltimore: Johns Hopkins UP, 1968.

——. *Selected Poems*. New York: Vintage, 1965.

——. *Selected Poems*. Centenary Edition. Manchester, England: Carcanet, 1987.

——. *The Selected Poetry of Robinson Jeffers*. New York: Random, 1938.

——. *The Women at Point Sur*. New York: Liveright, 1927, 1977.

Vardamis, Alex. A. *The Critical Reputation of Robinson Jeffers: A Bibliographical Study*. Hamden, CT: Archon, 1972.

ROBINSON JEFFERS

1

Robinson Jeffers: Poet of Carmel-Sur

Robert Brophy

> . . . the wholeness of life and things, the divine beauty of
> the universe. Love that, not man
> Apart from that, or else you will share man's pitiful confusions
> or drown in despair when his days darken.
>
> ("The Answer," *CP* 2: 536)

ROBINSON JEFFERS pursued a career-long quest for the wisdom that brings peace, as he sustained an unrelenting love affair with the indifferent but overwhelmingly beautiful god of the universe. His story has little of the dramatic in it, much of meditation, integrity, and dedication. From his vantage on the "Continent's End" (his poem which gave title to a collection of California poets edited by J. H. Jackson in 1925), he pondered the race's headlong rush toward apocalypse, and he looked outward to a cosmic, divine, and cyclic life that is ever renewed.

John Robinson Jeffers was born into a family of culture and modest wealth on January 10, 1887. His father, William Hamilton Jeffers, was a scholar and teacher, Professor of Old Testament Literature and Exegesis and of Biblical and Ecclesiastical History at Western Theological Seminary (Presbyterian) near Pittsburgh, Pennsylvania. A man of strong patriarchal authority and austerity, he was, as his son would be after him, master of many languages and well read in the classics and nineteenth-century philosophy. Robinson's mother, Annie Robinson, a beautiful and talented young woman, an orphan raised by cousins, had fallen in love with the visiting curate Jeffers, who was more than twenty years her senior. Robinson, their first of two sons, was clearly caught throughout his early life between two extremes—the distant, older, stern, taskmaster father and the emotional, youthful, vivacious, unfulfilled mother—the basis for later psychological angst and lifelong creative tensions.

The Jeffers family was financially able to travel freely, and in 1891, at age four, Robinson was launched into what was to be a succession of European sojourns. On this occasion he was introduced to kindergartens in Zurich and Lucerne. After his return home in 1893, the boy found himself relocated three times as his father sought, according to whim and the need for scholarly seclusion, a place where the boy's companions and other visitors would not intrude. Playmates were replaced by books and lessons.

From 1898 to 1902 the future poet and his younger brother, Hamilton, lived with their mother in Europe, Robinson being enrolled at schools in Leipzig, Vevey, Lausanne, Geneva, and Zurich. At twelve he was fluent in German and French and could read Latin and Greek. During these years he gained a reputation among his peers for solitariness and stoicism, the result of stern teachers, the awesome grandeur of the Swiss landscape, revulsion from some sexual perversion among his classmates, separation from family, and repeated relocations (his father, for reasons unexplained, visited from the United States to put him in successive schools).

In 1903, "westering" entered the family pattern. Because of the doctor's failing health or a growing polarization within the seminary faculty, the patriarch Jeffers retired and moved his family to California, first to Long Beach, then to Highland Park (Los Angeles), where young Robinson matriculated as a junior, age sixteen, at Occidental College, then a small Presbyterian school. Here with his native genius, wide classical background, and language expertise, he immediately excelled. He impressed peers and professors alike, taking courses in biblical literature, geology, history, Greek, rhetoric, and astronomy, the last a discipline featuring field trips to Mount Wilson and Echo Mountain observatories. For the first time in his life he made lasting friends and was able to take part in athletics and class hiking. At Occidental he began writing and publishing verse for *The Aurora*, his school literary magazine, which became *The Occidental* under his senior editorship. He graduated in a class of eleven in 1905, aged eighteen.

From there he immediately began graduate courses at the University of Southern California in central Los Angeles as a student of literature. Here in an advanced German class studying Faust, he met his future wife, Una, who was then married to a successful young lawyer, Edward Kuster. In April 1906 Robinson experienced another abrupt family relocation, an interlude in Switzerland where at the University of Zurich he took courses in philosophy, Old English, French literary history, Dante, Spanish romantic poetry, and history of the Roman Empire.

During the following semester he was back at the University of Southern California, translating German articles for one of the medical school faculty. In September 1907 he was accepted into the medical school, and, although he evidently did not anticipate a physician's career, he rose to the top of his class, becoming special assistant to Dr. Lyman Stookey and teaching physiology at the USC dental college. Una, meanwhile, was finishing a Master's thesis on "Mysticism" at USC and meeting her lover clandestinely at Hermosa Beach, Jeffers having moved nearby to be with her during the summer. The events of these years sound like a soap opera scenario: there was a code name "Theodosia" for phone calls, a painful "final separation" as Jeffers accompanied his family to Seattle and enrolled in forestry school there, a summer return to Los Angeles where they met by chance at a downtown intersection and began their affair again, an outraged husband discovering a love tryst, a five-month cooling-off period at Kuster's request during which Una agreed to go on a European tour, Kuster then falling in love with a teenage woman, and finally a divorce, which, though uncontested, made Los Angeles headlines.

For the year 1913 Robinson and Una found themselves in a waiting pattern, she at the University of California, Berkeley, pursuing more graduate work; he back at the University of Washington, again following forestry. After living together on Lake Washington for a few months awaiting the divorce finalization, they were married on the second of August at Tacoma.

The first months of married life were spent in the idyllic beach community of La Jolla, north of San Diego. There followed an eventful year, 1914: the Great War began in Europe (they had entertained plans for a future in Lyme Regis on the southwest English coast), a baby girl who lived only a day, a move to Carmel at the suggestion of a friend, and Jeffers's father's death.

It seems evident from his troubled, inconclusive writing at the time, and from the testimony of his wife, that the war years were troubled ones for Robinson. He was torn between an idealism that drove him toward enlistment despite domestic ties and the beginning of a philosophical pacifism. War was to be the matrix of many themes of his later poetry.

One must not underestimate the impact and influence of Carmel on Jeffers. Magnificent natural surroundings of mountain and sea, beaches, and cloud-scudded horizons were all but overwhelming. Life was simple, almost primitive: a rented log cabin amid pines, walks in woods and along the empty beaches, much reading, a few friends. In 1919 the young couple managed to buy land on a knoll overlooking Carmel Bay facing Point Lobos. There, apprenticing himself to a stonemason and contractor, Jeffers began work on the structure that was to be so formative in his imagination and expressive of his aesthetics, Tor House. The completion of this stone cottage was followed by his solitary construction of a four-tiered, forty-foot tower, five years abuilding, from which he could overlook the Pacific, the coastal landscape south toward Big Sur, and the night sky filled with brilliant stars. All the building stones were rolled up from his shoreline.

During his early adult years Jeffers had been writing poetry. Influenced by Keats, Shelley, Wordsworth, Swinburne, and Coleridge, he produced the romantic, imitative, melodramatic, and melancholic verse that filled his first two books, *Flagons and Apples* (1912) and *Californians* (1916). His wife testified that toward the end of this era Jeffers had a rather dramatic but otherwise undocumented conversion experience. In many ways it seems reminiscent of Whitman's, his writings shedding their "rhyme-tassels," as he called them, and turning thematically turbulent, ritualistic, mythical, and philosophically integrated under a kind of stoic, celebratory, devout pantheism. From time to time there were attempts at publication, but, when James Rorty found Jeffers in 1925 after the failure of *Tamar* at a New York publisher, he was intrigued by discovering one who was resigned to writing without an immediate audience but who felt himself compelled to "chronicle the human landscape of the Western Shore" (Brophy, *Myth* 281).

Returning to the East Coast, Rorty trumpeted his discovery to influential reviewers, Mark Van Doren, James Daly, and Babette Deutsch. A star was born. For the next ten years at least, Jeffers became the sensation of cocktail parties and literary circles of the eastern establishment. Yet from that point on, Jeffers's biography can easily become a mere listing of yearly publications (Melba Bennett, his only biographer so far, falls into this pattern). There were few dramatic events: no triumphal tours, no integration into new poetic schools, no great milestones, little domestic drama. Indeed he proved a self-effacing celebrity, almost indifferent to the newfound acclaim, except that it promised to put food on his table and justify his hermetic, contemplative, and poetic life above the Pacific.

Jeffers became a master stonemason, expanding Tor House year by year with walls and courtyard, garage and dining room, and, eventually, a separate residence for extended family. There were three trips to Europe (at Una's urging), a change in publishers (Liveright to Random House in 1933), sporadic summer trips to Taos, New Mexico, beginning in 1930, also at Una's instigation and only endured by Jeffers. Their twin sons, Donnan and Garth, born in 1916, educated first by Una at home, grew up and left home for the University of California, Berkeley, in 1935.

Recognition was muted after the first years of heady celebrity and came only intermittently: a Book of the Month award in 1935, a Doctor of Literature from Occidental in 1937, an honorary Phi Beta Kappa from USC in 1940, and election to the National Academy of Arts and Letters in 1945. There were no Guggenheims, and, inexplicably, no Pulitzer or Nobel prizes. Jeffers's one public appearance, a reading tour in 1941, had ironic beginnings. He had carefully insulated himself from the hamlet of Carmel, had methodically hedged his property on the three land sides with a dense wall of eucalyptus and Monterey cypress. He was almost fanatically intent on shutting out the hordes of humanity which he anticipated would overflow from Carmel to shatter his privacy. Developers led his list of villains. He managed to buy a whole block to moat his castle. Yet, Melba Bennett tells us (172), we owe his one reading/lecture tour to the department of sanitation's threatening to assess him $1,600 to extend sewer lines to take care of real estate development on Carmel Point.

The Second World War was a central life-concern for Jeffers in the 1930s; he saw it as a giant wave building toward a disastrous fall. Philosophically Jeffers believed in the inevitability of the grand processes of history; they had a fatalism in them that mimicked the seasons. Yet he was human enough to care and to protest the stupidity and chauvinism which brought war's inevitable destruction and cruelty.

He began to write anticipatory war poems as early as 1933; he was still writing them at his life's end. His postwar volume, *The Double Axe* (1948), produced a dramatic downturn in his critical reputation. The book was accompanied by an unprecedented Random House disclaimer; his verse was received with hostility from all directions. Jeffers had not changed his song; it was just that his bitterness had increased, and the age was bent on triumphalism and "Big Brother" imperialism, and the Cold War. It took fifteen years before critical attitudes could forgive *The Double Axe*. Meanwhile Jeffers received his son Garth back from the jaws of one war and looked ahead to the nuclear-bomb–fed apocalyptic conflict which might more finally and fatally claim his grandchildren. Amid all this, his life was filled with daily routines, a few crises, and gradual aging.

Jeffers's daily schedule, since the early 1920s expansion of Tor House, was unswerving: writing in the mornings, usually in the upper floor of his cottage, and stone work or tree-planting in the afternoons, with only an occasional pause to watch the Monterey sardine fleet slipping past the Point through the fog or airplanes droning out over the Pacific or a hawk circle his workplace. In the evenings there were awesome sunsets, walks under the constellations, reading by kerosene lamps (electricity came only in 1949), occasional trips to the tower parapet to attune his microcosm to the universe of stars and galaxies (as in "Night" and Margrave"). Jeffers's *Selected Letters* (1968) and Una's voluminous correspondence document this simple life, this centered, satisfying day-by-day life-celebration.

The family owned a succession of Fords, but travel, except for "pilgrimages" down the coast into canyons or down onto beaches, was exceptional. Besides summer trips to Taos and three cross-country journeys, two to Ireland in 1929 and 1937 and the third to the Library of Congress in 1941, there were only necessary jaunts to town, a supper party at Noel Sullivan's in Carmel Valley, and rare excursions to San Francisco or to Berkeley to retrieve their sons from college.

Often, for shorter trips, Una went without her husband. He preferred to keep his consciousness uncluttered and his solitude unperturbed. Tor House social life was almost exclusively orchestrated by Una, who was naturally gregarious and from all evidence a fine hostess and an informed, fluent conversationalist. There was no great stream of guests through Jeffers's gate, yet, since he would not come to them, celebrities did come to him, or at least visited him when they were in the Carmel area, appearing on the arm of George Sterling or Noël Sullivan or some other friend. Visitors represented a wide spectrum, mostly from the arts and letters: Edgar Lee Masters, Edna St. Vincent Millay, Lincoln Steffens, Irwin Cobb, Krishnamurti, James Cagney, Ralph Bellamy, Charlie Chaplin, Jo Davidson, Liam O'Flaherty, George Russell (AE), Bennett Cerf, Van Wyck Brooks, Louis Adamic, George Gershwin, Thornton Wilder, Jean Toomer, Langston Hughes, William Rose Benét, William Saroyan, Aldous Huxley, Toscanini, Salvador Dalí, and others. Many celebrities were periodically neighbors within a Carmel which drew artists and the wealthy because of its extraordinary beauty, its seasonal climate, its vacation facilities, and its artists' and writers' colony.

Much of his time with the family was spent in simple living—which included an intense intellectual life, filled with books and discussions ranging through philosophy and history, nature and art. To visitors, Tor House was a charming but rather austere household: a low-ceilinged, dark living room with a well-loved bulldog by the hearth, a tile-floored dining room with a rough-hewn table and benches beside another hearth, a tiny kitchen and then another made over from a garage, a colorful garden with an extensive herb annex, and, of course, the legendary tower.

At the war's end, Garth Jeffers returned with Charlotte, his Bavarian bride, then went to forestry studies in Oregon. Donnan, after a few wedded years in Ohio, rejoined the household of Tor House, married Lee Waggener, and raised four children there. Life remained simple and subdued. After the triumph of Jeffers's *Medea* on Broadway, starring Judith Anderson,[1] there was a trip to Ireland in 1948, during which Jeffers almost died of pleurisy. Then tragedy struck: in 1949 Una Jeffers became painfully ill with what she insisted was sciatica, but which was a devastating cancer. Jeffers took her to San Francisco in January 1950 for a month of intensive and experimental treatments at the University of California Hospital. No cure was obtained, and Una's remaining months were filled with general weakness and pain-relieving drugs. This harrowing time was the subject of Jeffers's most autobiographical poem, "Hungerfield" (1952/1954).

The declining years of Jeffers's life, following Una's death in September 1950, involved living out the pact he had made early in his career, not to take his own life but to drink it all, even to the dregs. His health and eyesight failed. He watched his grandchildren grow and thought grim thoughts anticipating world-annihilation as atom and hydrogen bombs, missiles and counter-missiles filled the news. During his final twelve years he wrote few poems. Significant for his culminating thought on various subjects, some were published posthumously, with problematic editing by Melba Bennett and by Random House, as *The Beginning and the End* (1963). He consented to help adapt *The Tower Beyond Tragedy* for Judith Anderson (1950) and began a re-creation of Schiller's *Mary Stuart* but stopped after completing one act.[2] There were still infrequent visitors, among them W. H. Auden. Jeffers died January 20, 1962; Carmel was covered with an almost unprecedented snow.

The themes of Jeffers's poetry follow his overview of life and remain consistent throughout his mature period.[3] He was a pantheist who believed that God is the evolving universe, a self-torturing deity who discovers himself in the violent change which is at the center of life's dynamism. Jeffers's images are reductively cyclic. To him cycle is the truth of the stars, the vitality of the planet, the fate of human, animal, insect, and flower life. Cycle moves inexorably through birth, growth, fullness, decay, and death. For him *Being* in all its manifestations necessarily involves change brought about by violence and pain, because every form resists its own dissolution. If these realities are customarily repugnant to humans, they are essential to beauty and divinity. For Jeffers there is only matter and energy, no spirit, no soul, no immortality. God endures forever; mankind is a temporary phenomenon, something of an anomaly in the universe because of the race's megalomanic fixations. But humans are also unique, able to reflect on God, capable of praise. In fact, they are, for the cosmic moment they endure, God's sense organs ("The Beginning and the End").

To him, consciousness is a universal quality of the cosmos, though humanity's participation in it will pass ("Credo"). Beauty survives the faculty to perceive it. Death is the end of each cycle, terminating individual existence as the material of each body is reassimilated into soil and air ("Hungerfield"). The world in its various rhythms is determined. The universe itself expands and collapses; oceans condense and evaporate; mountains and civilizations rise and fall; nations emerge and grow feeble. The mass of mankind is fated in its course, but the individual may choose to remove self from the downcycle, the breaking wave; he can stand apart and contemplate instead of being blindly caught ("Shine, Perishing Republic"). God himself (the pronoun is of course an abhorred anthropomorphism for Jeffers) is in no way like humankind; he is savage, unconcerned, and reckless, encompassing both good and evil, ever seeking new discovery ("Contemplation of the Sword"). If seen wholly, all things are sacred and in harmony. Evil itself is only part of the mosaic of beauty ("The Answer").

For Jeffers, the challenge of living a "good life" lies principally in detachment from insane desires for power, wealth, and permanence—in a measured indifference to pain, joy, or success, and in a turning outward to God, who is "all things." Wisdom, a word little used in his poetry except in irony ("Wise Men in Their Bad Hours"), means cosmic perspective ("Signpost"), an unfocusing from mankind (Jeffers's philosophy of "Inhumanism").[4] Peace, a cessation from strife, is an illusion in life. True peace is found in death. In life it can be anticipated in a stoic balance which discounts the innate prejudices for immortality, invulnerability, stability, and immunity from pain and sickness.

Saviorism, the great and most subtle temptation for the good person, is condemned for the implicitly self-aggrandizing notion that one can change the world at any level. Jeffers himself must have desperately fought this demon saviorism; he writes about it so often. He sees love as easily becoming an abnormality for an incestuous race, leading to many insanities. One love is pure: the love of God, who is indifferent to humanity. Piety lies in an undistracted regard for *Beauty*, earthly and cosmic. And terrible beauty is the God who implicitly commands worship.

The poet is one who creates as God creates ("Apology for Bad Dreams"), who reconciles existence for mankind, putting its preoccupations with sin, guilt, corruption, pain, and all other confounding fears and desires into saving context. The "good person" is not the religious leader, rebel, or savior, but the self-contained mystic, contemplating God and living out the necessary conspiracies of life with a certain aloofness, as Tamar reveals in her melodrama of family destruction.

Jeffers's art was his life, a consequence of his philosophy and of his sense of vocation. Once one grasps the dimensions of his beliefs, it becomes evident that Jeffers's poetry is impressively centered and predictable. His every poem's theme, one way or another, is the divine beauty of the cosmos and mutability of the individual. Jeffers reveals a deep sense of ritual, not only in nature's rites of death and renewal but in every rhythm of being. This focus is strikingly evident in a letter to his editor in 1929, in which he explains that the movement of his narratives is "more like the ceremonial dance of primitive people; the dancer becomes a rain-cloud, or a leopard, or a God. . . . the episodes . . . are a sort of essential ritual, from which the real action develops on another plane" (*SL* 68).

He embraces tragedy in its pre-Aeschylean sense of the inevitable, blameless fall which yields new beginnings. "All life is tragic" translates to "all life is cyclic." Though civilized humans flee the metaphysical implications of cycle, primitives seem to have accepted and celebrated them. Characteristically, in Mediterranean fertility cults, each year the cycle god, Attis, Osiris, Tammuz, or Dionysus, has to suffer the consequences of re-entry into being; each was born in order to die (and be reborn ten thousand times). Under this ultimate judgment, decline and death are not blameworthy or cataclysmic but inevitable and natural. Death may seem to be Jeffers's most frequent theme; it is a reality to understand, accept, and move within and beyond.

Inevitably, subordinate themes abound in Jeffers's poetry, but they all bear on the truth of the cycle: reconciliation with evil, confrontation with pain, indifference born of cosmic perspective, acceptance of God on his own terms, desirability of death and annihilation, inevitability of process, delusion of human effectiveness, presumptuousness of humanity's self-importance, the nature of the poet's art, the omnipresence and authenticity of tragedy.

Jeffers's poetics are simple and direct. His poetry embodies external landscape, not the landscape of the mind ("Credo"). After the lyrics and semi-narratives of his first two books, he consciously turned from meter and rhyme. He replaced the first with the larger, more supple accentual rhythms of Hebrew and Anglo-Saxon verse. Ten-beat lines are common in the narratives, although there are many variations; four-beat lines are more likely in the lyrics.

Much of Jeffers's poetic effect comes in word choice. He carefully selected words for their etymology and for their successive layers of meaning. He kept a large unabridged dictionary close at hand and pondered possibilities, sometimes for hours. His imagery makes a fascinating study. Most of it is taken from his immediate coastal experience: hawks, herons, wild swans, pelicans, cormorants, mountain lion, deer, and cattle; redwood, cypress, grass, wildflowers, rock, ocean, headland, clouds, sky, stars, and planets. His hawks are godlike totem birds, noble and fierce. Mountain lion and deer are predator and victim, metaphors for all victimhood, neither blameworthy.

Vegetative and animal life almost always fill a twofold function in his stories: they are part of the realistic backdrop for the action; they also foreshadow the tragedy imminent in all drama, recalling animal surrogates of the year-gods and the sacrificial flowers which sprang from the gods' blood. Rock is consistently a divine image, a mysterious, chthonic presence and stoic endurance; its volcanic origins make it "bones of the mother (earth)." The sea is mind-subduing expanse, life and death, matrix of all life. Mountain and headland are measure of the heavens and reminder of human life's precariousness. Storm represents elemental apocalyptic forces: earth, air, fire, water—in winds, quake, holocaust, and deluge—all are fearful agents in Jeffers's narratives. Clouds are dream media on which the poet projects human folly ("The Great Sunset"). Sky and stars are the universe beckoning. Stars are used both mythically, as in the constellation patterns of Orion and Scorpio in "Tamar," and, more often, scientifically—seen as gigantic nuclear fusion furnaces, whose lifespan predicts the fate of our sun and solar system ("Nova"). The far stars and galaxies are the actors of Jeffers's ultimate metaphor, the expanding and contracting universe which recycles itself every eighty billion years and is God's heartbeat ("The Great Explosion" and "At the Birth of an Age").

Of his poetics Jeffers wrote very little. His 1938 foreword to *Selected Poetry* (xiv) declares his intent to reclaim the subject matter which he thought poetry had surrendered to prose. He meant to write about permanent things or the eternally recurring ("Point Joe"). He promised to pretend nothing, neither optimism nor pessimism. He would avoid the popular and fashionable; he would create as he believed, whatever the consequences. He would write as though for an audience a millennium hence.

In an early *ars poetica*, "Apology for Bad Dreams," Jeffers indicates that he creates his violent verse-narratives principally for immunity and salvation. Focusing on the vignette of a woman beating a horse amid the magnificence of a coastal sundown, he attempts to reconcile human perversity with the essential beauty of things. The landscape, he says, demands tragedy (pain, sacrifice, horror); the greater its beauty, the stronger the demand. From this poem it would seem that the poet created these vicarious terrors in order to be spared the real terror of personal tragedy. Exactly what meaningful metaphysics was involved, Jeffers does not explain. He may mean he writes stories to educate himself to violence and the cycle, this taking some of the terror out of the pain that he, as everyone, must endure. Or he may write as a form of therapy, purging his inner violences, lest he act them out (and equivalently beat horses himself). Or he may see in his writing a way of participating in *Being's* ritual, making out a discovery-process that parallels God's own creative process—a kind of "magic" (as he calls it here and in the posthumous "But I Am Growing Old and Indolent").

The religious intent of Jeffers's poetry becomes clear in many a poem. For an early instance, one might read carefully the invocation in "Tamar," section V (*CP* 1: 32). Here he prays the god of beauty to enter into his "puppet" characters—a brother and sister botched with incest and the disintegrating family that surrounds them. God, Jeffers says, chooses the twisted and lame to be his signs and the agents of his revelation. The same kind of lyric interjection greets the reader in "The Women at Point Sur," Jeffers's most tortured and convoluted narrative (*CP* 1: 288–89). Here again his human grotesques are to praise God, "puppets" to speak of him; they "stammer the tragedy." Other writers, Jeffers announces in the Prelude to the poem, will tell tales to entertain; his vocation is to slit open the eyeholes of mankind's mask (*CP* 1: 240–41). Human resistance to God and to integration into the organic whole of the universe can be broken only by dramatic means: disorienting vision, limit-vaulting desire, unnatural crime, inhuman science, and tragedy. "These break [the mold], these pierce [the mask], these deify, praising their God shrilly with fierce voices: not in man's shape / He approves the praise" ("Roan Stallion," *CP* 1: 189–90). Later he will clarify this story-telling justification and further its religious context in the lyric "Crumbs or the Loaf" where, in a parallel to Jesus's story of the sower and the seed (Matt. 13), he characterizes his narratives as parables, as contrasted with the lyrics, which are his confrontive pronouncements.

A final statement on poetry comes toward the end of Jeffers's writing career. In 1948, amid the triumph of *Medea* and impending rejection of *The Double Axe*, he characterizes the truly great poet—in an article for the *New York Times*, "Poetry, Gongorism and a Thousand Years." The poet, he says, stands alone. He renounces self-consciousness, over-learnedness, labored obscurity (by which Jeffers would probably have characterized most of modern poetry as it followed Eliot and Pound). The poet is direct and natural, saying what he must say clearly, out of the spirit of his time but as understandable for all times.

In another place I have called Jeffers the "Metaphysician of the Continent's End" (*Robinson Jeffers* 44). Metaphysics is that most fundamental area of philosophy which studies *Being* itself. It has to deal with all that exists; it delves into the nature of all processes, of all that is—the workings and interactions of the universe and of the molecule and atom, of God and all that exists. "Of the Continent's End" means to suggest not only writing in and from the point of view of what Jeffers identifies as "west of the west" (*Flagons* 45–46) but also in using its scenes as setting. Jeffers does all these things, but his peculiar genius is his use of the West, this "drop-off cliff of the world" (in "Tamar," *CP* 1: 84) on which he perched his home, to explore the nature of *Being*, the relevance of the human race, and the bridge between humanity and the furthermost expanses of the cosmos.

In detail Jeffers is a realist; he represents his Western landscape exactly; specifically, it stretches from Point Pinos in the north to

Point Sur and Pfeiffer Beach in the south.[5] This twenty-five miles of storm-scoured promontories, precipitous headlands, wave-wracked points, wind-twisted trees, and precarious beaches was known intimately to him. It was the object of solitary walks and family "pilgrimages." The place-names of his poems are almost all right off the geological survey map: Points Pinos and Joe, Robinson Canyon, Carmel Beach, Point Lobos, Mal Paso Creek, Notley Landing, Palo Colorado Canyon, Rocky Point, Soberanes Reef, Bixby Landing, Mill Creek, Little Sur River, Point Sur. The terrain, the beaches, the weather, the flowers, the animals are all true-to-life re-creations. "Jeffers Country" is no mythical Yoknapatawpha County; only the characters' names are imaginary.

And Jeffers's characters too, in their own way, are authentic, arising as they do from the violent legends of this forbidding and isolating terrain. A psychological study once questioned whether the Big Sur country, because of something in its dynamism, causes madness or whether it attracts the mad, the grotesque, the macabre. Jeffers himself suggests the first in "Apology for Bad Dreams." Jeffers's characters are ranch families, self-exiled hermits in shacks, wandering Indian cowboys from a previous era who are caught in the land's struggle to realize itself.

This Carmel–Sur coast has never been domesticated; it is inconceivable, even now, that it ever will be. This is not so much remote backpacking country as impenetrable space, a precipitousness and storm-torn violence which, it seems, would reject human presence entirely. As one can see from the Sierra Club photo book of 1965, *Not Man Apart*, the coast is an almost continuous headlong precipice. The Coast Highway, an engineering triumph of the 1930s, strung a precarious ribbon of asphalt just above the drop-off, dynamiting through shoulders of rock, leaping over creek gorges with delicate butterfly bridges. During many a winter, a storm has carried a lane of the highway into the sea. Behind this coastal road are a few grassy knolls and fields, backed against wilderness. As one flies over it from Los Angeles to San Francisco, one sees tightly corrugated ridges and gullies choked with trees and brush—no roads, no lights, no water, no signs of life. This is wilderness in an almost mystic sense, a place to correspond to the empty spaces in the soul. One need not visit it; it was comforting to Jeffers just to know it was there and that it would ever resist being humanized, subdivided, asphalted, and fitted with sewer systems.

Very conscious of writing as a westerner, Jeffers perceived his land and his conscience as scarred with the vestiges of western expansion. All around him he pictured the ghosts of Indians who were too easy a victim of the white man's ambitions and diseases. During the Spanish occupation, San Carlos Mission, a mile or so southeast of Tor House, presided over the death of local tribes. A spade on his knoll may still turn over the remains of a tribal feast, abalone and clam shells and charcoal from their fires. In "Tamar" Jeffers imagines the nearby Carmel River mouth as a funnel to extinction of migrations which began millennia ago, first brown-skinned natives, then Spanish priests and soldiers, and finally English-speakers, following "the universal music . . . and were nothing" (*CP* 1: 34–35). Somehow this coast sums up all migrations and all that mankind has done for good or evil in human "progress." Jeffers's double, the self-stigmatizing hermit in "A Redeemer," summed it up thus:

". . . Not as a people takes a land to love it and be fed,
A little, according to need and love, and again a little; sparing the country tribes, mixing
Their blood with theirs, their minds with all the rocks and rivers, their flesh with the soil. . . .
Oh, as a rich man eats a forest for profit and a field for vanity, so you came west and raped
The continent and brushed its people to death." (*CP* 1: 406–07)

One must say that Jeffers is not a regionalist in the usual restrictive sense of the word—one who writes knowingly of his geographic section, reflecting its genius and foibles, relating its topographic and climatic peculiarities, recording its idiom and its philosophy. The California coast for him is not just a region; it is a final statement, a philosophical, metaphysical study. There are probably neither enough people in his mountains nor customs on his coast for regionalism, and the landscape is unearthly, not picturesque. The final frontier is an ontological statement, not a geographic or cultural one. It is final as the coast is final—to all of mankind's hopes and illusions and indirections. America's violence, its rape of the land, its betrayal of the indigenous peoples, its pillaging of resources—all of these must ultimately be faced here.

Any discussion of Jeffers's themes and aesthetics should somehow include some discussion of the objections to his writing—not to excuse his faults but to clarify his intent and identify his genre so that judgments may be better focused. Regarding his narratives, one can merely repeat what has been said above: Jeffers is a tragedian; he cannot write comedy, for he saw comedy as an unfinished story. His narratives are grotesque and usually end in blood. It seems clear from hints in the poems themselves that (whether he was successful or not) his intention was to write parables, to instruct and move himself and his readers beyond their limits. His genre is, at an important level, ritualistic; that is, each story represents a Dionysian process, illustrating the cycles of life and death. His dramatis personae, he says in "My Loved Subject," are the landscape: "Mountain and ocean, rock, water and beasts and trees / Are the protagonists, the human people are only symbolic interpreters" (*CP* 1: 484).[6]

Jeffers's human characters therefore are not primarily psychological or humanistic studies. Actually Jeffers consciously chooses a sort of stereotyping (he consistently called his characters "puppets"); his men tend to be Apollonian, stoic, stolid, and presumptuous that their power and plans will carry the day; his women are Dionysian and tend to follow the pattern of Agave's rending of Pentheus in *The Bacchae* (Jeffers's "The Humanist's Tragedy"); they are agents of violence and change. The reader should be cautioned: Jeffers should never be identified with his characters; their attitudes and statements are rarely or never his. He has no heroes, except perhaps Orestes and the Inhumanist, only maimed, floundering "idols."

Regarding the short poems, several additional cautions are suggested. Jeffers has many voices, the most prominent of which is that of prophet, a voice which may have come out of the Old Testament literature of his childhood. The prophet primarily proclaims the truth, no matter how bitter the consequences. The prophet is a person obsessed and desperate to communicate. Having a vision of holiness which he sees desecrated by those who love idolatry, injustice, and dishonesty, he deals in exaggeration, overstatement, and hyperbole, since this is the only way to reach the functionally blind and deaf. A prophet by definition must shock to communicate.

As Isaiah as prophet did not rant and excoriate all the time but also exhorted, comforted, and extolled, so Jeffers has other intonations and messages. At times he is pure mystic, adoring his god in the solitude of his tower as in "Night." At other times he is a teacher, reasoning and unfolding, suggesting how to live, as in "Signpost," "The Answer," or "Return." He can be a discerning philosopher as in "Theory of Truth." He can assume a sort of priesthood over the rituals of nature and celebrate their holiness and rhythms as in "Salmon-Fishing" and "To the House." He can turn himself inward to purify his art and sharpen his focus, always questioning the validity of his message and examining his poetic talents from the perspective of the eternal, as in "Self-Criticism in February" or "Soliloquy." Often his tones take on the gravity of the ecologist, lamenting the imbalance and guilts perpetrated by his own nation as in "November Surf," and even the apocalyptist, judging cities the ultimate idolatry and forecasting global purgation.

All of this is to say that Jeffers should be approached with some patience and an informed understanding of his intent. He cannot be summed up in one poem; nor is he heard well until he has been listened to in several voices. He has often been dismissed by his critics and the general reader as a misanthropist, pessimist, or nihilist. Isaiah might fall under the same charges. Jeffers's heavier poems ("Summer Holiday," "November Surf," or "Original Sin," for instance) should be balanced with lighter, more positive statements as "The Excesses of God" or "The Beginning and the End."

One last thought on Jeffers as Western writer. It is as if he instinctively came to grips with all the themes from the literature of the West. He deals with agrarian and pastoral types, the epic sweep of migration, hero archetypes, endemic violence, search for Eden, the failure of the American Dream, extermination of indigenous tribes, the grandeur of landscape, the mysticism of wilderness, immersion in nature, the folly of progress, the moral dilemmas of ownership, the ecology of land development, the rule of law, power, and greed. Grandson of an early pioneer of Ohio, he was inextricably involved in his nation's historical progress and in judgment upon it.

Jeffers reveals in his poetry a deep-seated ambivalence which amounts at times to self-contradiction, arising from the clash between mystic and prophet. On the one hand, he espouses an Eastern-type passivity and inner peace, assuming that nothing can be done about the world (yet seeing the universe as real and the mind as evanescent). War, betrayal, moral and political corruption are variations of a natural process of decay that inevitably follows the cresting of a nation's vitality and idealism. He can pronounce this process "not blameworthy" as in "Shine, Perishing Republic."

On the other hand, he can, and more often does, deal with humanity's errant ways with a heavy prophetic hand. Though he rejected the savior-syndrome, in many ways the redeemer whom he pictured in the short narrative by that title was alive in him "here on the mountain making / Antitoxin for all the happy towns and farms, the lovely blameless children, the terrible / Arrogant cities" ("A Redeemer," *CP* 1: 407). He tried to base his peace in the philosophy of Inhumanism. At times he seemed to reject not only American life but the life of the race as well. Yet he is ever conscious of his roots, every ready to pay his "birth-dues" to discover new meanings for his people (*CP* 1: 371).

Notes

1. Published separately in 1946, *Medea*, as a play, opened on Broadway September 20, 1947, to 214 performances. It inaugurated the Edinburgh Festival August 23, 1948, and was performed not only across the United States but in Denmark, Italy, France, and Germany. In 1982 Judith Anderson again appeared in *Medea*—on February 4 in Knoxville and then at The Kennedy Center, Washington, D.C., March 2, with Zoe Caldwell in the title role, Judith as Medea's nurse.

2. *The Tower Beyond Tragedy* was first adapted for the stage in 1933 at University of California, Berkeley, then produced in Carmel's Forest Theater in July 1941 with Judith Anderson as Clytemnestra. *The Tower* was adapted for The American National Theatre and Academy in 1950. In his adaptation of Schiller's *Mary Stuart*, begun in 1948, Jeffers intended to have leading actresses alternate roles on succeeding nights, playing Elizabeth and Mary Queen of Scots.

3. Much of the following discussion of themes, as well as the biographical overview, has been rather closely adapted from "Robinson Jeffers," my chapter in *A Literary History of the American West*, and from other such short summaries where I attempt to assess the poet and his work.

4. "Inhumanism," a key term toward understanding Jeffers's philosophy and poetics, first appears in his 1948 preface to *The Double Axe* (vii).

5. In an introduction to Horace Lyon's book of photographs, *Jeffers Country: The Seed Plots of Robinson Jeffers' Poetry*, Jeffers explains: "That is one reason for writing narrative poetry, and in this case a principal one: because certain scenes awake an emotion that seems to overflow the limits of lyric or description, one tries to express it in terms of human lives. Thus each of my too many stories has grown up like a plant from some particular canyon or promontory, some particular relationship of rock and water, wood, grass and mountain. Here were photographs of their seed-plots" (10).

Jeffers's incorporation of coastal landscape is attested to repeatedly in Carmel-Big Sur citations by Donald Clark's *Monterey County Place Names*.

6. The title, "My Loved Subject," was given by Bennett for inclusion in *The Beginning and the End* (50). *CP* indexes the poem, untitled in manuscript, by the first five words of its first line, "Old age hath clawed me."

Works Cited

CP *The Collected Poetry of Robinson Jeffers*. Ed.Tim Hunt. 3 vols. to date. Stanford, CA: Stanford UP, 1988, 1989, 1991.

SL *The Selected Letters of Robinson Jeffers*. Ed. Ann N. Ridgeway. Baltimore: Johns Hopkins UP, 1968.

Bennett, Melba. *The Stone Mason of Tor House: The Life and Work of Robinson Jeffers*. Los Angeles: Ward Ritchie, 1966.

Brophy, Robert. *Robinson Jeffers*. Boise: Western Writers Series No. 19, 1975.

——. "Robinson Jeffers." *A Literary History of the American West*. Fort Worth: Texas Christian UP, 1986. 398–415.

——. *Robinson Jeffers: Myth, Ritual, and Symbol in His Narrative Poems*. Cleveland: Case Western Reserve UP, 1973.

Clark, Donald T. *Monterey County Place Names*. Carmel Valley: Kestrel, 1991.

Daly, James. "Roots Under Rocks." *Poetry* 26 (August 1925): 278–85.

Deutsch, Babette. "Brains and Lyrics." *New Republic* 43 (May 27, 1925): 23–24.

Jackson, J. H. *Continent's End*. San Francisco: Book Club of California, 1925.

Jeffers, Robinson. *The Beginning and the End*. New York: Random, 1963.

——. *Californians*. New York: Macmillan, 1916.

——. *The Double Axe and Other Poems*. New York: Random, 1949.

——. *Flagons and Apples*. Los Angeles: Grafton, 1912.

——. *Hungerfield and Other Poems*. New York: Random, 1954.

——. *Medea*. New York: Random, 1946.

——. *Not Man Apart*. San Francisco: Sierra Club, 1965.

——. "Poetry, Gongorism and a Thousand Years." *New York Times Book Review* (January 18, 1948): 16, 26.

——. *The Selected Poetry of Robinson Jeffers*. New York: Random, 1938.

Lyon, Horace. *Jeffers Country: The Seed Plots of Robinson Jeffers' Poetry*. San Francisco: Scrimshaw, 1971.

Rorty, James. "In Major Mold." *New York Herald and Tribune Books* (March 1, 1925): 1–2.

Van Doren, Mark. "First Glance." *Nation*, 120 (March 11, 1925): 268.

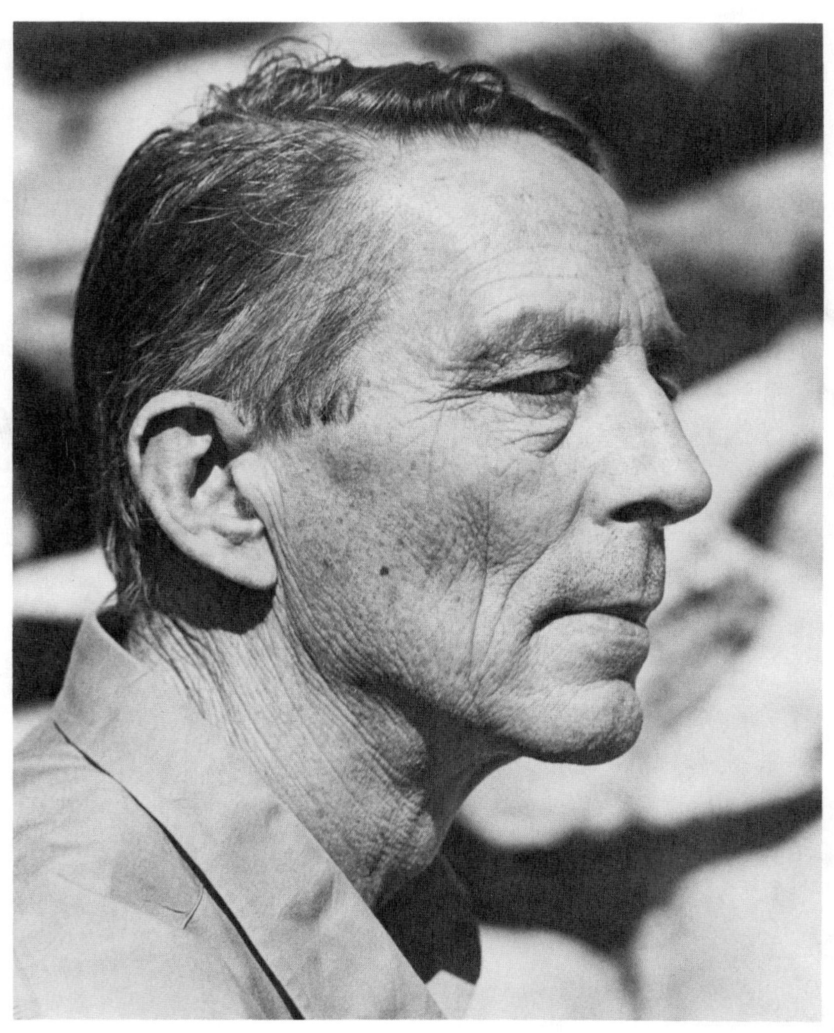

Robinson Jeffers. Photo by Morley Baer.

Above: Robinson and Una Jeffers, with dog "Billie," at site where Jeffers would build Tor House. Carmel, California, 1918. At left: Una Jeffers. Photo by Hagemeyer.

Bixby's Landing from north. Photo by Horace Lyon.

Notley's and Bixby's Landings from south. Photo by Horace Lyon.

Jeffers piling stones for Tor House and Hawk Tower. Photo by Herbert Cerwin. Archives of California State University, Long Beach.

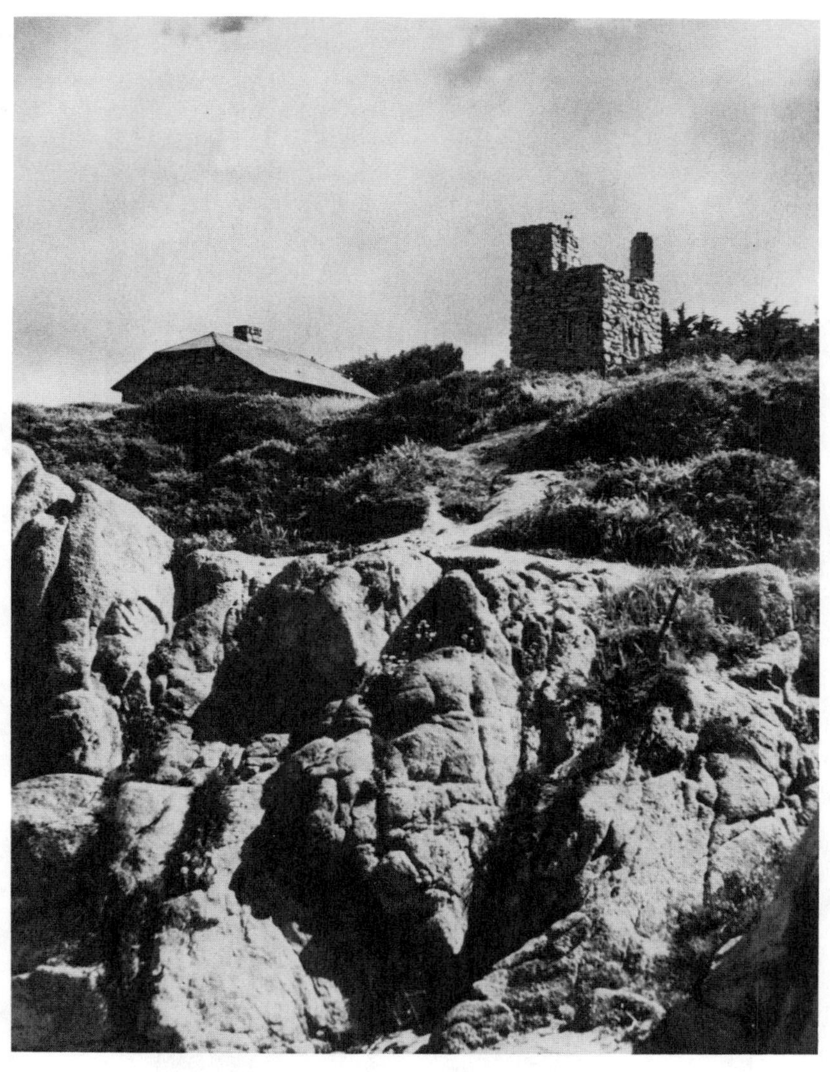

Tor House and Hawk Tower. Photo by Horace Lyon. Archives of California State University, Long Beach.

Living room, Tor House. Photo by Horace Lyon. Archives of California State University, Long Beach.

Una's reading nook, Tor House. Photo by Horace Lyon. Archives of California State University, Long Beach.

From left: Edgar Lee Masters, Gaylord Wilshire, Robinson Jeffers, sons Garth and Donnan, George Sterling. At Tor House, July 1926.

Salvador Dalí, Jeffers, and Ginger Rogers at a 1941 party in Monterey, California. By permission of the Monterey Peninsula Herald.

Robinson and Una Jeffers and their sons, Garth and Donnan, at Taos, New Mexico, 1938. Photo by A. A. Brill.

visions and other events,

As to my "religious attitudes" — you know it is a sort of tradition in this country not to talk about religion for fear of offending — I am still a little subject to the tradition, and rather dislike stating my "attitudes," except in the course of a poem. — However, they are simple. I believe that the universe is one being, all its parts are different expressions of the same energy, and they are all in communication with each other, influencing each other, therefore parts of one organic whole. (This is physics, I believe, as well as religion.) The parts change and pass, or die, people and races and rocks and stars; none of them seems to me important in itself, but only the whole. This whole is in all its parts so beautiful, and is felt by me to be so intensely in earnest, that I am compelled to love it, and to think of it as divine. It seems to me that this whole alone is worthy of the deeper sort of love; and that there is peace, freedom, I might say a kind of salvation, in turning one's affections outward toward this one God, rather than inward on one's self, or on humanity, or on human imaginations and abstractions — the world of spirits.

I think that it is our privilege and felicity to love God for his beauty, without claiming or expecting love from him. We are not important to him, but he to us.

I think that one may contribute (ever so slightly) to the

(over)

Letter from Jeffers to Sr. Mary James Power, October 1, 1934. Jeffers discusses his belief system.

beauty of things by making one's own life and surroundings
beautiful, so far as one's power reaches. This includes
moral beauty, one of the qualities of humanity, though it
does not appear elsewhere in the universe. But I would
have each person realize that his contribution is not important,
its success not really a matter for exultance nor its failure
for mourning; the beauty of things is sufficient without him.

— — There is nothing here that has not been more
feelingly expressed in my verses; but I thought that a
plain question deserves a plain answer. — Of course you
are welcome to ~~publish~~ photostat this at pleasure.

Sincerely yours,
Robinson Jeffers.

(The office of tragic poetry is to show that there is
beauty in pain and failure ~~since there are~~
as much as in success and happiness.)

Dear Blanche: Of course you can have this first draft if it
interests you — scribbled and incomplete — such answers are necessarily
incomplete as long as the mind goes on experiencing.

Affectionately,
Robin.

2

In the Poet's Lifetime

Alex Vardamis

DURING HIS LIFETIME, Robinson Jeffers's critical reputation underwent radical fluctuations. During the twenties the appearance of his work was heralded by both the avant-garde and the general reading public. And yet within less than two decades he was vilified by many of those who had initially praised his innovative daring. His poetry came to be largely ignored by both the literary establishment and the general readership. At the time of his death in 1962 the *New York Times* noted that "he was perhaps best known for his free adaptation of 'Medea,'" which, in the words of the *San Francisco Chronicle*, was "a truly great work of translation." To trace the ebb and flow of his fame is to explore the fashions of American thought in the years between, roughly, the First World War and the American involvement in Vietnam.

Initial, if limited, interest was aroused by the appearance of *Californians* in 1916. Now judged a somewhat immature work, atypical of the later Jeffers, *Californians* provoked critical judgments that would be echoed again and again in later years. The *Overland Monthly* in 1916 found that Jeffers handled the California background of his "descriptive narrative . . . with fine sense" and judged his work to be "worth while." Oscar W. Firkins, in the *Nation* in 1917, praised his "masculine fervor" and his "fine boldness." Yet, even in this early criticism, doubts arose that were to reappear with increasing frequency in the years to come. Firkins noted that Jeffers's "construction is *bushy;* he envelops, smothers, his idea in language, and the last deity to whom he could be coaxed to erect an altar is the god Terminus." In the same year the *New York Times*, in a discussion of "Recent Books of Verse by 'Minor Poets,'" saw Jeffers as a poet of "genuine talent." The anonymous critic added, however, that "Mr. Jeffers' gold is scattered through vast quantities of waste," adding that "If the present volume were only half as large as it is it would stand an excellent chance of being twice as good." Similarly mixed evaluations which recognized Jeffers's power while deploring his excesses were to reappear in future years.

The first important critical recognition followed the appearance, in 1924, of *Tamar and Other Poems.* Jeffers was forced to pay for publication of the book himself. The volume went unnoticed until Jeffers sent a copy to the California poet George Sterling, who found "Tamar" the "strongest and most dreadful poem" he had ever read, unique among "the unforgettable dreams of the art." Sterling recommended *Tamar* to James Rorty of the *New York Herald and Tribune*, who in turn introduced it to Mark Van Doren and Babette Deutsch. Rorty thought that *Tamar* was "a magnificent tour de force. . . . Nothing as good of its kind has been written in America." Van Doren, in the *Nation*, wrote that "few [volumes] are as rich with the beauty and strength which belongs to genius alone." In the *New Republic* in 1925 Deutsch found "thinking in these lyrics which lifts them . . . on to the plane of great writing." Other critics agreed that a poetic genius had arrived on the American scene. James Daly, in *Poetry*, said that "Jeffers is unsurpassed by any other poet writing in English," and *Time*, in 1925, finding Jeffers "unmistakably powerful," compared him to Whitman.

The following year Boni and Liveright published *Roan Stallion, Tamar and Other Poems* which included two additional long narratives, "Roan Stallion" and "Tower Beyond Tragedy," and several short poems. The new volume created a sensation. Reviews appeared in many prestigious publications. Deutsch in the *New Republic* ranked him "with the foremost American poets not only of his generation, but of all the generations that preceded him." In the *New York Times Book Review* in 1926, Percy Hutchison called Jeffers a mad genius comparable to the Greeks, and found parts of the new volume "equaled only by the very great." Edwin Seaver, in the *Saturday Review of Literature*, found "'Roan Stallion' . . . a magnificent achievement." H. L. Mencken, in *American Mercury*, saw "a fine and stately dignity in him, and the rare virtue of simplicity."

Praise extended to the popular press. Lillian Ford in the *Los Angeles Times* declared Jeffers "a major poet and one of the greatest America has yet produced." In 1925 the *Salt Lake City Telegram* saw in "the emergence of Robinson Jeffers . . . the outstanding literary event in years"; in 1926 the *Omaha World Herald* praised the elemental quality of the poetry, and Gremin Zorn in the *Brooklyn Eagle* proclaimed Jeffers a genius. With this one volume Jeffers had arguably become the most popular poet in America.

Nevertheless, adulation was not universal. Sidney L. Cox, writing in the *Sewanee Review* in April 1926, although acknowledging the volume's originality, complained about the "preposterous fantasies" and felt that Jeffers lacked both patience and restraint. Other voices condemned the "salaciousness," the decadence, and the "hideous wholesale destruction." From his first appearance in print detractors were shocked by Jeffers's immorality and violence. Religious conservatives objected vehemently to Jeffers's "Dear Judas" because of the poet's unorthodox interpretation of Jesus. But it was not only "Dear Judas" which offended some on moral grounds. Harriet Monroe, editor of *Poetry*, censured "Roan Stallion" for its concern with "abnormal passions." In 1929 Robert Hillyer, although acknowledging Jeffers's poetic skill, judged his material "revolting." Howard Mumford Jones in a review of *The Women at Point Sur* (1927) found in it an "excess of sex, insanity, and perversity," and Babette Deutsch in the *New Republic* in 1927 saw "irrelevant sordidness" in the volume. In a grass roots reaction to Jeffers's poetry in *Carnegie Magazine* in 1928, the reviewer, Samuel Church, complained of the "moral perversion in his long poems" and warned the public not to read Jeffers aloud in family circles. These judgments were not isolated.

In the 1920s, however, it was precisely Jeffers's "excesses" that attracted a devoted following. To many of the avant-garde, the poetry of Jeffers, shocking, radical and Nietzschean, seemed the quintessence of all their passions. Sterling, in describing Jeffers's poetry, employed the metaphor of "great serpents coiled around high and translucent jars of poison, gleaming with a thousand hues of witch-fire." Benjamin DeCasseres, in 1929, in *The Superman in America* found in Jeffers "the imaginative insanity of Blake, . . . the hallucinant chiaroscuro of De Quincy, the satanic joy in the hideous of Baudelaire, . . . the eeriness and incestuous motives of Wagner . . . and, beyond all, the defiant and aurealed wickedness of Nietzsche's Antichrist and Superman." Similarly in 1930 in the avant-garde Paris journal *Transition*, Eugene Jolas noted that "The will to illusion, in Nietzsche's sense, includes the will to penetrate into the darkest recesses of the human spirit. It is here where American poetry, with the exception of Jeffers, has not yet stepped out of the Calvinistic atmosphere."

Clearly, many among Jeffers's early admirers were radically anti-establishment romantics who took inspiration from Jeffers's iconoclastic, violent, and explicit narratives. Progressive journals such as *Masses* and *Nation* were among the first to pay Jeffers serious critical attention. Arthur Ficke, in 1928, proclaimed that

"Americans resent Robinson Jeffers blindly . . . because a secret part of them is aware of the terrible truth of all he writes. . . . The nightmare sex-designs . . . will of course repel the generality of human beings all the more because of their extraordinary eloquence and their unquestioned genius. His aim is to blast the human universe apart." Significantly, such bohemian figures as Eugene O'Neill, Edna St. Vincent Millay, and Mabel Dodge Luhan were among Jeffers's most loyal admirers in the lean years to come.

Jeffers's critical reputation and his popular fame grew with the appearance every year or two of new volumes of poetry: *The Women at Point Sur* in 1927, *Cawdor and Other Poems* in 1928, *Dear Judas and Other Poems* in 1929, *Descent to the Dead* in 1930, and *Thurso's Landing and Other Poems* in 1932. With the publication of *Thurso's Landing*, Jeffers's popularity crested. He appeared on the cover of *Time* magazine. Mabel Dodge Luhan dedicated to Jeffers her book on her adventures with D. H. Lawrence in Taos. Lawrence Clark Powell published his doctoral dissertation, *An Introduction to Robinson Jeffers*, and S. S. Albert's full-length bibliography of Jeffers appeared a year later. Henry Canby reflected general critical opinion when he declared that Jeffers was "among the few poets of unquestioned eminence writing in America." Several influential critics accorded him highest praise that year. Granville Hicks wrote that *Thurso's Landing* swept "forward on the wings of an imagery even nobler than that we have known." Percy Hutchinson, in the *New York Times Book Review*, found the new book Jeffers's "crowning achievement."

But the seeds of decline in Jeffers's literary reputation had already been planted. Some critics found fault with perceived deficiencies in Jeffers's style which was seen as loose, even sloppy, more prose than poetry. The New Critics, who dominated literary criticism from the 1930s to the 1960s, valued imagery, wit, irony, paradox, and ambiguity, and stressed close textual reading of tight, concentrated, shorter poems. Almost without exception they rejected Jeffers's verse, calling attention to the "looseness of rhythms," the absence, as Robert Penn Warren noted in 1937 in *Poetry*, of "concentration of interest in detail that gives a short poem its power." Warren judged the short poems in *Solstice* to be "turgid and feeble." The judgments of this influential group of critics ranged from Yvor Winters's savage attacks to Allen Tate's moderate defense, in which he concedes occasional "fine restraint and modulation of tone in his [Jeffers's] short poems." Blackmur, writing in the *Kenyon Review* in 1952, castigated "the flannel-mouthed inflation in the metric of Robinson Jeffers with his rugged rock-garden violence." Randall Jarrell wrote in 1963: "Jeffers' poems do not have the exactness and concision of the best poetry; his style and temperament, his whole world view, are to a surprising extent a matter of simple exaggeration." In an essay "The Progress of Hart Crane" which appeared in *Poetry* in June 1930, the California critic and poet Yvor Winters found "Whitman's poems, like Mr. Jeffers', . . . boundless catalogues. Both of these poets, and Mr. Crane, as well, are headed precisely for nowhere, in spite of all the shouting." In his *In Defense of Reason*, Yvor Winters summarized his views by saying that Jeffers's "writing, line by line, is pretentious trash." The disdain of the New Critics in the following decades, when they dominated the literary scene, resulted in the removal of Jeffers from serious consideration as a poet of the first rank.

Yet, Winters's criticism of Jeffers was to move beyond mere questions of style. Ad hominem attacks followed. Winters suggested, for example, that rather than force any more of his poetry on America Jeffers should consider suicide. Writing in *Poetry* in 1930 he found *Dear Judas* "revolting, maudlin, anecdotal." He rendered his *obiter dicta* on *Dear Judas* in comic detail, finding that the poem had no quotable lines "save perhaps three," and those "heavy with dross." In a review of *Thurso's Landing*, Winters stated his case more succinctly: "The book is composed almost wholly of trash." However, Winters was perhaps only the most conspicuous of the many hostile critics in the thirties and forties. Factors other than the quality of Jeffers's poetics contributed to his abrupt decline.

The Depression and widespread poverty in America in the thirties influenced reform-minded literary critics to demand socially and politically correct literature. Jeffers did not meet their expectation. Ruth Lechlitner, writing in the *New Republic* in 1936, mirrored the scorn that these critics directed against the poet of pessimism and doom. She chastised Jeffers for being above politics, saying that the "plain annihilation of humankind (followed by peace) will do Mr. Jeffers nicely. Provided, . . . that he can sit alone in his stone tower, surrounded by California scenery, while the whole disgusting business is going on, and dash off a last poem or two before peace gathers him to her bosom." Others criticized his lack of constructive social criticism. The early admirer James Rorty reversed himself in 1932, stating that Jeffers expresses "the death wish of a spent civilization," while "a new literature is emerging, the work of poets ardently partisan to human life. . . . Their ardors are just as valid as Jeffers' enthusiasm for basalt and grave maggots." In a review of *Such Counsels You Gave to Me* (1937), Eda Walton attacked Jeffers's antisocial anarchism. She saw him as one who has "removed himself too far from his own age to be seriously listened to as a prophet." Delmore Schwartz echoed many critics of the decade when he wrote in 1939 that Jeffers's poetry, because it rejected humanity, was "without interest and without value."

Although Marxist critics, writing in journals such as *Masses* and *Nation*, were among the first to pay Jeffers serious attention, their interest stemmed from what they saw as the poet's prophecy of the death of the capitalist system. Horace Gregory, expressing a typical Marxist ambivalence toward Jeffers, praised him in 1934 as a "superlative nature poet . . . who made us see the underside of a vast dream called American prosperity. . . ." Victor Francis Calverton declared that Jeffers's tragedies were a "reflection of the violent, toppling ruins of a dying civilization." Rolfe Humphries, on the other hand, condemned Jeffers in 1935 for making "no effort to show that the present horrible frustrations, deformations and agonies of men are due to the fact that they are for the most part still living under the degenerating capitalism of the 20th century," adding that Jeffers "served a very useful purpose to the governing class" by telling men that it is futile to protest against man's hard, inevitable lot.

Jeffers's isolationism was as unpopular in the forties as his lack of social commitment was in the thirties. In *Be Angry at the Sun*, 1941, Jeffers issued a passionate plea for the United States to avoid entanglement in another European war. His prefatory remarks to the volume served warning that the themes of his poetry were changing. "I wish to lament the obsession with contemporary history that pins many of these pieces to the calendar, like butterflies on cardboard. Yet it is right that a man's views be expressed, though the poetry should suffer for it." Stanley Kunitz, reflecting the mood of the times, warned Jeffers that if he did not "accept moral obligations and human values," he would "range himself on the side of the destroyers."

Violent attacks on Jeffers reached a crescendo with *The Double Axe* (1948). On receipt of the manuscript, Jeffers's editor, Saxe Commins, confided in a letter to Bennett Cerf on October 13, 1947, that "In all charity, I can only explain this melancholy book as proof of early senility. What the provocation for all these maledictions in our time and insane hatred of Roosevelt, I can't guess. . . . I don't see how we can do anything else but protest to Jeffers about the Roosevelt and isolationism passages that are manifestly obnoxious." Even after Jeffers complied with suggested revisions, the modified version of the text prompted a disclaimer from Random House absolving itself of responsibility for the material it contained. In *The Double Axe* Churchill, Stalin, and Hitler are frequently vilified as equally reprehensible warlords and Roosevelt comes in for special scorn. Reviews reflected general condemnation. R. I. Brigham in the *St. Louis Post-Dispatch* declared that "only the most devout followers of the right-wing nationalists, the lunatic fringe, and the most ardent of Roosevelt haters could, after reading *The Double Axe*, welcome the return of Robinson Jeffers." *Time*, in a review, "And Buckets o' Blood," condemned his pacifist stance and his implication "that no human kindness or decency would survive modern warfare." Gerald McDonald in the *Library Journal* found *The Double Axe* a "hateful book . . . a gospel of isolationism carried beyond geography, faith and hope." Politics, not poetry, engaged the critics.

Unfortunately for his critical reputation, Jeffers's isolationism and his distrust of New Deal social reform, as much as the apparent elitism and celebration of violence in his poetic themes, sometimes led critics to label him a fascist. The accusation first appeared in a review of *Solstice* in 1935 in which Philip Rice said that Jeffers's ideas resembled "good fascism." Babette Deutsch, in the *Virginia Quarterly Review* in 1942, similarly felt that *Be Angry at the Sun* gave "color to the suspicion that Jeffers has fascist sympathies." The accusation lingered. Michael Cohen, in his *The History of the Sierra Club, 1892–1970*, describes the controvesy that divided the Sierra Club when it considered using Jeffers's poetry as text for a photographic study of the Big Sur Coast. George Marshall, a member of the Sierra Club board of directors and a Jewish humanist and civil libertarian, in a memo dated December 23, 1964, wrote that Jeffers reminded him "of the over-sentimentalized anti–intellectualism . . . encountered in Germany . . . in 1933 in the midst of disintegrating minds which led more and more people to commit or accept vicious acts. . . . Much of Jeffers' writing strikes me as being anti-human or a-human and I should not like us to publish a book of this kind." David Brower, as editor, prevailed, and *Not Man Apart*, featuring the poetry of Jeffers, appeared in 1965.

The reasons for Jeffers's objection to American participation in the war were unambiguous, and they were not fascist. In "Shine, Empire," published shortly before the outbreak of the Second World War, Jeffers argued that America "Powerful and armed neutral in the midst of madness / . . . might have held the whole world's balance / and stood / Like a mountain in the wind. We were misled and took sides." Let the insanity of war rage abroad. "All Europe was hardly worth the precarious freedom of / one of our states: what will her ashes fetch?" Jeffers was consistent. He equally deplored America's involvement in the other two wars in his lifetime: World War I and the Korean War. Whatever cause the nation hid behind, the sword's reality was, for Jeffers, "Loathsome / disfigurements, blindness, mutilation, locked / lips of boys / Too proud to scream" ("Contemplation of the Sword").

Jeffers's next book, *Hungerfield and Other Poems* (1954), received scant critical notice. If not for generally successful East Coast stage productions of "Dear Judas" (1947), "Medea," (1947), "Tower Beyond Tragedy" (1950), and "The Cretan Women" (1954), Jeffers might have faded into obscurity. His adaptation of "Medea" opened on Broadway in 1947 to especially ecstatic reviews. Night after night, Judith Anderson played the title role to full houses. Jeffers was recognized finally—as a truly creative translator. Brooks Atkinson, in his review of "Medea" in the *New York Times*, noted "the literary style as terse, idiomatic and sparing. The imagery . . . austere and brilliant."

The death, in 1962, of Jeffers, who in the twenties had been proclaimed as the greatest American poet since Whitman, received first-page notice in only a handful of newspapers. Even in Carmel, coverage of the final day of the Pebble Beach Golf Tournament effectively eclipsed the passing of the poet who had helped make famous the central California coast.

And yet the cycle was not complete. In the decades to come some of the aspects of Jeffers's work that drew the most scorn eventually would lead to a revival in appreciation. Jeffers's pacifism, his vision beyond war and politics, would recommend him to the antiwar movement of the sixties and seventies. His cosmic rather than man-centered view of nature would inspire ecologists of the seventies and eighties. Serious critical reappraisals of his poetry would demonstrate that he was neither careless nor "flannel-mouthed." No longer an isolated voice crying, Cassandra-like, in the California wilderness, Jeffers would become the acknowledged mentor for a new generation of poets from William Everson and Gary Snyder to Robert Bly and Czeslaw Milosz. By the time the 1987 centennial of Jeffers's birth arrived, a vibrant renewal of interest was evident. And the second century has just begun.

Works Cited

Atkinson, Brooks. "Medea for Moderns." *New York Times* 26 Oct. 1947: Sec. 11, 1.

Blackmur, R.P. "Lord Tennyson's Scissors: 1912–1950." *Kenyon Review* Winter 1952: 1–20.

Brigham, R.I. "Bitter and Skillful Treatise in Verse." *St. Louis Post-Dispatch* 1 Aug. 1948: Sec. 6, 4.

"And Buckets o' Blood." *Time* 2 Aug. 1948: 79.

Calverton, Victor Francis. "Pathology in Contemporary Literature." *Thinker* Dec. 1931: 7–16.

Canby, Henry Seidel. "The Pulitzer Prizes." *Saturday Review of Literature* 23 Apr. 1932: 677.

Church, Samuel Harden. "A Pittsburgh Poet Discovered." *Carnegie Magazine* Nov. 1928: 180–82.

Cohen, Michael P. *The History of the Sierra Club, 1892–1970.* San Francisco: Sierra Club Books, 1988. 346–48.

Commins, Dorothy. *What Is an Editor? Saxe Commins at Work.* Chicago: U of Chicago P, 1978. 120–31.

Cox, Sidney L. Rev. of *Roan Stallion, Tamar and Other Poems. Sewanee Review* Apr. 1926: 243–47.

Daly, James. "Roots under the Rocks." *Poetry* Aug. 1925: 278–85.

DeCasseres, Benjamin. *The Superman in America.* Seattle: U of Washington Bookstore, 1929. 22–25.

Deutsch, Babette. "Bitterness and Beauty." *New Republic* 10 Feb. 1926: 338–39.

——. "Brains and Lyrics." *New Republic* 27 May 1925: 23–24.

——. "Or What's a Heaven For?" *New Republic* 17 Aug. 1927: 341.

——. "Poets and New Poets." *Virginia Quarterly Review* Winter 1942: 132–34.

Ficke, Arthur Davison. "A Note on the Poetry of Sex." *Sex in Civilization.* Ed. Victor Francis Calverton and Samuel D. Schmalhausen. New York: Macauley, 1929. 666–67.

Firkins, Oscar W. "Chez Nous." *Nation* 11 Oct. 1917: 400–01.

Ford, Lillian C. "New Major Poet Emerges." *Los Angeles Times* 11 Apr. 1926: Sec. 3, 34.

Gregory, Horace. "Suicide in the Jungle." *New Masses* 13 Feb. 1934: 18–19.

Hicks, Granville. "A Transient Sickness." *Nation* 13 Apr. 1932: 433.

Hillyer, Robert. "Five American Poets." *New Adelphi* Mar.-May 1929: 280–82.

Humphries, Rolfe. "Robinson Jeffers." *Modern Monthly* Jan.-Feb. 1935: 680–89, 748–53.

Hutchison, Percy A. “An Elder Poet and a Young One Greet the New Year.” *New York Times Book Review* 3 Jan. 1926: 14, 24.

——. “Robinson Jeffers' Dramatic Poem of Spiritual Tragedy.” *New York Times Book Review* 3 Apr. 1932: 2.

“In the Realm of Bookland.” *Overland Monthly* Dec. 1916: 570.

Jarrell, Randall. “Fifty Years of American Poetry.” *Prairie Schooner* Spring 1963: 1–27.

Jolas, Eugene. “Literature and the New Man.” *Transition* June 1930: 13–19.

Jones, Howard Mumford. “Dull Naughtiness.” *Chicago News* 3 Aug. 1927: 14.

Kunitz, Stanley J. “The Day Is a Poem.” *Poetry* Dec. 1941: 148–54.

Lechlitner, Ruth. Rev. of *Solstice and Other Poems*. *New Republic* 8 Jan. 1936: 262.

McDonald, Gerald. Rev. of *The Double Axe and Other Poems*. *Library Journal* 15 June 1948: 948.

Mencken, H[enry] L[oui]s. “Books of Verse.” *American Mercury* June 1926: 251–54.

Monroe, Harriet. “Pomp and Power.” *Poetry* June 1926: 160–64.

Obituary: “Robinson Jeffers.” *San Francisco Chronicle* 23 Jan. 1962: 34.

Obituary: “Robinson Jeffers Dead at 75.” *New York Times* 22 Jan. 1962: 23.

“Pacific Headlands.” *Time* 30 Mar. 1925: 12.

“Publication of Poems by Jeffers Creates Strong Demand for More.” *Salt Lake City Telegram* 29 Nov. 1925: magazine section, 1.

“Recent Books of Verse by ‘Minor Poets.'” *New York Times* 8 July 1917: Sec VII, 257.

Rev. of *Roan Stallion, Tamar and Other Poems*. *Omaha World-Herald* 24 Jan. 1926: magazine section, 6.

Rice, Philip Blair. “Jeffers and the Tragic Sense.” *Nation*, 23 Oct. 1935: 480–82.

Rorty, James. “In Major Mold.” *New York Herald and Tribune Books* 1 Mar. 1925: 1–2.

——. “Symbolic Melodrama.” *New Republic* 18 May 1932: 24–25.

Schwartz, Delmore. “Sources of Violence.” *Poetry* Oct. 1939: 30–38.

Seaver, Edwin. “Robinson Jeffers' Poetry.” *Saturday Review of Literature* 16 Jan. 1926: 492.

Sterling, George. “Rhymes and Reactions.” *Overland Monthly* Nov. 1925: 411.

Tate, Allen. *Sixty American Poets, 1894–1944*. Washington: Library of Congress, 1945. 55–59.

Van Doren, Mark. “First Glance.” *Nation* 11 Mar. 1925: 268.

Walton, Eda Lou. "Beauty of Storm Disproportionately. *Poetry* Jan. 1938: 209–13.
Warren, Robert Penn. "Jeffers on the Age." *Poetry* Feb. 1937: 279–82.
Winters, Yvor. "The Experimental School in American Poetry." *In Defense of Reason*. Denver: Alan Swallow, 1947. 30–74.
——. "The Progress of Hart Crane." *Poetry* June 1930: 153–65.
——. Rev. of *Thurso's Landing and Other Poems*. *Hound and Horn* July-Sept. 1932: 681, 684–85.
——. "Robinson Jeffers." *Poetry* Feb. 1930: 279–86.
Zorn, Gremin. "Books of the Moment Seen Critically by Prospectors in the Literary Mountains." *Brooklyn Eagle* 16 Jan. 1926: 5.

3

Robinson Jeffers and the Uses of History

Robert Zaller

"YOU HAVE DISFEATURED TIME for timelessness": so Robinson Jeffers apostrophizes himself in "Soliloquy" (*CP* 1: 215). Few poets have ever sought more distance from the quotidian, the ephemeral, the merely historical.

> Permanent things are what is needful in a poem, things temporally
> Of great dimension, things continually renewed or always present.
>
> Grass that is made each year equals the mountains in her past and future;
> Fashionable and momentary things we need not see nor speak of.
> (*CP* 1: 90)

Jeffers's conception of human history and its place in a wider cosmos is fully implicit in these lines. Value for him was above all perdurable; in contrast, the "fashionable and momentary" were beneath notice. But value did not imply stasis. There was no still point of the turning world for Jeffers as for Eliot, no imagined haven or transcendence beyond the vicissitudes of change, even for divinity. Existence *was* alterability, and endurance, the pathos of the temporal, could be predicated only of that which did not lapse rather than that which did not change.

The essential distinction in Jeffers's verse is therefore between the ephemeral and the perdurable rather than between the temporal and the eternal. The ephemeral is the *unrepeatable;* what succeeds it annuls it and extinguishes all trace of its existence. The sign of the ephemeral is singularity, the sport in nature; novelty, the fashion in culture. It appears in nature as a random flaw in design, an accident; in culture, however, it is an effect of morally deficient intention, of frivolity.

In contrast, the perdurable is continuous, whether through persistence or renewal; thus grass "equals" the mountain in its tenacity, though its mode of duration may differ. Duration is the result of effort, of resistance to the call of dissolution, and it is the quality of that effort rather than the length of duration that confers value, for all duration is relative:

> Mountains, a moment's earth-waves rising and hollowing; the earth too's an ephemerid, the stars—
> Short-lived as grass the stars quicken in the nebula and dry in their summer, they spiral
> Blind up space, scattered black seeds of a future; nothing lives long, the whole sky's
> Recurrences tick the seconds. . . . ("The Treasure," *CP* 1: 102)

From a longer perspective, the mountains celebrated in "Point Joe" are but a momentary buckling of the earth's surface, while stars and grass share the same brief summer from a standpoint sufficiently removed, and even nebular formation, the most extended spatial and temporal process known, subsides to mere "seconds" of duration. Clearly, duration itself, as a category of value, corresponds neither to time nor to substance but is ultimately a metaphor for what Jeffers calls in this poem "the treasure," the divine constancy in things.[1]

Because measure and duration are relative, and because all existence is equally permeated by the divine, Jeffers refuses to fetishize the natural world, or to privilege the human one. "Permanent things" are stable only from the perspective of the mortal observer; they are markers of continuance. Their importance is that they *manifest* greatly, and thereby constrain human pretension. Thus Jeffers notes in "To the Stone-Cutters" that rock will outlast the human inscriptions that "Scale in the thaws, wear in the rain," and in "Morro Bay" he contemplates the beauty of "That Norman rockhead Mont St. Michel . . . / . . . before it was built on" (*CP* 1: 5; 3: 400). Human effort does not create beauty—or, to use a more comprehensive term, value; it merely alters a value that already exists and is sufficient in itself beyond anything human agency can create. Indeed, the world's sufficiency might well exclude man altogether: no Western poet since Lucretius has looked more matter-of-factly than Jeffers at the human phenomenon, or more askance at human vanity. Perhaps, as he muses in "Margrave," the cosmos has, in man, "to dream, and dream badly, a moment of its night" (*CP* 2: 167).

Even consciousness, supposedly the characteristic feature of humankind, holds neither uniqueness nor advantage for Jeffers. He conceived it as the reflexive self-awareness of existence itself, a quality diffused generally through being, and as such neither confined to nor culminating in man, except as a point of extremity:

For often I have heard the hard rocks I handled
Groan, because lichen and time and water dissolve them,
And they have to travel down the strange falling scale
Of soil and plants and the flesh of beasts to become
The bodies of men; they murmur at their fate
In the hollows of windless nights; they'd rather be anything
Than human flesh played on by pain and joy. . . . (*CP* 2:161)

Jeffers ironically reverses the post-Darwinian progression of inorganic to organic matter and primitive to complex life-forms, calling the process (with a nod to Genesis) a "fall." There is, no doubt, a teleological element at work here, a sense of destiny threading itself through matter to arrive at exacerbated human consciousness. This consciousness, as Jeffers suggests in "Apology for Bad Dreams" (*CP* 1:208–11), enacts a parody of the divine agon, thereby mirroring but also estranging itself from it. It is a tortured paradox that seeks escape from itself in dogma and ritual, or more simply in pleasure and intoxication. Its mode of duration is history; and its history, essentially, is self-evasion.

In Jeffers's view the evolved consciousness of the human race and the intricate physiology through which it is manifested is radically unstable and fundamentally insupportable. Jeffers remarks somewhere that humankind cannot bear very much reality, by which he means both awareness of the conditions of existence and sensitivity to their impingement on the organism. These conditions are summarized in the Prelude to "The Women at Point Sur"—Jeffers's closest approach to a *summa* in verse—as "strain," the condition of locked tension that upholds universal structure:

Always the strain, the straining flesh, who feels what God feels
Knows the straining flesh, the aching desires,
The enormous water straining its bounds, the electric
Strain in the cloud, the strain of the oil in the oil-tanks
At Monterey, aching to burn, the strain of the spinning
Demons that make an atom, straining to fly asunder,
Straining to rest at the center,
The strain in the skull, blind strains, force and counterforce,
Nothing prevails. . . . (*CP* 1: 244)

As Jeffers remarks, to apprehend the strain of universal process, to "feel" it in all its immense simultaneity, would be to share the consciousness of God; but the more evolved creaturely consciousness is, the greater its nervous sensitivity, the more transient its perceptions, and the less its experiential capacity. What humans feel they feel acutely; without mediation they would be consumed. Jeffers suggests that this is, ontologically considered, the human function:

> Humanity is the mould to break away from, the crust to break through, the coal to break into fire,
> The atom to be split. ("Roan Stallion," *CP* 1: 189)

Considered on an individual level, this is the function of tragedy, "the white fire," as Jeffers puts it, that both proceeds from and consumes the human actor. If for the Greeks tragedy was an affirmation of order through the enactment of transgression, for Jeffers it is a rapture, a quest for origins that spends itself to "shine terribly against the dark magnificence of things" (*CP* 2: 278). Transgression is its mode of expression, for only by defying the natural order can existence be breached to reveal divinity: "unnatural crime, inhuman science, / . . . wild loves that leap over the walls of nature, . . . / . . . These break, these pierce, these deify, praising their God shrilly with fierce voices" (*CP* 1: 189). The orthographic closeness of "defy" and "deify" suggests the paradoxical nature of the tragic enterprise; by violating the boundaries of natural process, the tragic actor seeks the creator through the crust of his creation. The act of transgression is simultaneously one of defiance and exaltation; thus, while Jeffers's intransitive use of "deify" almost suggests an aggrandizement of divinity, it is tempered at once by the shrill but subordinate cries of "praise." The result is an *acclamation* of the divine, for in Jeffers's fiercely monistic universe God cannot be dissevered from any of his manifestations in the phenomenal world—even from humanity.

The tragic protagonist thus functions in Jeffers as a kind of lightning rod for the divine. His sign is the impulse to transgression. Tamar, the first of these protagonists, begins with a simple violation of the incest taboo, but comes to understand that she must "revoke" relationship as such if she is to overcome her essential contingency. The freedom she finally seeks is the divine afflatus itself, the unconditioned desire that transcends any object and can be resolved only in annihilation. This, too, is the quest of the Reverend Arthur Barclay in "The Women at Point Sur," where annihilation is figured as "the black crystal" for which divinity itself longs. Barclay himself, the most ambitious of Jeffers's heroes, comes closest to embodying this ineffable paradox when, as he lies dying, he experiences the elation of renewal: "I am inexhaustible" (*CP* 1: 367).

These are, in fact, Barclay's final words, and the closing words of the poem. Humanity is consumed in the ultimate hubris of imagining itself divine; but this hubris is, in some sense, its destiny. The poet himself plays this game at one remove, forging "idols" whose function is "praise":

> . . . I sometime
> Shall fashion images great enough to face him
> A moment and speak while they die. These here have gone mad:
> but stammer the tragedy you crackled vessel. (*CP* 1: 289)

The line between "stammer" and "speak" in this passage is essentially a rhetorical one; in either case, the speaker is consumed in his utterance. Jeffers is closer to Dionysian ritual in his conception of the tragic protagonist than Aristotle and perhaps even the classical playwrights themselves, if not to even older and more buried layers of sacrifice (see Hughes; cf. Brophy). Indeed, he suggests quite openly in "Apology for Bad Dreams" that his protagonists were burnt offerings meant to "magic / Horror away from the house" (*CP* 1: 209). One need not gloss this too literally to be struck, as readers from Benjamin DeCasseres to Czeslaw Milosz have been, by Jeffers's affinity with primitive states of mind, and with the aura of danger he conjures.

Jeffers would no doubt have been a priest rather than a poet had his imagination been limited to the ecstasies of sacrifice. But his heroes of transgression are balanced by those of renunciation; Dionysian abandonment, by Apollonian withdrawal. If Tamar is the prototype of the former hero, the figure of Orestes in "The Tower Beyond Tragedy," Jeffers's free adaptation of the Oresteia, most fully embodies the latter. For Orestes, transgression appears in the shape of duty, the appointed task of slaying the Tamar-like heroine who is his mother Clytemnestra. Having performed it, he is tempted to incest, the "sin" of Tamar herself, by his sister Electra; but, rejecting the trap of inversion, he chooses the mystic's path—ultimately, Jeffers's own—of *contemplatio* and *devotio*, the love that goes "outward" (*CP* 1: 178).

The hero of renunciation represents not the negation of the hero of transgression, however, but rather the opposite pole of an identical quest. The white fire that "flies" out of the tragic mask in "Roan Stallion" and is described as the "essence" of the divine epiphany later in the same poem is the vision also vouchsafed to Orestes, not in action but by passionate contemplation:

> . . . they had not made words for it, to go behind things,
> beyond hours and ages,
> And be all things in all time, in their returns and passages, in the
> motionless and timeless centre
> In the white of the fire. . . . (*CP* 1: 177)[2]

The type and antitype of the tragic hero thus represent two approaches to the same reality in Jeffers, just as the "white fire" of divine peace and the "black crystal" of annihilation are two aspects of phenomenal transcendence. We can see in Jeffers's protagonists, posed thusly, the force and urgency of his own religious quest.[3] It is a force that threatens to pull the narratives and verse dramas which embody it apart, conceding as it does little room and less value to the accommodations of ordinary experience. Tamar ends in a holocaust and Barclay in a wilderness, while Orestes, rejecting both love and power, meets his death in "high Arcadia"—a striking contrast to the Oresteia itself, in which he is absolved in a court of law and lives to found the classical city.

With Tamar, Orestes, and Barclay, Jeffers would seem to have established his tragic prototypes, leaving little for him to do but ring changes on them or, like Wordsworth, to lapse into discursive or hortatory modes. But by creating a third prototype, the hero of negation, he was able to recover his narrative pulse and to extend his dramatic range in the large-scale works of his middle period, "Cawdor," "Thurso's Landing," and "Give Your Heart to the Hawks." In fashioning this new prototype Jeffers gave voice to the skepticism of his age, and it is perhaps for this reason that these works have been less problematic to some of his admirers than the more overtly questing earlier narratives. Cawdor, Reave Thurso, and Lance Fraser are all men of doggedly practical disposition, less nonbelievers than the kind of men—common in all ages, but typical in those of lost faith—for whom religious questions simply do not arise. When tragedy befalls them (for none seeks it) they respond with stoic endurance, acknowledging no appeal beyond themselves whether for judgment or surcease. Reave Thurso speaks for all of them when he describes the cosmos as a harrowing void:

> ". . . I'll tell you
> What the world's like: like a stone for no reason falling in the
> night from a cliff in the hills, that makes a lonely

Noise and a spark in the hollow darkness, and nobody sees and nobody cares. There's nothing good in it
Except the courage in us not to be beaten. It can't make us
Cringe or say please." (*CP* 2: 260–61)

Yet it is by his very skepticism that the hero of negation is enabled to participate in the divine agon. What Thurso, Cawdor, and Fraser endure is pain: in the first case, that of physical maiming; in the latter two, of grief and guilt. Reave's physical pain is unremitting, but he refuses to dull it with opiates or end it with suicide: it is what he has and what he is, his "last inch" as he grimly puts it, and he will not yield it. For Cawdor and Fraser, who have killed respectively son and brother, there is no opiate *except* pain: Cawdor gouges his eyes out (and reproaches himself for weakness in doing so), while Fraser rakes his hands over barbed wire. These heroes of negation reduce the world to nothing but the experience of pain, despising solace and denying release. But in this they exemplify in flesh and spirit the agony of "strain" that is the lot of all material existence, and by embracing what they suffer, they mimic the self-inflicted torture of Heautontimoroumenos, the Promethean god whom Jeffers invokes in "The Women at Point Sur" and describes at length in his dramatic poem "At the Birth of an Age." Their willful rejection of any comfort and forgiveness, human or divine, might be seen as blasphemous in the context of a salvific god; but mercy is hardly to be sought of a divinity who creates the world whose body he is by an act of self-torment.[4] It is thus only by denying god that the hero of negation attests him. The cry of his pain is the hymn of his praise; his ignorance of the greater anguish he shares is the condition on which he partakes of it.

By whatever description and in whatever mode—whether seeking divinity through action or contemplation, or rejecting it in stoic denial—the Jeffers hero is, above all, a solitary whose destiny is defined only when, by transgression or tragic experience, he is removed from ordinary human intercourse, abstracted from the space of history, and raised upon the pyres of the divine agon. In the radical case of Tamar it is not only "relationship" that is rejected but temporality as such, as Tamar searches for "the muddy root under the rock of things" that will abrogate process and succession (*CP* 1: 63).[5] Such is the single-minded intensity of Jeffers's vision that it seems at moments to pass over the dimension of history entirely, as his earth-girdling eagle does in "Cawdor":

> . . . time relaxing about it now, abstracted from being, it saw the eagles destroyed,
> Mean generations of gulls and crows taking their world: turn for turn in the air, as on earth
> The white faces drove out the brown. It saw the white decayed and the brown from Asia returning;
> It saw men learn to outfly the hawk's brood and forget it again; it saw men cover the earth and again
> Devour each other and hide in caverns, be scarce as wolves. It neither wondered nor cared, and it saw
> Growth and decay alternate forever, and the tides returning. (*CP* 1: 512)

Between the tragic protagonist who seeks (or suffers) transcendence and the masses who endure the cycles of historical recurrence there was clearly a gap to be bridged. Historical change might be seen as analogous to, implicit in, or subsumed by natural process as a whole; but it could not occur without agency nor be compassed by mere scientific explanation. Jeffers was the heir of a rich psychological and epistemological tradition of the will; it was, he felt, man's defining characteristic, the paradoxical urge that led both to self-affirmation and to self-transcendence. The tragic protagonist was simply the one in whom the impulse of will was predominant over all else, but even among those in whom it beat most faintly its powers were still latent. Civilization itself was a conspiracy against the anarchy of the will, but a conspiracy that longed to fail, and periodically did. "You are tired and corrupt," Jeffers apostrophized his own postwar generation,

> You kept the beast under till the fountain's poisoned,
> He drips with mange and stinks through the oubliette window.
> The promise-breaker war killed whom it freed,
> And none living's the cleaner. ("The Women at Point Sur," *CP* 1: 241)

As will goaded civilization into being, so too it renewed it at the end of the culture cycle when a new vision arose to supplant the one whose force had been sapped by convention and staled by interpretation. Vision was thus the animating force of civilization, arising from a perceived need that was collective but realized through individual genius. Only an act of will could break through the impasse of failed belief to renewed vision, and only an act of equal force could impose it on the waiting world, which would fix it as dogma and legitimate it as authority, thus inaugurating the new cycle.

These separate processes of will fused, for Jeffers, in the figure of the savior. The tragic hero, breaking through his personal "mask," found his goal in transcendence like Orestes or endurance like Thurso or destruction like Tamar, but his witness was a solitary act: he attested the world, but did not (except in his own unrepeatable example) aspire to change it. The savior's larger but fundamentally compromised quest was not only to find truth but to signify it; unassuaged by personal vision, he was compelled to engender belief. This compulsion drove him into the arms of history.

Jeffers considered the phenomenon of the savior in two reflective poems, "Meditation on Saviors" (1928) and "Theory of Truth" (1938).[6] Unlike the prophet, who emerges from solitude and returns to it after discharging his limited function, the savior must stay to impose his vision, and, if necessary, immure himself within it to ensure its efficacy. This was the destiny of Jesus:

> . . . the young Jew writhing on the domed hill
> in the earthquake, against the eclipse
>
> Frightfully uplifted for having turned inward to love the
> people:—that root was so sweet O dreadful agonist?—
>
> . . .
>
> Among the mild and unwarlike
> Gautama needed but live greatly and be heard, Confucius needed
> but live greatly and be heard:
>
> *This* people has not outgrown blood-sacrifice, one must writhe
> on the high cross to catch at their memories;
> The price is known. (*CP* 1: 397, 400)

Jeffers's Jesus is a man of power, "A man forcing the imaginations of men, / Possessing with love and power the people." His "love" is an act of aggression, deflected (as Jeffers suggests both here and in the dramatic poem "Dear Judas") from its original, incestuous object; and it is suitably if terribly returned in the act of crucifixion. At the same time a complicity in violence is suggested between Jesus and his audience ("*This* people has not outgrown blood-sacrifice. . . . / The price is known"), and that in turn contrasted with the idealized, not to say idyllic, image of Gautama and Confucius persuading "the mild and unwarlike" by virtuous example. In "Theory of Truth," however, the savior is viewed as "tormented," whether in the person of Lao-tze, Jesus, or the Buddha:

Here was a man [Lao-tze] who envied
the chiefs of the provinces of China their power and pride,
And envied Confucius his fame for wisdom. Tortured by hardly
conscious envy he hunted the truth of things,
Caught it, and stained it with his private impurity. He praised
inaction, silence, vacancy: why?
Because the princes and officers were full of business, and wise
Confucius of words.

Here was a man who was born a bastard, and among the people
That more than any in the world valued race-purity, chastity,
the prophetic splendors of the race of David.
Oh intolerable wound, dimly perceived. Too loving to curse his
mother, desert-driven, devil-haunted,
The beautiful young poet found truth in the desert, but found
also
Fantastic solution of hopeless anguish. The carpenter was not his
father? Because God was his father,
Not a man sinning, but the pure holiness and power of God. His
personal anguish and insane solution
Have stained an age; nearly two thousand years are one vast
poem drunk with the wine of his blood.

And here was another Savior, a prince in India,
A man who loved and pitied with such intense comprehension of
pain that he was willing to annihilate
Nature and the earth and stars, life and mankind, to annul the
suffering. He also sought and found truth,
And mixed it with his private impurity, the pity, the denials.(*CP*
2: 609)

Jeffers's schematic readings of these historical figures need not detain us here. What all share in common is the quest for transcendence, a quest spurred by personal frustration or anguish because "only tormented persons want truth." Truth, however, cannot resolve anguish; as we have seen, for Jeffers truth is inseparable *from* anguish, the divine agon of self-torment that constitutes the material world. But divine truth and anguish are complementary; the latter is the instrument by which the former is clarified and made known to itself. In the case of the savior—the human case *in extremis*—these conditions are reversed: anguish is not the servant but the master of truth, and therefore "the great answers" appear to the truth-seeker only through his tormented subjectivity, stained by "impurity" and twisted with "strands of insanity."

As much might be said of the tragic hero or of the prophet, but the savior projects his crippled self-esteem into the world as love and pity, demanding discipleship and belief in response. Because the savior's vision, if powerful enough to touch others, must partake of truth, it can impose itself under favoring historical circumstances; we must assume a thousand failed heretics for each successful visionary. These visions are the axes of history, the metaphors that forge religions and shape cultures, for although the tormented few alone seek the wine of truth, the many must have the bread of doctrine.

Jeffers's view of history is thus partly Hegelian and partly Nietzschean. His religious founders, like Hegel's world-historical figures, are the agents of historical transformation. Like the Hegelian hero, the Jeffersian savior, acting from private interest or desire, achieves more than he purposes, and his passion is complicit with a power but dimly perceived and an intention beyond his knowing. Whereas Hegel's Spirit grounds itself in history, however, for Jeffers humanity is only one of the stages on which the divine agon unfolds. Since, moreover, divine self-actualization is for Jeffers fully present at every moment and in every manifestation of the created world, no theater is privileged, and no form definitive. Thus, there can be no counterpart in Jeffers to Hegel's vision of history as progressive.

Instead of subordinating the cosmos to history as in both Christian and Hegelian eschatology, Jeffers followed Nietzsche in assimilating the latter to the former. Recurrence, the tidal force that flowed through all phenomena, was the sole meaning of events, weaving humanity into the huge pattern that rocked the oceans and lit the heavens. No more than the constellations could the stations of history endure:

> . . . our Pacific has pastured
> The Mediterranean torch and passed it west across the
> fountains of the morning;
> And the following desolation that feeds on Crete
> Feed[s] here. . . . ("The Cycle," *CP* 1: 14)[7]

Jeffers's conception of history as a pattern of recurrent cycles, though clearly indebted to nineteenth-century natural science as well as his own idiosyncratic cosmogony, had classical roots as well. From Thucydides and Polybius through the Roman historians and in Renaissance thought from Machiavelli to Vico (the latter an influence specifically cited by Jeffers), history was seen as cyclical, a view advanced again in Jeffers's time by the Egyptologist Flinders Petrie and by Oswald Spengler. But Jeffers was constrained by none of these models. He avoided the shoals of positivism by emphasizing the self-determining quality of human experience, contrasting it with what he called the "sonambulism" of natural process. Nor in the end, despite the use of organicist metaphors in such poems as "Shine, Perishing Republic" ("Out of the mother; and through the spring exultances, ripeness and decadence; and home to the mother" [*CP* 1: 15]), would he subscribe to the biological determinism of a Spengler. In a 1943 letter to Frederic Ives Carpenter, he noted that: "Civilizations rise and fall, ours has risen and will fall, so will others in the future. . . . [But] the conceptions of adolescence and maturity [in a culture] seem to me a little too specialized" (*SL* 295).

Jeffers was willing to concede, with Vico, that from a certain standpoint civilization might be regarded as "a single cumulative process." But this did not constitute progress in any significant sense:

> It [civilization] tends to grow richer and bigger—because some knowledge is inherited across the gaps—but not therefore better—nor worse. Greek civilization was poorer and smaller than Egypt's before and Rome's after, but certainly not worse than either. Ours is immensely richer and bigger; but not better. All I can conclude is that "Each for its quality / Is drawn out of this gulf."(*SL* 295)[8]

The notion of "inherited" knowledge spanning the gaps between culture cycles again suggests Vico, as the idea that each cycle exhibits its own specific and unique value suggests Herder. Herder's notion of history as a process of ascent is, of course, quite foreign to Jeffers, for whom truth was gained only by tragic hazard and the concept of a generalized spiritual advance was absurd. At best, the lessons of history might inculcate wariness and skepticism, and the desirability, as Jeffers put it in "Meditation on Saviors," for each man to make his health in his own mind.

"The Broken Balance," like "Meditation on Saviors" a poem of the late-1920s,[9] exhibits both Jeffers's classicism and his sense of the West's impending decline:

> The people buying and selling, consuming pleasures, talking in
> the archways,
> Were all suddenly struck quiet
> And ran from under stone to look up at the sky: so shrill and
> mournful,
> So fierce and final, a brazen

Pealing of trumpets high up in the air, in the summer blue over
Tuscany.
They marveled; the soothsayers answered:
"Although the Gods are little troubled toward men, at the end of
each period
A sign is declared in heaven
Indicating new times, new customs, a changed people; the
Romans
Rule, and Etruria is finished;
A wise mariner will trim the sails to the wind."

I heard yesterday
So shrill and mournful a trumpet-blast,
It was hard to be wise. . . . (*CP* 1: 372)[10]

The trumpet-blast, for Jeffers, had been the Great War. From the first it had for him the character of an apocalyptic event, and in his earliest large-scale poem, "The Alpine Christ," he envisioned it as the occasion for a (failed) Second Coming. A decade later, "The Women at Point Sur" begins, as a hawk is crucified on a barn wall, with the comment "'It is necessary for someone to be fastened with nails.'" The thirst for redemption has been debased into a futile, symbolic act of cruelty that merges with the general climate of violence so vividly evoked in "The Prelude." The poem's narrative traces the disastrous career of its savior-hero, Arthur Barclay, whose charismatic powers can focus the latent violence around him but not resolve it. Barclay is no charlatan—"he touched his answers," as Jeffers comments in "Theory of Truth"—but he is unable to communicate them, and they are lost finally in "the glimmer of insanity." With the character of Barclay and in "Meditation on Saviors," Jeffers firmly puts aside his own Christological yearnings, and in "The Broken Balance" he confronts a world incapable of salvation and reduced to mere "soothsayers." He remains wedded, that is to say, to a theophanic conception of history, but he sees the West of his own time as at an impasse, too materially powerful and sophisticated to fall, too spiritually enervated to regenerate itself. What remained, he felt, would be a long career of decline, "starred with famous Byzantiums and Alexandrias," but incapable of fundamental renewal (*CP* 3: 14).

What remained for the poet—other than the vanity of prophecy—was honest custody and ethical fortitude. In "To the Stone-Cutters," Jeffers had found "the honey of peace in old poems"; twenty years later, in "Prescription of Painful Ends," the valedictory note was his own, and he spoke of producing "poems for treasuries, time-conscious poems." The goal was not merely to speak of "permanent things," but also to fix in memory, to *make* permanent, those values that the West had signified and which would be inevitably lost with the cultural matrix that had embodied them.

In the dozen years following "Meditation on Saviors" and "The Broken Balance," Jeffers produced three dramatic poems with historical settings and a fourth set in the historical present: "Dear Judas," a Noh-like evocation of the passion of Jesus; "At the Fall of an Age," based upon the legend of Helen; "At the Birth of an Age," a commixture of Teutonic, Norse, and Christian mythology; and "The Bowl of Blood," a masque on the contemporary theme of Hitler's conquests. Jeffers himself indicated the culturally retrospective nature of these poems:

> I was considering the main sources of our civilization, and listed them roughly as Hebrew-Christian, Greek, Roman, Teutonic. Then it occurred to me that I had written something about the Hebrew-Christian source in *Dear Judas*, and that *The Tower Beyond Tragedy* might pass for a recognition of the Greek source. About the Roman source I should probably never write anything, for it is less sympathetic to me. Recognition of the Teutonic source might be an interesting theme for a new poem, I thought . . . and the Volsung Saga might serve for fable. (*SP* xviii)

The "fable" was "At the Birth of an Age," which depicted the movement from Mediterranean to Nordic culture. Its real companion was not "The Tower Beyond Tragedy" but (as the related title suggests) "At the Fall of an Age," which addressed the transition between Mycenaean and Athenian culture. What unifies the three poems of the historical trilogy, however, is less the schema of transition between culture cycles than the common theme of efficacious sacrifice: of the savior Jesus in "Dear Judas," of the ageless Helen in "At the Fall of an Age," of the Self-Hanged God in "At the Birth of an Age." In each case, the sacrifice is both a symbol and an instrument of renewal. But in "The Bowl of Blood" the figure of Hitler ("the Leader") is inadequate, "a sick child / . . . invoking destruction and wailing at it," as Jeffers describes him elsewhere ("The Day Is a Poem," *CP* 3: 16); and the values of blood and soil he evokes, an anachronism. Although the Jesus of "Dear Judas" falters humanly in the Garden, he summons too a fierce pride ("'no man shall live / As if *I* had not lived'") and a final confidence in the purity of his vision ("'I have known his glory . . . I have *been* his glory'"). In contrast, Hitler turns away from the sight of blood, and at the height of his power curses his existence ("'I wish my mother had died in that night / When she conceived me'"). He is an agent of dissolution, and even in defeating him (as Jeffers never doubts the West will do), the process of decay will only be hastened, because no countervalue is called forth.

The core value of the West was, in Jeffers's view, freedom, the reason and condition of its existence:

> The quality of these trees, green height; of the sky, shining, of
> water, a clear flow; of the rock, hardness
> And reticence: each is noble in its quality. The love of freedom
> has been the quality of Western man.
>
> There is a stubborn torch that flames from Marathon to
> Concord, its dangerous beauty binding three ages
> Into one time; the waves of barbarism and civilization have
> eclipsed but have never quenched it.
>
> For the Greeks the love of beauty, for Rome of ruling; for the
> present age the passionate love of discovery;
> But in one noble passion we are one; and Washington, Luther,
> Tacitus, Aeschylus, one kind of man. ("Shine, Republic," *CP*
> 2: 417)

Freedom had been the West's "passion," its "steep singleness," but in the mass societies of abundance freedom could have no place. "The beauty of modern / Man," Jeffers wrote in "Rearmament," "is not in the persons but in the / Disastrous rhythm, the heavy and mobile masses, the dance of the / Dream-led masses down the dark mountain." In "The Purse-Seine" he likened the populations of cities to fish trapped in a net, "incapable of free survival, insulated / From the strong earth, each person in himself helpless, on all dependent" (*CP* 2: 515, 517–18). The very memory of freedom would wither in the wars of order:

> Men will fight through to the autumn flowering and ordered
> prosperity. They will lift their heads in the great cities
> Of the empire and say: "Freedom? Freedom was a fire. We are
> well quit of freedom, we have found prosperity."
> ("Hellenistics," *CP* 2: 526–28)

For the chorus of maskers in "The Bowl of Blood," freedom is already a legend that belongs to a distant past and, perhaps, an imperceptible future:

I have heard a story about freedom, a vain vain tale
Told by some Greeks, by some slave-holding Greeks
And a few Roman authors . . .
Freedom must wait.
This is the hour of masses and masters. (*CP* 3: 94, 95)

In the face of inexorable decline, Jeffers could only counsel a soldierly resignation: "Sad sons of the stormy fall, / No escape, you have to inflict and endure" ("Flight of Swans," *CP* 2: 419). Consolation was to be sought not in historical experience—which, as we have seen, was based at best upon partial and fragmented vision—but in an integrated view of humanity and the cosmos. Had Jeffers succeeded in his own counsel of detachment, had he forsworn freedom for mere solitude, he would be perhaps a more perfected but surely a less interesting poet to us. This was his temptation, but not his goal; he had pledged himself, as he wrote in "Meditation on Saviors," "not to seek refuge, neither in death nor in a walled garden," nor to separate himself from the destiny of his time: "This people as much as the sea-granite is part of the God from whom I desire not to be fugitive." The agon must be shared, for there was no other reality; in the words of the Self-Hanged God of "At the Birth of an Age":

. . . On earth rise and fall the ages of
man, going higher for a time; this age will give them
Wings, their old dream, and unexampled extensions of mind;
and slowly break itself bloodily; one later
Will give them to visit their neighbor planets and colonize the
evening star; their colonies die there; the waves
Of human dominion dwindle down the long twilight; another
nature of life will dominate the earth . . .
. . . and accuse me of inflicting what
I endure. These also pass,
And new things are, and the shining pain. . . . (*CP* 2: 483)

The prose of history, the patient knitting of cause and effect, the clash of interests and the movement of classes, peoples, and empires, concerned Jeffers little as such. Nor did he ever seek to resolve the tension in his thought between the radical agency of saviors in cultural formation and the seemingly volitionless tides of historical change. For Jeffers each age was, as he put in "Theory of Truth," a vast poem, which actualized the power of the single great metaphor on which it was founded. He did not regard this as a sufficient theory of history—as he wrote to Carpenter, "One may be reckless in verse, but there ought to be some system about history or philosophy" (*SL* 295)—but it was sufficient to his purposes, and served his own metaphor of the eternal, immanent God who suffered all change on the Nessus shirt of his own created flesh.

Notes

1. Cf. the lines in "Night": "To us the near-hand mountain / Be a measure of height, the tide-worn cliff at the sea-gate a measure of continuance" (*CP* 1: 115).

2. Cf. the image of the caged eagle's spirit coming to final rest in "Cawdor" and striking "Peace like a white fawn in a dell of fire" (*CP* 1: 513).

3. William Everson has even gone so far as to see Jeffers as primarily a religious figure for whom verse was the instrument and discipline of a quest, and poetry—the only verbal access to the divine for someone who rejected creed and dogma—the result. See Everson, and, for my commentary on his position, see Zaller, "The Giant Hand."

4. Cf. the divine self-apostrophe in "Apology for Bad Dreams": "'I bruised myself in the flint mortar and burnt me / In the red shell, I tortured myself, I flew forth, / Stood naked of myself and broke me in fragments, / And here am I moving the stars that are me'" (*CP* 2: 211).

5. For a more extended discussion of this point see Zaller, *Cliffs of Solitude,* 15–23.

6. The dates are those of publication. "Meditation on Saviors" (originally entitled "Note on 'The Women at Point Sur'") was to have been included in *The Women at Point Sur* (1927), but was omitted from that volume together with several other short poems, presumably for reasons of space, and published with its new title the following year as part of *Cawdor and Other Poems.* See Tim Hunt, "Textual Note" to *The Women at Point Sur and Other Poems* (New York: Liveright, 1977), a volume which prints the entire manuscript as Jeffers submitted it. Both "The Women at Point Sur" and "Meditation on Saviors" are importantly modified by each other, and need to be read in that context. When "Meditation on Saviors" was reprinted in *The Selected Poetry of Robinson Jeffers* (1938), "The Women at Point Sur" was omitted but for a single brief section, further removing the two poems from their original context. They are separated again in Hunt's edition of *The Collected Poetry*, where the "Meditation" is grouped with a series of poems around "Cawdor" that also includes all but one of the poems (two of which were substantially rewritten as well as retitled for the *Cawdor* volume)

originally part of the "Women at Point Sur" manuscript. Hunt's guiding principle has been to print the collected poems in chronological order, grouping them around major poems and/or published volumes. In view of the complex textual and literary history of Jeffers's poetry this decision cannot be faulted, but (like every editorial judgment) it entails compromise. Volume IV of *The Collected Poetry*, now in preparation, will include textual variants. "Theory of Truth," a poem also related to "The Women at Point Sur," as its subtitle ("Reference to Chapter II, *The Women at Point Sur*") directly indicates, was first published in *The Selected Poetry*. The importance Jeffers attached to it as a summation of his work is indicated by the fact that he chose it to conclude the volume.

7. "Feed" is used in earlier printed versions of the poem as well, including *SP* 80. See Tim Hunt's discussion of this apparent solecism in his commentary on "The Cycle" in *CP* 4 (in press). I am grateful to him for sharing it with me in advance of publication.

8. The quotation is from Jeffers's "Woodrow Wilson" (*CP* 1: 106–07).

9. The fifth of the poem's seven sections was originally intended as part of the *Point Sur* volume, under the title "Day After Tomorrow." It was first published in *Dear Judas and Other Poems* (New York: Liveright, 1929).

10. The lines are based on a passage in Plutarch's *Life of Sulla*.

Works Cited

CP *The Collected Poetry of Robinson Jeffers*. Ed. Tim Hunt. 3 vols. to date. Stanford, CA: Stanford UP, 1988, 1989, 1991.

SL *The Selected Letters of Robinson Jeffers, 1897–1962*. Ed. Ann N. Ridgeway. Baltimore: Johns Hopkins UP, 1968.

SP *The Selected Poetry of Robinson Jeffers*. New York: Random House, 1959 (1938).

Brophy, Robert J. *Robinson Jeffers: Myth, Ritual, and Symbol in His Narrative Poems*. Hamden, CT: Archon, 1976.

Everson, William. *The Excesses of God: Robinson Jeffers as a Religious Figure*. Stanford, CA: Stanford UP, 1988.

Hughes, Dennis D. *Human Sacrifice in Ancient Greece*. New York: Routledge, 1991.

Zaller, Robert. *The Cliffs of Solitude: A Reading of Robinson Jeffers*. Cambridge: Cambridge UP, 1983.

——. "The Giant Hand: William Everson on Robinson Jeffers." *Perspectives on William Everson*. Ed. James B. Hall, Bill Hotchkiss, and Judith Shears. Eugene, OR: Castle Peak, 1992.

4

Telling the Past and Living the Present: "Thurso's Landing" and the Epic Tradition

Terry Beers

> It seems to me that *great poetry* gathers and expresses the whole of things, as prose *never can*. Its business is to contain a whole world at once, the physical and the sensuous, the intellectual, the spiritual, the imaginative, all in one passionate solution.
>
> ROBINSON JEFFERS, *Themes*

IN 1932, at a time when Robinson Jeffers enjoyed considerable popular and critical success,[1] he published one of the most significant works of his career, *Thurso's Landing and Other Poems*. The title poem of this volume marked a new creative direction in Jeffers's verse, one noticed at the time by many reviewers. Granville Hicks, writing for *Nation*, found it "'Perhaps the most human poem he has written'" (qtd. in Vardamis 87). Jeffers evidently agreed, and he ventured, for him, some extraordinary claims for it:

> It is about as long as *Cawdor* and it seems to me to be the best thing I have yet written. The scene is a canyon of the coast south of Monterey, widened by an episode into the Arizona desert. The time is perhaps more distinctly near the present than usual in my verses; the persons seem to me to be a little more conscious of what they do (qtd. in Alberts 72).

Jeffers may or may not have regarded "Thurso's Landing" as the best thing he had written.[2] But by remarking upon the comparative self-consciousness of the characters in his latest poem, for the first time Jeffers himself explicitly raised important issues about the motivations of his characters and, by implication, how these affect the telling of his narratives.

One way to approach these issues is to study how the characters in "Thurso's Landing" illustrate the intricate syntax of human cause and effect by telling their own versions of past events, compacted stories that embedded within the larger narrative of "Thurso's Landing" explain how these characters choose to live in the present. These stories lend dimension to the characters by introducing separate narrative voices that must accommodate and be accommodated by the authorial voice of the poem. Recognizing how these various narrative voices then fit within the larger compass of the poem provides a trailhead for a new route across the literary terrain of "Thurso's Landing," a work which in the tradition of literary epics ultimately prescribes "one passionate solution": a view of the world that provides a way of thinking and acting that is not, in the words of Helen Thurso, "'at last contemptible'" (*CP* 2: 240).

Like others of his narrative poems, Jeffers's inspiration for "Thurso's Landing" came from the wild coastland of central California. In his Preface to the *Selected Poetry* Jeffers claimed that he did not remember planning the story, that it "was suggested entirely by the savage beauty of the canyon and sea-cliff that are its scene, and by the long-abandoned lime-works there" (xvii). In "Thurso's Landing" these lime-works transform into the rusty artifacts of human failure, and perhaps of human cowardice, a pathetic inheritance for the characters who continue to inhabit the canyon's rough terrain.

These lime-works torture the poem's protagonist, Reave Thurso, whose father built them and who later committed suicide after their failure. Reave, an unsentimental and unforgiving man, interprets his father's suicide as cowardly and longs to rid the canyon of its rusty reminders of his failed father. His wife Helen—impatient with the solitary life led by Reave, his lame brother Mark, and their withered mother—runs off with itinerant construction worker Rick Armstrong, a friend of Reave's. Reave subsequently pursues Helen and brings her back a year later. Soon after, Reave suffers a terrible accident while dismantling a rusty cable stretched across the canyon by his father, an accident that leaves Reave impotent, painfully crippled, and entirely dependent. In the meantime Mark, haunted by ghostly visions of his father and racked by his forbidden desire for Helen, hangs himself. Living now in constant pain, Reave manifests a courage and endurance that earns Helen's admiration, But, wishing him freed of his ceaseless pain, she has Reave moved to the abandoned landing platform overlooking the violent Pacific coastland, and there she slits his throat and poisons herself, leaving the indomitable old mother as the last survivor of the family.

Such is the essential action of the poem, the telling of which creates an omniscient point of view sometimes only subtly distinct from the consciousness of individual characters. Early in the poem, for example, Rick Armstrong, on his way to the Thurso ranch house,

. . . remembered the great cable
That spanned the gorge from the hill, with a rusted iron skip
Hanging from it like a stuck black moon; relics,
With other engines on the headland, of ancient lime-kilns
High up the canyon, from which they shot the lime
To the promontory along the airy cable-way
To be shipped by sea. The works had failed; the iron skip
Stuck on its rusted pulleys would never move again
Until it fell, but to make desolate creaking
In the mountain east wind that poured down the gorge
Every clear night. (*CP* 2: 177)

The revelation that Armstrong "remembered" the cable is an important point of omniscient privilege, but the balance of the description almost imperceptibly veers away from Armstrong's specific thoughts. While the authorial voice economically provides exposition, it eventually emerges to establish a more or less objective attitude toward past events: in this version of the past, old Thurso receives no mention. The works had failed, not the man.

In other moments, the separation of the authorial voice and character is more distinct, as in the narrator's description of Helen's "dream" after she seduces young Armstrong:

She lay but half quieted, still hotly
longing,
Her eyes morbidly shuttered like the sleep of fever showed
threads of the white and faint arcs of the crystalline
Violet irises, barred across by the strong dark lashes; the night of
the lids covering the pupils,
Behind them, and under the thick brown hair and under the
cunning sutures of the hollow bone the nerve-cells
With locking fibrils made their own world and light, the
multitude of small rayed animals of one descent
That make one mind, imagined a mountain
Higher than the scope of nature, predominant over all these
edges of the earth, on its head a sacrifice

Half naked, all flaming, her hair brown like a fire through the
level skies. . . . (*CP* 2: 186)

Not only is Helen's dream—of "the superstitiously worshipped spirit of love" (*CP* 2: 186)—made available by dint of the omniscience of the authorial voice, but so also are the physiological mechanisms of its generation, something well beneath the consciousness of the impassioned Helen. Here the narrative does not so much establish a view toward the past events of this fictionalized world (as it does in the example above) as it begins to establish the ground for an almost scientific objectivity toward human beings and their self-deluding dreams. But the distance between character and narrator is never so great as in those moments when the authorial voice seems to be addressing the reader directly, passing judgment upon action to come or action only recently related. There are only a handful of these moments throughout the poem. One is an important observation offered just after an episode where Helen desperately attempts to provoke Reave into violently losing his self-control (by comparing her own naked body to that of the wraith-like runaway Hester Clark, whom Reave picked up as mistress and servant after Helen ran off with Armstrong):

It is certain that too violent
Self-control is unlucky, it attracts hard events
As height does lightning; so Thurso rode up the canyon with a
little death in himself,
Seeing in his mind Helen's naked body like a red bird-cage
Welted with whip-stripes; and having refused the precious relief
of brutality, and being by chance or trick
Cheated of revenge on her desert lover, he endured small deaths
in his mind, atrophied spots, like mouse-holes
For the casual malice of things to creep in uncountered: so
shortened by refusal of a fair act, Thurso
Rode up from the shore in the frown of fortune. (*CP* 2: 227)

The passage begins with an overt statement offered to the reader, one commenting on the unfortunate consequences of an extreme, and hence unhealthy, self-control. But soon it shades into a more oblique narrative, one that traces the contours of Reave's thinking and returns attention to the action of the poem. The narrator's aside, only briefly maintained, is nevertheless important because it not only comments upon a quality of the character but overtly urges, away from the action of the poem and without challenge, a particular observation about human nature. Moments like these, coupled with the occasional detachment of the authorial voice, establish a sometimes god-like point of view against which authority the characters—as they reveal their motivations by telling their own versions of past events—must be understood.

When usurping the role of narrator, it is the characters, not the authorial voice of the narrator, who create distance and establish their apparent independence. The clearest way to illustrate this is to compare the ways in which Reave and Helen each tell the story of the failed lime-works.[3] Reave's version comes first. He has destroyed the long-suffering family dog with a gunshot. Helen uses the occasion to wonder why Reave should be so ready to have "helped" the animal and yet so condemning of his father who had helped himself:

> "We may help out the beasts, but a man mustn't be beaten.
> That was a little too easy, to pop himself off because he went
> broke.
> I was ten years old, I tried not to despise the soft stuff
> That ran away to the dark from a touch of trouble:
> Because the lime-kilns failed and the lumber mill
> Ran out of redwood.
> My mother took up his ruins and made a farm;
> *She* wouldn't run away, to death or charity. Mark and I helped.
> We lost most of the land but we saved enough." (*CP* 2: 190–91)

Later, when returning from the hospital where Reave was taken after the accident, Helen asks him how his father died. Reave's only answer: "'Leave that'" (*CP* 2: 241).

As Reave relates it, the story vibrates with contempt for old Thurso's suicide, but it is a contempt based upon Reave's own will to live and of the courage that sustains it. Reave makes this clear by juxtaposing the responses of his parents to troubled times: the father is made of "'soft stuff / That ran away, to the dark'"; the mother "' . . . wouldn't run away, to death or charity.'" There is more than a young man's bitterness for a past abandonment; there is a touch of admiration for the spirit of a mother who "made a farm," a commitment to work and to life that Reave consciously emulates. If Reave is too hard on his father—he will not even talk directly of the suicide—he balances this negative intolerance by embracing the positive values demonstrated by his mother. This version of the story, then, confirms Reave to be a man with a fierce will shaped by an inflexible and an unforgivingly strict code of behavior.

Later in the poem, Helen tells a partial version of the story to Hester:

> Helen looked up, cliff over cliff, the great naked hill
> All of one rifted rock covering the northwest sky; and said: "It's called Thurso's Landing. That's something,
> To have the standing sea-cliffs named after you. His father used to swing down the barrels of lime
> From the head of that to the hulls of ships. The old wrecks of rusting engines are still to be seen up there
> And the great concrete block that anchors the cable. I hope you'll stay
> To see it come down." (*CP* 2: 223)

Where Reave sees only failure, Helen sees accomplishment, admiring the remains of what old Thurso built in his lifetime. For her, even old Thurso's ruins left a more lasting legacy than what she has from her own father: "'*My* dad never owned anything. / While I worked in a laundry and while I crated fruit / He ate my wages and lived as long as he could / And died crying'" (*CP* 2: 191). Her version also displays more imagination than Reave's, focusing partly on old Thurso as an active man who ". . . used to swing down the barrels of lime / From the head of that to the hulls of ships." Helen's narrative creates a more vital version of Reave's father. But it also establishes what at this point is a fundamental difference between her and Reave, since in her version she does not take the trouble to condemn the elder Thurso's suicide.

These versions of the past—that given by the authorial voice, that given by Reave, and that given by Helen—more or less agree as to the facts of old Thurso's failed business and his suicide, but the attitudes conveyed by the narrators of these stories are much different. Reave is bitter and condemning, Helen is admiring and apparently understanding, and the omniscient narrator's stance (unsurprisingly) is disinterested, focused on the failure of the works, not the man. These differences certainly explain something about the values that motivate the characters, especially Reave's respect for courage and endurance and his tolerance for pain that results from that respect. But these differences also establish separate narrative points of view that, on first glance, are not easily reconciled one with the others. In this way, "Thurso's Landing" appears to take the form of a dialogical narrative in which the individual characters resist the authority of a single, unifying authorial voice.[4] Or do they?

One important obstacle to reading the poem exclusively as a dialogical narrative is that the independence of the characters is compromised by those moments in the poem when they unconsciously share figurative language, either with each other or with the authorial voice. Helen, for example, declares a desert auto-camp to be like a ship, "'everything smells / In spite of neatness'" (*CP* 2: 207). Not long after, she fears that people who will die dream of a ship (*CP* 2: 208). She relates her fear to her confidant Mark (*CP* 2: 214) and fulfills the metaphor later, when she tells Hester, "'If I could just imagine what's good, or even / What's bad, you'd see the machine move like a ship'" (*CP* 2: 221). For Helen, the ship metaphor conveys forward movement and culmination, but also death.

Against this background, the reader finds Reave unconsciously echoing the same theme when he chooses the identical vehicle to convey a different idea. Referring to a future moment when he will cut the cable, Reave tells his mother, "'Our ship sails when I cut the cable'" (*CP* 2: 229). Reave means to say that the job of removing the offending relics of his father's failure will liberate himself and his family. But thanks to Helen's earlier words, Reave's choice of figure portends something entirely different and clearly links the fate of the two characters together. More important, however, when characters share figurative language in this way, readers are reminded of the artifice of the poem and so are not likely to regard the voices of individual characters as autonomous, in dialogue with and equal to the authorial voice of the poem.

This kind of link occurs not only horizontally between characters but also vertically between characters and the authorial voice. Early in the poem the narrator describes Mill Creek Canyon:

> . . . like a crack in the naked root of a dead pine when the bark peels off. The bottom
> Of the fissure was black with redwood, and lower
> Green with alders; between the black and the green the painted roof of the farmhouse, like a dropped seed,
> Thurso's house, like a grain of corn in the crack of a plank, where the hens can't reach it. (184)

The description lends perspective to the cabin and the landscape surrounding it by comparing them to a grain of corn in a crack, effectively conveying the distance of the narrator from the immediate scene of events. Helen, who has sometimes shared this kind of perspective,[5] also shares the language. To Hester (banished by Reave from the headland after his wife's return) Helen declares, "'You wouldn't stay in this wretched crack / Between two rocks?'" (*CP* 2: 222).

Of course Helen cannot achieve the same degree of distance, cannot see into the consciousness of others, cannot transcend her own drama. But her use of figurative language does demonstrate an essential sympathy with the authorial voice of the surrounding narration, which itself compromises her autonomy once again by reminding readers of the artifice of the poem. As the characters and the authorial voice share figurative language, this essential sympathy develops among them, a sympathy that becomes a positive unity as Reave and Helen respectively espouse and accept the explicit values expressed throughout the poem by the authorial voice. As we have seen, these values are chiefly expressed through narrative intrusions, two of which are here especially significant. The first occurs just as Reave Thurso is being fetched back to the Mill Creek farm after his hospital stay. As the farm truck approaches the headland, the narrator's voice turns aside from the action to address the reader:

No life
Ought to be thought important in the weave of the world,
whatever it may show of courage or endured pain;
It owns no other manner of shining, in the broad gray eye of the
ocean, at the foot of the beauty of the mountains
And skies, but to bear pain; for pleasure is too little, our
inhuman God is too great, thought is too lost. (*CP* 2: 242)

For Jeffers—and presumably for the authorial voice he creates here—nature is literally the sensible sign of the vital processes that lace the "weave of the world" with no discernible purpose. Compared to the inhuman God, no single human being nor even all of humanity can claim significance, especially since beside the "gray eye of the ocean" and the "beauty of the mountains / And skies" even human thought is lost, too puny to have a lasting impact. The theme of human insignificance is already apparent in the perspective that Helen and the authorial voice have shared throughout the poem. Here that perspective is stated in starkly unequivocal terms, and in terms that place in relief Reave's tragedy against the imposing backdrop of natural phenomena.

Something of the same perspective is conveyed in a second important intrusion near the end of the poem. Helen has poisoned herself and left the mother to carry on with the wearying business of life and misfortune:

> "The platform is like a rough plank theatre-stage
> Built on the brow of the promontory: as if our blood had labored all around the earth from Asia
> To play its mystery before strict judges at last, the final ocean and sky, to prove our nature
> More shining than that of the other animals. It is rather ignoble in its quiet times, mean in its pleasures,
> Slavish in the mass; but at stricken moments it can shine terribly against the dark magnificence of things." (*CP* 2: 278)

This second passage compares the headland to a theater stage, a conceit that is extended to personify the ocean and sky as "'strict judges.'" But it is the authorial voice itself that lends to the human drama the strictest judgment of all: humanity is ignoble, mean, and "slavish in the mass." Yet the language also lends a positive shading to two human capacities, the extraordinary ability to tolerate pain and the quality of courage. Both these capacities have already been exemplified by Reave's rejection of his father's suicide and his own painful, unalleviated suffering after his accident.

Reave, of course, is bound by his own beliefs to a kind of aggressive vitality. After Mark's suicide, Reave compares the world to a stone, "'. . . for no reason falling in the night from a cliff in the hills, that makes a lonely / Noise and a spark in the hollow darkness, and nobody sees and nobody cares. There's nothing good in it / Except the courage not to be beaten'" (*CP* 2: 261). Reave thus renews his intention to bear his own pain and decries the seductive peace of self-inflicted death. At the same time he recognizes that in the eyes of an inhuman god such courage will win no approval since "nobody sees and nobody cares." Through such declarations and through his willingness to suffer, Reave achieves a kind of integrity that fulfills his strict code: he will not even take drugs for the pain lest he dull that sensation by which his life takes its meaning.

The authorial voice has declared that too violent self-control is unlucky; but through that self-control—and the unwavering rejection of his father's and Mark's suicide—Reave becomes the self-conscious exemplar of a life that has no other manner of shining "but to bear pain." In his actions he has fulfilled the potential that the authorial voice has sketched for humanity. Eventually, and despite his implacable self-control, his own voice and his actions come to reflect closely the same values declared by the narrator. Indeed, at times Reave's pronouncements to other characters are indistinguishable in kind from those directed to the reader by the authorial voice. By the end of the poem, even Helen—who once wished only for jewels and furs (*CP* 2: 246)—seems to choose actions in tune with these values.

Living with the Thurso family is to live in isolation: not much activity, not much to nurture the imagination of a woman like Helen. Under these circumstances, to call her self-absorbed is perhaps extreme. Yet throughout most of the poem her mind centers on herself, on escaping the confining circumstances of her marriage and living once again in a world that the Thursos, in Mark's words, are "well without . . ." (174). After Reave returns with her from the Arizona desert, her smoldering contempt for him directs her purpose. She tells Mark, "'I used to think / That the only good thing is a good time: I've got past that . . . / Into the dark. I need something, I can't know what it is.' She thought in her heart: 'I know. / To humble your strong man, that's what I need'" (*CP* 2: 215). But after Reave's accident, Helen begins to see Reave's native determination with more clarity, understanding that a powerful conviction as well as a powerful stubbornness moves him to proclaim, "'I have my own law / That I will keep, and not die despising myself'" (*CP* 2: 248). And though she still feels contempt, her purposes become more complex, even as she resolves to end Reave's suffering by killing him with a rifle.

She fails to carry through, for Reave, "damning her act with remote absolute merciless comprehension," tricks her into moving too close and knocks her off balance (253). Robert Zaller has recognized that Helen's motives are various: "Love and hate are now inextricably mingled in her, pity for Reave's agony, shame for his helplessness, rage at his persistence" (102). Her motives become more focused, however, as the poem continues, and Helen ultimately demonstrates a new faithfulness to Reave, one that she had earlier proclaimed, perhaps with some irony: "'I'll never leave him. I promised him never to leave him and I've grown faithful / At last'" (245).

Helen cancels this irony at the end of the poem. After having Reave carried to the top of the headland where he can see the Pacific stretching westward, she offers him a kiss, and as their lips meet, she drags a knife across his throat and thereby ends Reave's terrible suffering. At the same time Helen accepts his burden: she tells Reave's mother that she has swallowed an especially caustic poison—"'The little tablets / I used for fear of having a baby, in our happy time'" (*CP* 2: 276)—in order to feel for a little while before her death the intensity of pain that Reave had struggled to tame. Helen's death is not an escape from life; she thinks of it as a tribute to Reave. As she expresses her only disappointment, she also demonstrates how completely she has accepted Reave's values, even as she falls short of fulfilling them: "'I can't / Be silent in pain like Reave: Oh, I did hope to'" (277).

At the end of the telling of "Thurso's Landing," Reave, Helen, and the authorial voice have shown themselves more or less in accord: by recognizing and valuing the terrible beauty in the "shining" suffering of human beings, their sometime tolerance for pain, their potential for the stubborn endurance required by living, these voices together emphasize an important theme of the poem, "death often desirable, but always to be resisted" (Jeffers, *Themes* 4). That Helen fails the ultimate test by choosing suicide is not an individual challenge to this idea; it is instead a demonstration of human weakness and an illustration that not everyone shares the same capacity for great suffering, whatever one may believe about its value. In this light and despite its undeniable dialogical dimensions—the competing narrative voices and their initially differing values—"Thurso's Landing" ultimately is less like a dialogical narrative and more like a story that on its own terms significantly borrows from an older tradition, that of the epic. Let me close by telling why I think this is the case.

One of the abiding critical challenges of reading Jeffers is coming to some conclusion about the relationship of his work to that of his (these days more canonical) contemporaries. In his Foreword to the 1938 *Selected Poetry*, Jeffers himself emphasized the differences: "[Modern poetry] was becoming slight and fantastic, abstract, unreal, eccentric; and was not even saving its own soul, for these are generally anti-poetic qualities" (xiv). But recent critics have begun to notice the similarities. Robert DeMott speaks in terms of kinships: like T. S. Eliot, Jeffers believed in the decline of the West; like William Carlos Williams, he attempted to see life without the obstructions of religious belief, to see nature as a constant force in human life, to use the principle of "decreation" (408–09). John Elder has also noticed the kinship with Eliot, pointing out that both poets reject urban, technological culture (14). These kinships derive from a common negative impulse, a shared disgust with modern civilization and an attendant desire to clear it away, the ecological idea of "breaking down" (Elder 209). But in Jeffers's case there is, I think, something else, too: an urge to express a positive set of values that adopted would help readers see how to avoid the civilized corruption that in

"Shine, Perishing Republic" Jeffers claims "Never has been compulsory" (*CP* 1: 15).

In this aspect of affirmation, Jeffers shows himself to be kin to another of his contemporaries, Ezra Pound, with whom he shared an abiding faith in the rhetorical power of poetry. Compare the epigraph to this essay with this declaration by Pound: "Most good prose arises, perhaps, from an instinct of negation; is the detailed convincing analysis of something detestable; of something which one wants to eliminate. Poetry is the assertion of a positive, i.e. of desire, and endures for a longer period" (324).

Jeffers's "passionate solution" is kith and kin to Pound's "assertion of a positive," each in its way a formulation of the didactic potential of verse. Together these formulations suggest the spiritual sympathy of these two poets for the unfailingly didactic tradition of epic poetry. That Pound purposefully sought to extend this tradition is a commonplace: his famous definition of an epic—"a poem including history"—undergirds the structure of the *Cantos*. In the case of "Thurso's Landing," Jeffers can be thought to be participating in the epic tradition in his own way.[6]

The most important element of an epic is its didactic dimension, which, if arguably present in all poetry, is, according to Michael Bernstein, deliberately stressed in the epic (14). As we have seen in "Thurso's Landing," instruction is accomplished by means of the narrative asides and by the voices of the characters themselves, as they come to accept and to demonstrate the values asserted by the authorial voice. Reave Thurso, moreover, provides a kind of epic hero—flawed by native stubbornness but redeemed by a strict code of behavior—by which readers can measure their own attitudes, especially about their place in a larger, indifferent cosmos and their capacities for understanding and coping with a civilization better "kept out."

Two other elements of the epic tradition also emerge from reading the poem, but these are substantially transformed. From the *Iliad* and *Odyssey* to *Paradise Lost*, an epic poem features a dominant voice upholding the values significant to its community while it speaks to an audience of this community's citizens. How can this be the case with "Thurso's Landing," a poem with precious little sympathy for any human community? The answer lies in considering what the notion of community might mean in Jeffers's poems.

In his poetry, as in his life, Jeffers usually focused his attention upon family relations, exploring the tensions and the rewards of this most basic and, with all its faults, this most natural and successful form of human congress. In this respect, the family represents a kind of community that despite its small size achieves the kind of scale natural to epic verse: for not only is the family a universal expression of relationships of biology and blood, in Jeffers's verse it becomes the only possible platform for declaiming and upholding transcendent values, because, in Jeffers's view, larger human communities are foredoomed human communities. Helen Thurso expresses this clearly: "' . . . sometime / San Francisco and New York and Chicago will fall / On the heads of their ghosts . . .'" (*CP* 2: 236). In the world of "Thurso's Landing," great human achievements pale beside the shining of a single human being, whose own suffering is significant because it exemplifies an attitude toward living and dying that is not contemptible. The epic scale and the notion of community are naturally readjusted, then, to accommodate the immediate world of Jeffers's inhumanist hero and the value of the family community.

Regarding "Thurso's Landing" as a poem that borrows significantly from the epic tradition is not, of course, to claim it to be the same thing as an epic poem. Jeffers's narrative poems generally and "Thurso's Landing" particularly are too complex to be served well by sorting them according to a single scheme.[7] But attending to the narrative voices contained in the poem and considering their didactic implications does suggest that thinking of other Jeffers poems in terms of epic criteria will have at least a provisional and heuristic value. And it also suggests a new way to think of the congruencies between Jeffers's work and that of contemporaries like Pound, both of whom shared a faith in the power of poetry to convey their respective values.

Notes

1. In 1932 *Time* magazine featured Jeffers's face on its cover, claiming that "a considerable public now considers [Jeffers] the most impressive poet the U.S. has yet produced" ("Harrowed Marrow" 63); in the same year Lawrence Clark Powell brought out the first book-length study of Jeffers's work; and soon after, in 1933, S. S. Alberts produced his *Bibliography of the Works of Robinson Jeffers*, which Frederic Carpenter notes was issued by a commercial publisher just eight years after the publication of Jeffers's first book of poems, "a fact perhaps unique in the history of literature" (43).

2. Before the publication of *Thurso's Landing and Other Poems*, Jeffers wrote to T. R. Smith of Liveright revealing a possible motive for his

claim: "I want 'Thurso's Landing' to be published promptly, partly because it seems to me the best thing I have written yet and I don't want it lying around so long; partly because too long a vacation is not good advertising; my income has been cut a little, like other people's, while taxes increase" (*SL* 185).

3. For an analysis of another important dimension of these stories see Robert Zaller (57–61; 100–04) who fully traces the Freudian implications of Reave's relationship to his dead father.

4. Here I refer to Mikhail Bakhtin's influential description of dialogic narrative, which regards characters as independent of authorial control and ultimately indeterminate. In dialogical works, then, characters and author deploy different but equal voices in a continuing dialogue. Many of Jeffers's narratives are certainly susceptible to this kind of reading. Patrick Murphy's analysis of some Jeffers narratives reveals that no ultimately totalizing authorial voice is in control. But to me, using Bakhtin's ideas finally leads to limited readings of poems like "Thurso's Landing," since, as I intend to show below, the apparently autonomous characters eventually embrace the inhumanist values of the narrator. Nor should this be held against Jeffers as a modern creative artist. As Tzvetan Todorov makes clear in discussing the aesthetic merits of dialogic works, "There exists no literary method whose use obligatorily produces an aesthetic experience" (68).

5. Helen often remarks on the perspective lent by distance. For example, looking from atop the headland upon Reave, who has been searching somewhere below for a wounded deer, she says to Rick Armstrong, "'Look down there: / What size Reave Thurso is really: one of those dirty black ants that come to dead things could carry him / With the deer added'" (*CP* 2: 180–81).

6. Discussions of epic often founder upon apparently rigid criteria ultimately derived from the traditional epics of Homer: a grand style, a setting ample in scale, a hero of great importance who performs superhuman deeds and in whom the gods take an interest, and a public voice directed at the citizens for whom the epic embodies the beliefs of their community. But J. B. Hainsworth argues that such criteria are derived from very few examples and are really wide generalizations (4). Michael Bernstein overcomes these problems by adopting an approach to defining "epic" inspired by Wittgenstein's analogy of "family likeness." He names four "characteristics"—that the epic presents a narrative of the audience's own heritage, that the dominant narrative voice will function as speaker for values generally significant for communal stability, that the audience will be a citizen in a social nexus, and that the element of instruction will be deliberately foregrounded. But in the spirit of Wittgenstein, Bernstein argues that no single epic need exhibit all the

qualities usually associated with the genre and that the presence of one feature does not ensure that a given poem will qualify as an epic (14). The subsequent discussion, then, will adapt slightly these ideas developed in greater detail by Bernstein in his study of the *Cantos* (12–15).

7. Allan Rodway notes that typing a poem according to some particular genre scheme is less important than using genre criteria heuristically, to see what emerges in the analysis (91).

Works Cited

CP *The Collected Poetry of Robinson Jeffers*. Ed. Tim Hunt. 3 vols. to date. Stanford, CA: Stanford UP, 1988, 1989, 1991.

SL *The Selected Letters of Robinson Jeffers, 1897–1962*. Ed. Ann N. Ridgeway. Baltimore: Johns Hopkins UP, 1968.

SP *The Selected Poetry of Robinson Jeffers*. New York: Random, 1959 (1938).

Alberts, S. S. *A Bibliography of the Works of Robinson Jeffers*. 1933. New York: Franklin, 1968.

Bakhtin, Mikhail. *The Dialogic Imagination*. Trans. Michael Holquist and Caryl Emerson. Ed. Michael Holquist. Austin: U of Texas P, 1981.

Bernstein, Michael. *The Tale of the Tribe: Ezra Pound and the Modern Verse Epic*. Princeton: Princeton UP, 1980.

Carpenter, Frederic. *Robinson Jeffers*. New York: Twayne, 1962.

DeMott, Robert. "Robinson Jeffers' 'Tamar.'" *In the Twenties: Fiction, Poetry, Drama*. Ed. Warren French. Deland, FL: Everett/Edwards, 1975. 405–25.

Elder, John. *Imagining the Earth: Poetry and the Vision of Nature*. Urbana: U of Illinois P, 1985.

Hainsworth, J. B. *The Idea of Epic*. Berkeley: U of California P, 1991.

"Harrowed Marrow." *Time* 4 April 1932: 63–64.

Jeffers, Robinson. *Themes in My Poems*. San Francisco: Book Club of California, 1956.

Murphy, Patrick D. "Reclaiming the Power: Robinson Jeffers's Verse Novels." *Western American Literature* (1987): 125–48.

Pound, Ezra. *Literary Essays of Ezra Pound*. Ed. T. S. Eliot. Norfolk, CT: New Directions, 1954.

Powell, Lawrence Clark. *Robinson Jeffers: The Man and His Work*. Rev. ed. Pasadena: San Pasqual P, 1940.

Rodway, Allan. "Generic Criticism: The Approach through Type, Mode, and Kind." *Contemporary Criticism*. Stratford-Upon-Avon

Studies 12. Ed. Malcolm Bradbury and David Palmer. New York: St. Martins, 1970. 83–105.

Todorov, Tzvetan. *Introduction to Poetics.* Trans. Richard Howard. Minneapolis: U of Minnesota P, 1981.

Vardamis, Alex A. *The Critical Reputation of Robinson Jeffers.* Hamden, CT: Archon Books, 1972.

Zaller, Robert. *The Cliffs of Solitude: A Reading of Robinson Jeffers.* Cambridge: Cambridge UP, 1983.

5

Jeffers's "Roan Stallion" and the Narrative of Nature

Tim Hunt

Robinson Jeffers's narrative poems were in large part the basis of his initial success in the mid-1920s. The sweep of their long lines was in striking contrast to the compressed, fragmented surface of much Modernist experiment, and their plots—often turning on incest and sexual violence—were compelling at least in part because they were shocking. But, overall, the narratives have been a problematic factor in Jeffers's reputation. For one thing, by the mid-1920s most serious readers of poetry no longer considered the narrative a viable form, and Jeffers's use of it seemed to mark him as a poetic reactionary in a generation of poetic radicals. For another, later generations of readers have been less shocked by the narratives' actions and correspondingly more bothered by their seemingly excessive nature and tone. As a result, some have rejected Jeffers altogether as a serious figure, while others, Robert Boyers, for instance, have chosen to defend his work by trying to shift attention from the narratives (which Jeffers assumed were his main claim to significance) to his lyrics and short meditations. This impulse is certainly understandable; the best of the shorter pieces do have an exemplary austerity and an impressive control of rhetoric and pace. But dismissing the narratives is a mistake, in spite of the problems they present. If they are the main impediment to establishing Jeffers as one of the major poets of his generation, they are, at the same time, the best means to make that case.

Various readings of the narratives have been advanced in recent years. Robert Brophy has explored their mythic elements and ritual structures; Robert Zaller has developed a psychoanalytic reading of them; Patrick Murphy has suggested they be approached dialogically as "verse novels"; and most recently William Everson has argued that the narratives are for Jeffers (and through him for the reader) a form of religious action. Much, though, remains to be done. I suspect, for instance, that we would learn a good deal about the nature of Jeffers's narrative practice and its implications by following out his own hints in later years (in the Introduction to the 1935 Modern Library reissue of *Roan Stallion, Tamar and Other Poems*, for instance) that his turn to narrative was at least partly shaped by his rejection of Imagism and early Modernist attempts at a poetry of collage. Such an investigation might well show us that Jeffers thought of narrative—at least his approach to it—as a radical aesthetic gesture, however much it might differ from the radicalism and experiment of his Modernist contemporaries. In this piece, though, I want to concentrate on the way Jeffers's sense of nature helps explain his particular approach to narrative. In particular, I want to suggest that his sense of nature and his strategies for narration are inextricably linked, that recognizing this link can give us additional ways to account for the violence of the poems, and that this can help us clarify what our stake in this violence may be as readers. For the sake of space my focus will be one of Jeffers's briefer and most admired narratives, "Roan Stallion," first published in 1925 in *Roan Stallion, Tamar and Other Poems*.

Jeffers's view of nature was likely shaped in part by his graduate work in biology while a medical student, his graduate work in forestry, and his general interest in the discoveries of astronomy and physics in the early years of the century. These encounters immersed him in systems that celebrated levels of order and conflict beyond the human will, and his investment in them likely complicated his search for his voice as a poet. His earliest collection, *Flagons and Apples* (1912), shows him straining to adopt the aestheticism of the Pre-Raphaelites and turn-of-the-century verse, a gesture fully in character for poets of his generation in their apprentice work, but one complicated for him by such antithetical lessons as Darwin's. While art affirmed (or was supposed to) that imagination and human making were central, science did not. And the often stilted, self-conscious quality of these early poems may reflect not simply Jeffers's uncertainties about the nature and validity of poetry in a world defined partly by the perspective of science but also his tendency at this point to write poems more as an attempt to escape these uncertainties than to engage them.[1] It took Jeffers some years to realize that he could incorporate the perspectives of science into his poetry—that indeed his double allegiance gave him little choice in the matter. And in part his turn to narrative reflects his search for a mode that would allow him to explore the complexities of his desire to affirm beauty and human meaning and yet also affirm his recognition of the insignificance of human desire and will in the natural order that science revealed.

By the time of "Roan Stallion," the view of nature Jeffers had derived at least partly from his engagement with science had become fundamental, both thematically and formally, to his narrative work. In the mature poems nature figures as a kind of ultimate reality that comprehends the physical world and life's different orders into a single all-encompassing organism that we know, to the extent that we can know it, both by its materiality and by its perpetual alternation of destruction and renewal.[2] In particular, Jeffers is compelled by this quality of transformation, and his focus on it is largely the way he moves beyond the positivism of late nineteenth-century science to formulate a "nature" that is both scientific and aesthetic. In a key 1920 lyric, "Continent's End," he images nature as both an ultimate material process—"tides of fire"—and simultaneously as a unifying awareness—"the eye that watched"—produced by this flux, bound to it, yet comprehending and transcending it. Nature, that is, is more than matter and process; it is the energy behind them and an awareness emerging from them. As such it is (at least at this level of abstraction) both material and ideal.

The dualism in this vision of nature (nature as a material process/nature as transcendent awareness) helps shape Jeffers's approach to narrative. Nature's vision of itself—that full simultaneity of participation in the flux of being and transcending consciousness—is only partially and intermittently available to us as individuals. Only nature at its ultimate, as God, can unify experiencing and knowing, and even for God, knowing cannot be separated from the experience of destruction and renewal, a process which we can imagine at the human level only as a kind of suffering. And even at this ultimate level that Jeffers imagines, nature cannot fully know itself; it cannot translate itself into knowledge, since that would require being able to escape the transformations that are its basic condition. Jeffers's sense of nature, that is, allows the action of knowing but does not allow translating knowing into something as final and fixed as knowledge; that would abstract knowing from being. Knowing can only emerge from experience and is dialectically bound to it.

At the human level, our ability to be and to know nature is necessarily less than nature's own, and human knowing is further compromised in Jeffers's view by our desire to blind ourselves to our participation in the flux of being and to substitute the illusion of knowledge for the risk, pain, and redemption of knowing (a knowing that is at best partial and temporary because of our human limits). As such, knowing is most likely when circumstances compel us to confront the flux of our being—our immersion in the "tides of fire." The other possibility is to enter these "tides" willingly, and this is a key to Jeffers's narrative practice. Through imaginative imitation (a form of participation in nature), we can imitate nature and partly discover/experience its terms, its paradoxical unity. We can enter the "tides of fire" and momentarily know "the eye that watched." Partly because of its capacity for scope and partly because it could be used to enact process, narrative offered Jeffers this potential for imitation and discovery.

Narrative was for Jeffers, then, a way to probe the limits of our ability to experience nature's reality and our capacity to become conscious of it. It was a strategy for using the figures of the poem to imitate and enter nature's process and thereby draw both poet and reader into moments that might temporarily approximate nature's simultaneity of being and knowing. As such, his narratives are not, as most narratives are, stories about characters but rather "stories" about nature. As Jeffers himself later noted,

> one reason for writing narrative poetry . . . [is that] . . . certain scenes awake an emotion that seems to overflow the limits of lyric or description, [and] one tries to express it in terms of human lives. Thus each of my too many stories has grown up like a plant from some particular canyon or promontory, some particular relationship of rock and water, wood, grass and mountain. (*Jeffers Country* 10)

The characters, that is, serve to express nature, not the reverse; they are images that reveal nature's flux, their actions enact that flux, and the pain of their being exists to engage us in nature's process and bring us through it to the momentary and partial simultaneity of being and knowing which is as close as we can come to nature's ceaseless simultaneity of the "tides of fire" and "the eye that watched."

As such the characters and their acts are a means to nature, not ends in themselves, and we seldom identify with them as people even when they are at their most compelling. In a way this relative lack of identification seems to invite a kind of passive speculation that would undercut the process of participation the poems must enact to be successful, but the poems, as Jeffers suggests, take their basic emotion, not from the characters, but from "scenes" and from what they "awake" for the poet and through the poet for the reader. The consciousness at stake in the narratives is not, that is, the consciousness of the characters so much as the consciousness of nature, poet, and reader, and becoming too involved in the characters as individuals would actually tend to reinforce the exclusively human perspective, the blindness, the poems attempt to counteract. The key point here is that Jeffers's narratives are, in effect, dramas of consciousness, and they take their particular energy from the tensions Jeffers finds in human consciousness.

For Jeffers consciousness figures as both a kind of redemption and a kind of damnation—perhaps more a redemption intertwined with a damnation. It awakens us to nature's beauty and gives us the power to identify with and participate in its transcendence. But this identification—and the transcendence—is always partial and temporary since consciousness is also self-awareness. Unlike the organisms and objects about us, we are always at least partly aware of ourselves; we know nature from our individual and collective perspective as one of its parts. We can see neither the whole nor what it would be like to see as the whole, and our sense of the beauty comes only from participating in nature's flux. As a result, the actual transcendence of knowing is always rooted in our recognition of the pain of being, mortality, and our own insignificance as individuals and species. In Jeffers there is no final escape from being, and this sense of being beyond time yet in it prevents us from participating fully in the flux of the moment. It alienates us from the being it enables us to know and celebrate. Just as being precludes full knowing, knowing precludes full being. Only God (the power that acts through and is nature) escapes the paradox and is fully both. At best, as Jeffers said in a different context, we are "the ape of that God" ("Apology for Bad Dreams"). We can imitate but not attain God's being and awareness. This is both the despair of the human condition and its significance. For in our aping we may momentarily realize nature—our pain in it and the beauty of and beyond it. By glimpsing the whole, we may at moments grasp, yet escape, our mortality.

As such, the narratives deflect the kind of identification we expect to have with the characters as a way of relocating human intensity, not denying it. In the narratives, that is, we identify less with the characters Jeffers creates than (through them) with the poet's and our own struggle to enter nature's flux through his imaginary characters. Thus, much of the actual force of the poems comes from our participation in the narrator's evolving relationship to his characters and changing distance to them. This is what draws us into nature and consciousness and convinces us that the poems start from Jeffers's own intensity (as they must if they are to reach the pitch of knowing). This does not mean, however, that the narratives are a kind of covert confession or the sort of self-reflexive gesture we associate with more recent literary experiments. If they were either, the focus would be, finally, on the poet's personality, and the poems would leave us as locked in the human world, as isolated from nature, as focusing on the personality of the characters would. What it does suggest is that the poems are a real process, though an imaginary world, through which we join the poet as he apes God and through which we come to exist and know within the same general limits he does.

Many of Jeffers's narratives explore characters whose views of the world deny nature's fundamental force. These are often ranch people a generation removed from the frontier and their parents' Protestant certainty. In spite of the intense beauty of the landscape they inhabit (the Big Sur coast and mountains of California), their world has been shaped more by society, culture, and history than by the land they work, and as a result they experience the land (or at least the society it supports) as constriction and deprivation, even when they value the escape from town and city that it seems to afford. In these poems the central characters typically discover the nature they have denied and are destroyed by it when its power shatters the false consciousness they have erected between themselves and it. In "Roan Stallion," though, Jeffers uses a different sort of figure to approach nature: a woman, California, who seems so fully part of the landscape through which she moves that she all but embodies it. For her, society is the distant abstraction, nature the immediate presence, and she, unlike her counterparts in the other narratives, has experienced the terms of being, not denied them. But in spite of this grounding, she too must suffer and discover. Although she participates in nature, she has not actually faced its problematic implications—she has not yet become conscious. Nature for her is still something to be known, and she must, like the figures in the other narratives, discover the fracture between being and knowing. For her, though, her different route to the moment of vision alters both what she suffers and what she discovers. Instead of the violence of nature, she suffers what might be termed the violence of consciousness, and for her the fracture between being and knowing is something she experiences as a momentary realization of what Jeffers would call God.

Ironically, California's simplicity as a figure is the basic problem in writing the poem and reading it. Although California's immediacy, her lack of introspection, immerses her in nature's flux, it also makes her largely unknowable to herself and others. It (including her relatively limited resources for self-expression) stands as a kind of preconsciousness that poet, narrator, and reader are already too distanced from nature and too self-aware to experience directly; we can only infer something of her world from her actions. Actually, it would be more accurate to say that we know her through the narrator's (largely implicit) actions, which make the poem, in effect, two processes: a tracing of California's discovery of the terms of being as she enters consciousness through her desire for the stallion and the narrator's own attempt to evoke her discovery in such a way that he (and we as readers) sufficiently set aside our own consciousness—yet without losing it—to enter her world. As such, the poem is paradoxically an attempt to lose, but not lose, consciousness through the process of California's gaining hers. As readers we can enter fully into neither process, but the interaction between the two becomes a kind of refraction that makes the process of consciousness (both the narrator's and California's) sufficiently real that we too confront the fracture between being and knowing. Through California (or, more properly, the poet's attempt to imagine her) we realize something of the tragic world (at least from the human perspective) of God's knowing through its own ceaseless transformations, its unfolding and dissolutions.

This complexity of narration in "Roan Stallion" is, as it must be, something we all but overlook. If we were to focus on it while reading the poem, we would lose our sense that California's struggle is real. But if we do not sense the narrator's attempt to imagine the character, project her world, and confront it, we would remain, finally, alienated from the poem's process. The poem, that is, must establish the "reality" of both the character's world and the narrator's (though subordinating the latter) if the poem is to work.

The poem's opening paragraphs demonstrate how Jeffers posits California's world as real yet invented, interpreted, and to be interpreted. Emphasizing sound and action, the opening lines treat the physical world as immediately present and all but transparent: "The dog barked; then the woman stood in the doorway, and hearing iron strike stone down the steep road / Covered her head with a black shawl and entered the light rain; she stood at the turn of the road" (*CP* 1: 179). Most obviously, this unit asserts

California's immediate reality; she hears and stands in the rain. Less obviously it signals our distance from this world. Although the dog's bark presumably calls the woman out, the narrator does not link sound and act. We are onlookers, not participants. We have the details, but not the context to interpret them, and for the narrator to offer California's thoughts at this point (for instance, California heard the dog bark and realized the wagon would soon be there) would lessen both the immediacy of this physical world and the impression that she (in her all but unconscious state) embodies and expresses it. These opening lines, that is, push us to suspend momentarily our habit of fitting whatever we encounter into a human and social frame, and to that extent they push us toward the immediacy of the perceptual world and are a first, if minor step, outside the world of consciousness into the world of being (though it should be noted that this world of being is not actually California's).

In part, though, the success of this opening unit is also a measure of its failing. Uninterpreted actions and details cannot draw us into California's world or establish its implications, but neither can interpretation, since its appeal to known patterns and values undercuts the immediacy of perception. Here again the opening lines are suggestive. A second look shows that they do not actually set interpretation aside altogether. Although the narrator simply juxtaposes the bark and the woman in the doorway, he does link her stepping into the rain to her "hearing iron strike." In part this marks the difficulty of setting aside our habits, but it also demonstrates how the narration itself becomes a part of the action. By offering the link, the narrator moves toward the world of his character and gives us what he imagines to be her perception and her reaction. He then leaves us to infer (as he has presumably done but as she does not need to do, since we react to our own perceptions more than we note and interpret them) that the sound of iron is a wheel of an unseen wagon. We are, that is, moving into a curious realm where we are in part outside the character and aware of a reality physically immediate and distinct from her yet inside and seeing through her perceptions (perceptions that are immediate enough that they seem, appropriately enough for the poem, prior to thought).

By itself the shift within the opening lines might seem inadvertent, or not there at all, but it anticipates the narrator's greater presence in the rest of the opening verse paragraph. The woman, we discover in the third line, is "nobly formed . . . erect and strong as a new tower" (*CP* 1: 179). These qualities help define her particular presence, but do so by stressing the kinds of abstractions the opening avoided, abstractions that reflect the narrator's world as much as the character's and that help justify the way the narrator next reifies her into a kind of regional emblem:

> . . . she was only a fourth part Indian; a Scottish sailor had
> planted her in young native earth,
> Spanish and Indian, twenty-one years before. He had named her
> California when she was born;
> That was her name; and had gone north. (*CP* 1: 179)

The narrator attributes the naming to the sailor, but the merger here of genealogy, history, and name—the hybrid California of the present and the earlier "native earth"—brings us out of the world as the character knows it, beyond the world of the sailor, and toward an allegorical dimension that can originate with the narrator, or poet. (The sailor may also have meant the name allegorically, but if so, the narrator's allegory here erases—rather, supplants—that earlier gesture.) This passage, then, extends our ability to interpret more than our ability to participate. It replaces perception with abstraction. But the effect is not, finally, of abstraction, because the implicitly interpretive motion within the first two lines has prepared us to experience interpretation as itself a motion that retrospectively extends the narrator's stake in his own material back to the beginning. We experience the narrator, that is, not simply as a source or place of interpretation but also as an action in the way he moves from recognizing a quality, "nobly formed," to interpreting it through the greater abstraction of the simile "strong as a new tower," to creating the incipient allegory that closes the passage. And taken as a whole the first verse paragraph casts the act of perception (which opens it) and the act of interpretation (which closes it) as complements that ground and intensify each other.

The narrator's changing relationship with his own imagining is an important part of the power of the "Roan Stallion." The process, though often implicit, creates the sense that we participate in California's world even as we know we stand outside it. This is something the opening of the second verse paragraph demonstrates. Like the poem's first lines, it imitates the sequence of California's perceptions as it presents the nearing horse and wagon, but these lines are richer because we read them as a kind of reaction to the first part's all but allegorical conclusion. Without seeming to violate California's perspective, the details are both her perceptions and the narrator's (and her own) implicit interpretations of them. For California the figure on the buggy seat, her husband Johnny, is literally twisted around to hold the stallion's halter. To us, the word "twisted" (suspended at the line's end for emphasis) and his eyes, "burnt-out" with "fortune in them" (*CP* 1: 179), combine to evoke his moral squalor and alienation from the vitality California represents even before we observe his exploitation of her. Moreover, Jeffers's approach to narration (whether we respond to it explicitly or implicitly) is more than a strategy to enrich our participation in the character and the details of her world. It is also a thematic factor. The narrator's interaction with the figures he presents makes him an implicit character in the poem; he exists not simply to relate an already made and interpreted set of elements but as a device to experience, discover, what is latent, inherent in the set. The story, that is, becomes two stories: the story of California and the stallion (foregrounded through most of the poem) and the story of the narrator who invents the elements of the first story, immerses himself in them, and struggles toward vision by means of them.

The second narrative (implicit early in the poem) becomes increasingly visible and significant as the narrator progressively deepens California's conflicted relationship to being and consciousness and as she and the narrator each move toward their intertwined moments of crisis and vision. In the first phase of the poem, the narrator is least involved and least visible. He invokes the figures, then (largely) stands aside as an observer and lets the realistic elements of California's basic situation drive the poem forward. The initial situation is a relatively simple one. Her husband, "an outcast Hollander . . . shriveled with bad living," wins a stallion by "luck" (*CP* 1: 180). For her, its power and beauty become an intensely troubling presence that measures the pathetic Johnny and her own compromises. Whether these compromises are by chance or design is not important; either way, the stallion confronts her with the limits of her own being, and her desire for it, or what it represents, impels her toward recognizing nature's power. Most simply the stallion leads her to discover that she can only be alive to her world, including the stallion's beauty, through consciousness (both the pain that produces it and the pain of consciousness itself).

At first, California desires the stallion but fails to recognize this. Instead, she resents it as an emblem of her own exploited condition. Like the tired buckskin mare Johnny leaves in her care, she works, goes without, and passively accepts male vanity and privilege. Although she does not yet consciously admit the implications of this, the narrator progressively fuses mare and woman into a single figure, as California first prepares the mare for the trip to Monterey and then returns. This is, again, in a sense the narrator's action; he draws an equivalency California would not (at least yet) accept or recognize. But in crossing the storm-flooded ford she responds in ways that presume the equivalency. Touching the mare's "animal surface" as it shakes "like the beat of a great heart," she imagines a "water-stallion" about to, as she puts it, "'curl over his woman'" (*CP* 1: 184). And for her the crossing becomes an experience of nature as a kind of sexual violence writ large (the water stallion's mating), even as it becomes an attempt to deny that realization through the appeal to the guiding innocence of baby Jesus (her vision of a baby surrounded by angels with "birds' heads, hawks' heads" and holding "A little snake with golden eyes" underscores the intensity and ambivalence of her vision) (*CP* 1: 185).

As the ford scene suggests, the identification of mare and woman is by no means a simple matter. It involves more than simile or metaphor. The woman is not like a mare; nor is she a mare (or the other way around). Either way of understanding the identification, for us as readers or for the woman herself, would impose human terms on it, reduce it to a symptom to be explained by some system or other, and thereby deny the vision's significance. Rather, mare and woman are alike in each expressing a more comprehensive, fluid, and powerful dynamic, in which the ongoing process of destruction and renewal, or energy becoming matter and matter energy, is like the sexual dynamic (rather the dynamic is like it). In this sense, the equation between mare and woman points to a reality that is neither of them but in which each participates. Significantly, California need not recognize this archetypal alignment for it to call forth water stallion (and possibly the archetype, if that is the best term for it, works only if she does not recognize it). But recognize it or not, the water stallion constellates the desires and fears the stallion represents but which she can neither express nor act on nor deny. The water stallion expresses, or, rather is, nature as power, and California's immersion, her figurative coupling with it, is a baptism into nature that then leads to the need for consciousness, and the beginning of consciousness brings her conflicts to the surface but in no sense resolves them.

In the first phase of the poem, then, the stallion initiates California's discovery of nature as power, but we see this discovery primarily through the narrator's imagery and her actions, because she herself is still not prepared to set aside her ambivalence and recognize what the stallion is and represents. In addition, she thinks through her senses. This, the root of her participation in nature, enables her to respond to the stallion but means she has few terms to represent her relationship to it or her confusion. The ford scene, though, not only confronts her with the world she has entered through her desire but also offers her for the first time metaphors, a vocabulary, to explore it, and this initiates the poem's second phase in which California's attempt to express the issues through the images she has experienced drives her further into her own being, further into consciousness, and to a second and more comprehensive merger with nature's power and a second and more volatile moment of vision.

In California's initial meditation after the ford scene (the start of the poem's second phase), she hates but does not hate the stallion; sees it as part, but not part, of Johnny's vanity; dismisses it as a mere animal, "too cheap to breed," yet fantasizes it "rang[ing] in freedom, / Shaking the red-roan mane for a flag on the bare hills" (*CP* 1: 187). Her growing awareness of her confusion and ability to express it is particularly evident when she describes her experience at the ford to her young daughter. A mare has been brought up to be serviced; California, though she wants to watch, stays indoors and tries to distract the child by telling "once more about the miracle of the ford" (*CP* 1: 187). However, in her account of how "the little Jesus" lighted her way to save her, she substitutes terms that evoke the water stallion, the figure that mediates her sense of the actual stallion. She inadvertently refers to the Virgin Mary as "'the stallion's wife,'" and God becomes first "a red-roan mane" "'rang[ing] on the bare blue hill of the sky,'" then "'the shining and the power. The power, the terror, the burning fire [that] covered her over,'" and then "'the hooves'" and "'terrible strength'" to which the Mary/stallion's wife gives herself "'without thinking'" (*CP* 1: 187–88). The account conflates California's vision at the ford, the biblical annunciation, her own intuition of the archetypal mating of divine and human as an inexpressible covering of power, and it fuses these elements into a story that begins to express the dynamic of being and define her possible participation in it. As such, it testifies to her increased awareness, but this awareness is itself complex and conflicted. As she comes to recognize nature's inherent power and flux, the "tides of fire," she also begins to sense that accepting this power means being "covered" not simply with "the shining and the power" but also the "burning." Her growing awareness of this potentially alienates her from being even as it draws her more fully, more consciously, into it; unlike the Mary/stallion's wife of her story who gives herself to "the hooves" "without thinking," California is already enmeshed in a form of thinking—her attempt to tell the story of her vision (more her attempt to tell her vision as a story?).

The way California nervously disavows these substitutions as she tells the story indicates both her partial understanding of what she senses and her intense ambivalence about it. She desires the flux of being yet intuits that "shining" and "strength" can be "terrible." The scene outside in the corral further intensifies her ambivalence; it is both an occasion for the stallion to be "The power, the terror, the burning fire" and yet an exploitative denial of that power—a mere transaction that celebrates (even as it indicts) Johnny's degraded and degrading pretense to the stallion's power. Ironically, Johnny himself underscores this disparity when he, after the stallion finishes, confronts California. His "face reddened as if had stood / Near fire, his eyes triumphing," he brags that he will return the following night and "'show her how the red fellow act, the big fellow'" (*CP* 1: 188). Johnny here confronts California with the split between his own debased use of the stallion to gratify his desire for personal power and her own sense (and selfless recognition) of its power as a form of beauty. Doing so, he inadvertently catalyzes her to act and precipitates her (and the narrator's) second visionary moment. Least important, he sets in motion the forces that destroy him.

In the scene that follows, California's actions again initially testify to her partial awareness of the nature and conflicted implications of her desire. Most simply, she wants to deny the cheap lust and mere reality of Johnny's world that constricts her much as the stallion's corral constricts its freedom. She wants to escape both the constriction and her own sense of the contradictions that enmesh her. She wants to escape to the "shining open" hills and the "enormous night" where she imagines she may find God "brooding his night" (*CP* 1: 190). In effect, she wants the ecstasy of the ford without the terror. She wants the peace outside the flux of being, the transcendence of "the eye that watched," a world with the "Father himself" that is prior to (or beyond) both the mating of the Mary/stallion's wife with the "burning fire" and her own empty servicing of Johnny—acts which, like the stallion serving as stud, evoke the larger flux that sexual desire points to and in part expresses. At the same time her choice of the stallion to carry her to see "the Father . . . brooding his night" shows that her flight is also toward the dimension of the vision at the ford which was its terror and which she now in part desires. She wants not only to see God but to become the stallion's wife, to mate with God. This, though, is something she cannot explicitly admit without confronting the stallion's beauty and power as both the agency of her desire for God and the God she desires. She cannot, that is, admit that the stallion has come to be for her God's embodiment or God itself (a distinction perhaps significant for us as readers but not for her) without also affirming a desire to immerse herself in the "tides of fire." Still, it is no accident that her image of God quickly shifts from a "brooding" "Father" sitting "cross-legged, chin in hand" to a figure "Leaping the hills, shaking the red-roan mane for a flag" (*CP* 1: 190).

Simply describing California's story (both the one she imagines and the one she acts out) and her images for it suggest that "Roan Stallion" is inherently allegorical, but these elements do not, finally, construct an allegory; that would imply that the narrator (or the poet) had a godlike ability to stand outside the flux of being and use the mediation of the work to interpret the world from a secure and transcendent position. Such authority, though, would divorce being from knowing and deny their interdependence. It would affirm one at the expense of the other. This is not to argue that "Roan Stallion" is without an allegorical dimension but to suggest that it functions as a means to an end. It is not a frame containing the poem's significance. Instead, the allegorical is a capacity the narrator uses to begin to bring nature's terms into consciousness, and these terms then become, like the terms he has California invent for her own conflicted desire, both potentially enabling and disabling. They can be evaded, or they can be engaged and overturned through the risk of action, violational action. The allegory, that is, exists to be outstripped, and it must be if the poem is to imitate nature's process and enable narrator/poet/reader to approach God's simultaneity of being and knowing. This means that the poet must refuse the temptation to use the poem to enact meanings in the usual sense and instead use it to enact himself through the figures he creates. Moreover, he must do so by immersing himself (in as total and voluntary a manner as God does) into their being and consciousness—including the violational excess—and committing himself to it. Failing to do this would reduce the poem to encoded (and false) knowledge and make it a trap, an illusory escape from the conditions of being and consciousness.

In "Roan Stallion" the narrator/poet's moment of crisis coincides with California's own and takes the form of two extended passages that interrupt the narrative. The first provides the transition to the poem's third phase and bridges between Johnny's threat to be "the big fellow" on his return and California's ride into the hills. The second coincides with (actually substitutes for) California's momentary and violational union with the stallion/God. In both, the narrator speaks in his own alternately lyric and declamatory voice. In part the comments gloss the process California enacts, but, more important, these breaks in the story invite us to see it as something the narrator has invented (and is inventing) out of his own need to push beyond his own conflicted desires. As such, the narrator's telling of the story—the flashes of insight, the evasions, the momentum and falterings—are analogous to California's own attempt to discover yet control her story as she tells it to her daughter. And even though the abstract assertions about "Humanity" and "Tragedy" in these passages (especially in the first) might seem to make this the moment when the poem becomes fully (if obscurely) allegorical, it is actually the point where the poem escapes (one might say consumes) its allegorical tendency and where the narrator (more properly the poet) commits himself to the risk of "aping" the knowing which is God by committing himself to the fire of being.

The placement of the first intrusion suggests how it functions. Having brought California to her conflicted desire to become the Mary/stallion's wife, her terror at the prospect, and her all but recognition of her own contrasting and degraded mating with Johnny, the poet must choose what is to happen to her and what his stake in it will be. Like California, he must decide whether or not to mount the "bare" and "shining" hill. Although the speaker's language here tends toward the abstract and cosmic (and thus differs fundamentally from the language he has given California and into which he has made her), it is nonetheless (significantly and appropriately) a language of crisis, and his attempt in the passage to summarize God, violence, and tragedy is less an attempt to explain what the poem means or has meant than his attempt to will himself fully into the process of the poem and complete it. Thus, when the narrator declares that "Humanity is the start of the race . . . the coal to break into fire," the claim stands not simply as a proposition but as a testimonial gesture revealing his own need to "break into fire" if he is to make a "praise"—to become the "praise" of the God that "walks lightning-naked on the Pacific." As the narrator recognizes, "humanity" (including the poet) is "the last / Least taint . . . of the solution" of being, but "the praise" is something "He approves" (*CP* 1: 189–90).

Here, as in the poem's beginning (even though the tactic differs), the character's world and the narrator's elicit, shape, and constitute each other. The narrator's metaphors extend our sense of California, but his own reactions demonstrate that she herself (her desire, passion, and confusion) is a metaphor, a figure rather, impelling his own motion toward accepting the tides of fire and attaining a moment of consciousness beyond the usual abstraction or convention that passes for knowing. She is the "vision that fools him / Out of his limits" (*CP* 1: 189), just as her "desire" fools her out of hers (and just as the poem perhaps fools us out of ours). And as such, the narrator must decide whether to risk the vision she represents. To risk the violation, though, he must do more than simply invent what his character will experience and then distance himself from it through his ability to interpret it psychologically or symbolically. Instead, he must commit himself through his full power of imagination to experience the violation he creates for his character as if his own. And the language of this intrusion, thus, marks the beginning of a kind of simultaneous implosion (in which the figures of the poem collapse into the narrator and the narrator into the poet) and explosion as the violational leap beyond norms and limits into the beauty of nature's flux "Slit[s] eyes in the mask" of the invented structures that usually protect and alienate us from what "walks lightning-naked on the Pacific" and "laces the suns with planets, / The heart of the atom with electrons" (*CP* 1: 189). With the intrusions the poet not only violates his narrative, his poem, but commits himself to his characters and rises to the risk of violation in and through them.[3]

The intrusions also mark a commitment to something that outstrips language and its categories. Words, metaphors, and the figures we construct from them can point to being's flux and power; they can even enact processes that confront us with our conflicted, partial relationship to it and trigger moments of vision. They cannot, however, become or control that being; and this is particularly apparent in the second intrusion, which closes this phase of the poem and which pushes the limits of language and knowing even further, all but erasing the distinction between California's story and the act of imagining it. The passage follows the narrator's brief description of California and the stallion on the "calvary" of the hilltop, where she kneels to the stallion, "draggled" but "brokenly adoring" and "pray[ing] aloud." She addresses it as "God," "fear," "strength," and above all "clean Power," then lies "weeping" before It (*CP* 1: 193). The narrator then modulates into his own moment of vision, a vision that corresponds with hers, derives from his attempt to imagine hers, yet is finally not hers, since hers cannot, he claims, be known. But out of that unknowable "lightning," he imagines "a crucified man [that] writhed up in anguish" and then "A woman covered by a huge beast in whose mane the stars were netted . . . [that] Smiled under the unendurable violation, her throat swollen with the storm and blood-flecks gleaming / On the stretched lips" (*CP* 1: 194).

In one sense, the narrator's failure to offer California's "actual" thoughts or actions contradicts his ability (and willingness) to do so earlier in the poem, and this failure is even more problematic in that this intrusion does not simply bridge between two moments in the plot but effaces one of its most crucial moments. However, the narrator is not simply being coy or choosing for the sake of decorum to leave what happens between California and the horse unsaid. Rather, to describe it (whatever the it might be) would either force the reader to treat it as a literal event and psychologize it or to treat it as symbolic and push it toward the realm of myth. Either would turn the poem toward a statement of knowledge and away from participation and discovery. For the moment, to be fully violational it must be the speaker/poet enacting and experiencing it. And this must happen at a pitch where what is imagined and the act of imagining outstrips language and where language (as it consumes itself) becomes a momentary light. At this level it does not matter whether the vision is first her image of Christ and then the actual mating with the stallion, her image of Christ and her dream of mating with the stallion, or the narrator's own violational imagining of both imposed on the figure of California. The competing explanations (as with the vision at the ford where the vision might be hysterical hallucination, allegorical emblem, etc.) do not really count, even though the need to explain and the possible explanations paradoxically intensify the passage's reality even as they reveal it as an imagined act. What becomes real in the passage is the narrator's (and our) discovery of the different realities and the correspondences that modulate yet unify them, and through this strategy the poem evokes as a reality (yet does not contain or embody) a simultaneity of "unendurable violation"/absolute and transcendent vision which is beyond time, yet is in time and momentary and on the verge of collapse even as it attains its greatest pitch.

It is, thus, no surprise (in fact, the logic of Jeffers's narrative practice in part determines this) that, as powerful as California's vision is (rather, the vision of the fused figure of narrator and California), neither the vision nor the fusion can be sustained, and this limit shapes the final phase of "Roan Stallion," a coda to the vision on the "calvary" of the hilltop. When Johnny, the next night, tries to fulfill his boast that he can "'show her how the red fellow act'" California leads him to the corral where she allows the stallion to trample him, then, "moved by some obscure human fidelity," shoots the stallion (*CP* 1: 198). California's reasons (though presumably they are experienced more as a kind of impulse) for standing by while the stallion reduces Johnny to "A smear on the moon-lake earth" are easy to imagine; her reasons for then shooting the stallion perhaps less so, though the "human fidelity" seems to be the daughter who pleads with her to shoot. But whatever California's precise motivation, the significance of the moment is clear. In the moment before she shoots the stallion, "Each separate nerve-cell of her brain flaming the stars fell from their places / Crying in her mind" (*CP* 1: 198). In this moment she again becomes human, and the stallion again becomes a horse. In the narrator's vision of California's vision, her skull is "a shell full of lightning," and her vision is like the "atom bounds-breaking" that, in its release of energy, becomes "self-equaling, the whole to the whole" (*CP* 1: 194). The vision itself, the ecstasy, has been the release of the individual nerves from the bounds of identity, and here the tug of the human link ravels the nerves (and identity) together again. Similarly in the same passage, the narrator has imagined her as "A woman covered by a huge beast in whose mane the stars were netted," and as the stars fall, the image falls, both for her and for him. She has lapsed, as inevitably she must, back within the limits of human visions. The slits of the mask have closed, and she "turn[s] on her little daughter the mask of a woman / Who has killed God" (*CP* 1: 198).

In this final moment of the poem we see the narrator's full stake in it. Simultaneously, killing the stallion is an act to release the energy, the spirit, and a rejection of it. Appropriately, the gesture is loaded and paradoxical for both character and narrator. For California, killing the stallion is tragic enough, but the last sentence indicates it is equally, yet differently, tragic for the narrator. The "smell of the spilt wine [that] drift[s] down hill" (*CP* 1: 198) at the close suggest how much the poem has been about sacrifice: the sacrifice of Johnny to the stallion, the sacrifice of the stallion to the daughter and human limits (or to God), the sacrifice of California to the narrator.[4] But California's lack of self-awareness and language (though it enables her to experience her desire so completely) means she neither sees this fully nor realizes its implications. The narrator, though, does. For him, it does not matter that California's act can be explained, since its significance is not what it reveals about the human world and condition but what it reveals (or allows us to glimpse) about nature and God. For if "the essence" is "the white fire" that forms and consumes itself, all incarnations are partial and temporary, and all vision (fated or chosen) an act of self-sacrifice. In a primary sense this is the "tragedy" of the poem, not the violence or pain, not even the destruction, but that vision, the appreciation of the beauty beyond the violence, is at best partial and temporary. As such, the narrator imitates—but only imitates—God's own perpetual coming into consciousness and God's own sacrifice; and our participation becomes not only a recognition of a world beyond our own limits and suffering but a recognition of the world's own unending destruction and renewal in which the only transcendence is itself incarnation, limit, pain—and beauty.

Notes

This essay is an extension of "Nature, Narrative, and Knowing: Jeffers and the Mode of 'Roan Stallion,'" the introduction to The Yolla Bolly Press edition of *Roan Stallion*. I would like to thank the press and James Robertson for permission to publish the reworked sections.

1. For more on this point see Hunt, "Nature" 1–2, and *CP* 1: xxi–xxiii.
2. For a discussion of how Jeffers seems first to have adapted this sense of nature in the lyrics of the early 1920s, see Hunt, "Problematic."
3. Murphy suggests that these intrusions function dialogically and that Bakhtin's emphasis on narrative as a process and form of action can be usefully applied to "Roan Stallion" and the other narratives. This, I would suggest, is partly true. In a dialogical reading the characters are presumed each to have a kind of ideological independence, and the narrative is imagined as the site where these perspectives compete and play out. The author does not dictate which perspective should be privileged or authoritative. Although California is more than simply a counter illustrating some predetermined meaning and although the poem's stress on participation and confrontation subverts translating it into final statements or a single, static interpretation, the poem remains largely gov-

erned by the author's perspective. The poet (or his narrator) invents and projects the narrative figures not for the sake of their own dialogue but in order himself to act through them. The poem retains an authorial center, and what dismantles monological authority is less the competing voices of the characters than the way they become counters in an oddly hybridized meditative ritual or ritualized meditation that enmeshes us in our problematic relationship to the dynamic of being and knowing. In "Roan Stallion," for all its indeterminacy, it is the sense of an authorial center that makes the process seem sufficiently real to be compelling, and the poem's indeterminacy derives in part from the way we sense that this authorial presence is in the process of becoming through the action of the poem.

4. For a discussion of the sacrificial patterns of "Roan Stallion," see Brophy 75–110.

Works Cited

CP *The Collected Poetry of Robinson Jeffers*. Ed. Tim Hunt. 3 vols. to date. Stanford, CA: Stanford UP, 1988, 1989, 1991.

Boyers, Robert. "A Sovereign Voice: The Poetry of Robinson Jeffers." *Centennial Essays for Robinson Jeffers*. Ed. Robert Zaller. Newark: U of Delaware P, 1991.

Brophy, Robert. *Robinson Jeffers: Myth, Ritual, and Symbol in His Narrative Poems*. Cleveland: Case Western Reserve UP, 1973.

Everson, William. *The Excesses of God: Robinson Jeffers as a Religious Figure*. Stanford, CA: Stanford UP, 1988.

Hunt, Tim. "Nature, Narrative, and Knowing: Jeffers and the Mode of 'Roan Stallion.'" *Roan Stallion*. By Robinson Jeffers. Ed. Tim Hunt. Covelo, CA: Yolla Bolly P, 1990.

——. "The Problematic Nature of *Tamar and Other Poems*." *Centennial Essays for Robinson Jeffers*. Ed. Robert Zaller. Newark: U of Delaware P, 1991.

Jeffers, Robinson. *Flagons and Apples*. 1912. Cayucos, CA: Cayucos Books, 1974.

——. Introduction. *Roan Stallion, Tamar and Other Poems*. By Robinson Jeffers. New York: Modern Library, 1935.

——. Introduction. *Jeffers Country: The Seed Plots of Robinson Jeffers' Poetry*. Ed. Horace Lyon. San Francisco: Scrimshaw P, 1971.

Murphy, Patrick. "Reclaiming the Power: Robinson Jeffers's Verse Novels." *Western American Literature* 22 (1987): 125–48.

Zaller, Robert. *The Cliffs of Solitude: A Reading of Robinson Jeffers*. New York: Cambridge UP, 1983.

6

"Divinely Superfluous Beauty": Robinson Jeffers's Versecraft of the Sublime

David J. Rothman

SINCE THE 1930s, a few perceptive scholars (Klein, Powell, Nickerson, Hymes) have realized that Robinson Jeffers's versecraft was highly original, and crucial to the success of his mature work.[1] Their investigations have gone relatively unheeded except by a few other committed Jeffers scholars, but the material reasons for this general neglect will soon come to an end, when Stanford University Press brings out the fourth and final volume of *The Collected Poetry of Robinson Jeffers*. This volume includes Tim Hunt's painstaking editing of the unpublished and rarely reprinted early poems, and its arrival will give all readers the opportunity to examine a chronological arrangement of the entire range of Jeffers's work for the first time.[2] This arrangment makes it clear just how hard Jeffers worked to transform his craft (as well as his subject) during the late 1910s and early 1920s, between *Flagons and Apples* and *Roan Stallion, Tamar and Other Poems*. When we read *The Collected Poetry* side by side with Jeffers's own commentary on the evolution of his forms, in letters and other prose works, we now have substantial evidence of what he was trying to do when he abandoned the regular and rhymed versification of his early work.[3]

My argument is that Jeffers was one of the two or three greatest innovators of versecraft in twentieth-century poetry in English. Although his influence has not been as obvious as that of Hopkins, Pound, Lawrence, Williams, Marianne Moore, Cummings, or Olson, he understood the general questions of prosody more deeply than any of them. More important than any display of interest or knowledge, however, is the fact that Jeffers succeeded—where most of the others failed—in formalizing a system of versification that contrasts markedly with accentual-syllabic meter. Further, like all strong poets, Jeffers comprehended that versification is not the adornment of sense, but one ground of its making, and accordingly drew upon this aspect of his craft in a highly self-conscious way. We are unlikely to understand Jeffers's evolution as a poet, or even the success of his individual poems, without a grasp of the crucial role of versecraft in his art.

At a time when Jeffers's reputation appears to be improving, attention to this aspect of his craft is particularly important, because it has been so misunderstood. Jeffers's mature poetry (from the early 1920s on) is emphatically not free verse in the Modernist tradition (as many critics have assumed); nor is it accentual-syllabic. Avoiding these two poles, Jeffers developed a system of unrhymed, non-alliterative, accentual verse. To begin with a simple description that I will return to and complicate throughout this essay: Jeffers's accentual system requires counting the number of strong stresses in each line, but not counting the syllables, and avoiding rhyme. He pursued this model more assiduously than any other poet, with the possible exception of Longfellow, since the alliterative revival of the fourteenth century. Jeffers is thus one of the few poets—perhaps the only one—whose verse has been called free, when much of it is highly regular, although not accentual-syllabic.[4]

Questions of versecraft are inevitably technical, and fraught with methodological difficulties. Yet no understanding of Jeffers's poetry can be thorough if it ignores his sophisticated innovations in this area. If we wish to understand these innovations, we need to strive to meet Jeffers on his own ground, which means paying precise critical attention to the craft that was so intimately bound up with his success. The rewards of such a discussion are a better understanding of a major poet's overall project.

I

One can hardly blame readers who argue that Jeffers would have preferred to forge poems from eternity and stone, "nothing wrought nor remembered," rather than words. Given what appears to be systematic hostility to language in much of his work, it is no surprise that critics and scholars have focused on his lurid, violent plots, sublime descriptions of the natural world, philosophical ideas, and didactic and spiritual programs, tending to ignore questions of craft. Typifying this view, Robert Hass has written, in an essay that praises Jeffers, that "[l]anguage itself is simply not one of Jeffers' subjects" (xl).

Yet Jeffers continuously invoked his ideas about language in his poems at the same time as he worked them out in practice. Consider Jeffers's version of the Oresteia, "The Tower Beyond Tragedy" which first appeared in *Roan Stallion, Tamar and Other Poems*, the volume that made him famous in 1925. Near the end of the play, resisting his sister Electra's attempt to seduce him, the character Orestes says "I have fallen in love outward" (*CP* 1: 178). By this he means he has turned away from self-absorbed humanity, which is symbolized by his sister's incestuous longings, to embrace the external, "inhuman" world of nature and the void. For Orestes, language is insufficient to express the sublime immensity of this inhuman cosmos:

> . . . they have not made words for it, to go behind things, beyond hours and ages,
> And be all things in all time, in their returns and passages, in the motionless and timeless center,
> In the white of the fire . . . how can I express the excellence I have found, that has no color but clearness;
> No honey but ecstasy; nothing wrought nor remembered; no undertone nor silver second murmur
> That rings in love's voice, I and my loved are one; no desire but fulfilled; no passion but peace,
> The pure flame and the white, fierier than any passion; no time but spheral eternity. . . .

Again and again throughout his work Jeffers plays variations on this manifesto of inarticulable sublimity, in which the inhuman world, and the even greater void in which it rides, transcend consciousness and every means of expressing it, especially language. Yet to write "They have not made words for it, to go behind things," is not an avoidance of language, but rather the opposite: a theory of it.

Jeffers's goal was not to purify the dialect of the tribe, like so many of his contemporaries'. Yet we should take a more sophisticated approach to Jeffers's denials of language, for Orestes's denial (and Jeffers's) is only comprehensible as language; both rely on language in order to deny it. However anti-linguistic, Jeffers's inhumanist vows did not lead to silence, but to voluminous, extravagant, sensual writing. In a sense, Orestes's denial of language works like the Cretan paradox: "The Cretan saith 'All Cretans always lie.'" Like this self-destroying statement, Orestes's generative "no" to language only makes sense in language.[5] Jeffers's work is first and foremost poetry, not its negation. We should not confuse what it says with what it is.

This confusion is exactly what has occurred in most Jeffers criticism, and his reputation has suffered as a result. He tricked many readers into thinking that he did not care about his craft, because he insistently denied language in this way. While the critics' confusion is an historical (if backhanded) compliment to the poems, it ultimately has not served Jeffers well. Rarely has the craft of a poet of such stature been so misconstrued—one would have to go back as far as Whitman, and before him perhaps Milton, to find a comparable example. Oddly enough, in both of the earlier cases, the accusations were surprisingly similar in at least one crucial regard: like Jeffers, both Milton and Whitman were accused of lacking poetic "technique," and writing prose, not verse, or "verse only to the eye," as Johnson famously quipped on a similar debate that once raged over *Paradise Lost*.

As a first, practical step, therefore, to focusing attention on Jeffers's versecraft, let us perform an old experiment, rewriting verse as prose in order to reveal in what ways the versification meshes with sense. When we do this to Jeffers, we find a different case from that presented by either metrical verse (rhymed and unrhymed) or free verse. Here is "Divinely Superfluous Beauty," one of Jeffers's earliest lyrics in his new metric, as prose:

> The storm-dances of gulls, the barking game of seals, over and under the ocean . . . divinely superfluous beauty rules the games, presides over destinies, makes trees grow and hills tower, waves fall. The incredible beauty of joy stars with fire the joining of lips, O let our loves too be joined, there is not a maiden burns and thirsts for love more than my blood for you, by the shore of seals while the wings weave like a web in the air divinely superfluous beauty.

In what way does this version differ from the poem Jeffers published? Obviously, none of the words or punctuation marks are different. Yet without rhyme, and an obvious metrical scheme, it is virtually impossible to reconstruct the lineation of Jeffers's poem.

"Divinely Superfluous Beauty" is not free verse, however, in the sense of being prosodically unpredictable from line to line. In Jeffers's poem, the verse works in groups of three lines: one long line of six strong stresses (five in the very first line), followed by two lines of three each:

> The storm-dances of gulls, the barking game of seals,
> Over and under the ocean . . .
> Divinely superfluous beauty
> Rules the games, presides over destinies, makes trees grow
> And hills tower, waves fall.
> The incredible beauty of joy
> Stars with fire the joining of lips, O let our loves too
> Be joined, there is not a maiden
> Burns and thirsts for love
> More than my blood for you, by the shore of seals while the
>   wings
> Weave like a web in the air
> Divinely superfluous beauty. (*CP* 1: 4)

I do not think there is any way that either a reader or a listener unfamiliar with what Jeffers wrote would be likely to lineate the prose paragraph I presented above in this way. The chances, at any rate, are a good deal less than with a Yeats poem, or even an excerpt from Milton.

Indeed, Jeffers's patterning of the lines seems random—after all, any piece of English prose whatsoever could be similarly lineated, as there is no rhyme in Jeffers's poem, and no limit on the number of syllables per line, only on the number of lines. Yet the 6 3 3 pattern of stresses is undeniably there in Jeffers's poem—so the question remains: Why choose 6 3 3 for a pattern of stresses? Why not 6 4 2, or 3 6 6, or any other of a virtually infinite number of such combinations? Assuming all the lines are filled out at the end of the poem, Jeffers could choose any pattern at all—unlike the much tighter and (at first glance) more technically demanding accentual-syllabic forms, which would impose many more rules on him. The language of his poem would not resist any word at any point in the way iambic pentameter would have resisted Shakespeare if he wanted to use the word "afternoon" beginning in the tenth-syllable position of a line such as "Shall I compare thee to a summer's [day]."

In short, the metrical organization of sounds in Jeffers's lines (whatever their diction), is no different from what it is for prose. What this means is that rewriting Jeffers's poem as prose does not disturb the modulation of relative stress-values, a modulation that lies at the heart of accentual-syllabic meter in English (as Jesperson demonstrated long ago in his essay "Notes on Meter," collected in Gross, ed., 105–28). Indeed, such modulation is not a principle of Jeffers's versecraft to begin with. Nevertheless, Jeffers's verse is still not technically "free" in the Whitmanian or Imagist sense, because each line involves counting stresses in a way that those poets abjured.

It is tempting to search for a numerological key to the 6 3 3 arrangement in this poem, one that has something to do with Jeffers's ideas about beauty and its proportions. This kind of occult approach (very popular among students of versification) is wrongheaded. The problem is that such an approach always enslaves versification to the propositional sense of poems, as if that sense existed before the actual words were written, and the verse-form only reflects what the words say. In contrast, I think that Jeffers, like all strong poets, drew upon versecraft to make his poems, not the other way around. If anything—to show my hand somewhat—it may be that his sense of the "superfluous" beauty of verse is one source of this poem.

Jeffers did not arrive at the mature craft of "Divinely Superfluous Beauty" and his subsequent works either quickly or easily. Like Whitman, Masters, Sandburg, and Lawrence, he began as a competent metrical versifier, but then, already past the age of 30, he shifted to a radically different verse technique which accompanied a much more successful poetry. The conversion that unleashed Jeffers's creative power in the 1920s was no less formal than thematic, and included a decision "To shear the rhyme tassels from verse" ("Mal Paso Bridge," *Roan Stallion* 172),[6] and to tap a metric more profound than the sea:

> Mother, though my song's measure is like your surf-beat's
> ancient rhythm I never learned it of you.
> Before there was any water there were tides of fire, both our
> tones flow from the older fountain. ("Continent's End," *CP* 1: 17)

These tides of fire, as Jeffers reiterates throughout his mature work, are not only the natural forces of space but, more, the oblivion beyond anything we know of nature. They transcend both representation and traditional metric.

As we have seen, this decision involved not only a shearing of rhyme, but also of syllable count, leaving only the non-metrical stress-counts to organize each line. Jeffers began with what he had learned, an accentual-syllabic line (such as iambic pentameter or tetrameter), in which he counted both syllables and stresses, and which he usually rhymed. He eventually eliminated syllable counts, and then also jettisoned rhyme, retaining only stress-counts.

The early poems show that Jeffers experimented with different kinds of techniques before coming to his solution. "Divinely Superfluous Beauty" was written in 1920, but in the same year Jeffers was trying to finish a poem that he eventually called "Decline of the West." This poem is composed in rhythmically free but endstopped, rhymed couplets. It begins (in its final version):

> Where the fields are paved with gold-eyed poppies and blue-
> flame lupine flowers
> From the turbulent free headland to the cloudy coast-range
> towers,
>
> We were sorrowful in the morning and the morning of the year
> And the morning of the world's truce, for a hope gone from
> here.

Much of Jeffers's mature subject matter swirls through this poem of disillusionment with politics, and love of classical beauty and nature:

> For myself I have the hills and the stone belts of my own house,
> Casements opening west over salt water and south to the coast-
> range brows.
>
> Walls on a rock above the sea and granite ecstasy kept clean
> From the breath of multitude, the bondage of submitting men.

What is missing, of course, is the force of the vision, which Jeffers only tapped when he forged the craft not yet evident here. This quest for a new versification cannot be separated from his visionary aspiration; indeed, Jeffers put a great deal of work into both, and it is arguable that he could not express his new vision until he built the instrument that could play it. By this point, he was mature enough as an artist to realize this, and this is no doubt why he left this weak poem unpublished.

Klein, in the mid-1930s, was the first to realize what Jeffers was doing in his mature work, and also to realize that Jeffers was not the only poet who had ever imagined this kind of verse. When Klein wrote to Jeffers to ask him if Bridges's comments on accentual verse at the end of the 1901 version of *Milton's Prosody* were a source for his accentual versification, he responded favorably, claiming that he had read Symons on Bridges's poetry, and was familiar with the ideas, although he had not actually read Bridges's book.[7] The key theoretical passage that Klein excerpted from Bridges and sent to Jeffers describes pure accentual verse exactly as Jeffers used it, and as I have summarized it above. In the crux of that lengthy passage, Bridges writes:

> Now the primary law of pure stressed verse is, that there shall never be a conventional or imaginary stress: that is, *the verse cannot make the stress, because it is the stress that makes the verse* [emphasis in original]. . . . If the number of stresses in each line be fixed, (and such a fixation would be the metre,) and if the stresses be determined only by the language and its sense, and if the syllables which they have to carry do not overburden them, then every line may have a different rhythm; though so much variety is not of necessity.[8]

Jeffers responded to Klein:

> People talked about my "free verse" and I never protested, but now I am quite touched to hear that someone at last has discovered the metrical intention in it. Thank you. ("KJC" 15)

He then discusses Coleridge's meter in *Christabel* (which Bridges had shown is more syllabic than either Coleridge or Jeffers thought), questions of syllabic quantity (which Jeffers raises but does not claim to have solved), and several other points. Later, after reading Klein's study, Jeffers comments:

> Of course you have noticed that (chiefly in my narrative poems) many lines are of irregular length—"free" no doubt—as are many lines in Elizabethan dramatic verse—but it seems to me there is a metrical pattern—if only, at most irregular, as a background from which to measure departures from the pattern ("KJC" 20).

The key word here is "measure," not "free." Klein responds by sending Jeffers a summary of Bridges's seven rules of accentual verse from the revised 1921 volume of *Milton's Prosody* ("KJC" 22), for which Jeffers again thanks him. Thus, despite some indication that Jeffers was also playing with classical scansion as he thought about his new metric, the underlying principle of his verse is stress unmodified by regular syllabic counts, exactly as Jeffers, Klein, Powell, Ghiselin, Nickerson, and several others have described it, and as Hymes has set about analyzing it in the shorter poems.[9] As Hymes and others have shown, and any reader who bothers to start counting can soon realize, Jeffers was extremely inventive with his stress-count verse, endlessly spinning out new patterns.

Recently recovered evidence further indicates Jeffers's intentions, and shows him clearly echoing Bridges's formulation that in stress-based verse "the verse cannot make the stress because it is the stress that makes the verse" more than a decade after his initial exchange with Klein. This is the entire text of "Rhythm and Rhyme," an unpublished poem Jeffers worked on during the late 1940s:

> The tide-flow of passionate speech, breath, blood-pulse, the sea's waves and time's return,
> They make the metre; but rhyme seems a child's game.
> Let the low-Latin languages, the lines lacking strong accents, lean on it;
> Our north-sea English needs no such ornament.
> Born free, and searaid-fed from far shores, why should it taggle its head
> With tinkling sheep bells, like Rome's slaves' daughters?

Jeffers makes his original technical sources clear, alliterating frequently (especially in line 3, on "l"), and yet also displays his original technique, as he forges the lines in alternating lengths of 9 and 5 strong stresses. A naïve reader might at first think that this poem justifies an organicist program, because of the sources for craft that Jeffers cites in the first line; but Jeffers ultimately cites "strong accents," a purely linguistic feature, as prior to all these other phenomena. Jeffers fully understood that only languages which have such accents to begin with can make "metre" from passionate speech, breath, blood-flow, and so on. Not only does this poem exhibit the craft it describes, both innovatively and deeply informed by tradition, it shows in what way Jeffers saw that craft as an essential ground of his poetics. For, ultimately, this poem says that the source of "The tide-flow of passionate speech, breath, blood-pulse, the sea's waves and time's return" in poetry is "strong accents."

The versification of "Divinely Superfluous Beauty" exemplifies Jeffers's mature practice as he alludes to it in this later poem, and as we have been examining it. All modulation of the kind that characterizes accentual-syllabic lines has been junked, except for the collection of stress groups (sixes and threes in this case). But such groups have to be taken as wholes for the patterns to become apparent. The modulations do not inhere in terms of syllable count, but only rhythmically, as Bridges foresaw. There is no accentual-syllabic grid, or norm, only variation based on a generative scheme that is no different from that for prose. Writing the words as verse only highlights patterns that exist in any event, no matter how they are lineated. And, unsurprisingly, Jeffers has often been accused of writing prose cut into lengths, like Whitman, and before him, Milton.[10]

Jeffers's verse does retain patterns of number, not only in lineation, but because the strong stresses are regularly counted. These numberings, however, are arbitrary, in no way modulating the utterance as even the loosest accentual-syllabic meter does. I use the term "arbitrary" in a purely technical sense, to indicate patterns of counting; Jeffers's choice of words is anything but arbitrary, but his freedom to place any word he chooses at any point in the line is absolute. His system of versification imposes an order on his lines, but it is an order that in no way restricts his word choice.

Because of this arbitrary system of counting, Jeffers can afford to jettison the figures of grammar that Whitman relied on to shape his free verse. He has developed a way of counting that is quite literally "superfluous"—the poems manifest an orderliness that appears unnecessary, or whimsical, and that makes sense only to the eye. The sense of pattern is a function of the tension between the poem's non-modulating utterance and its appearance on the page in lines.

II

The writing of non-modulating, unrhymed accentual verse provided Jeffers with the creative ground necessary for his mature work. It is not irrelevant to his poetry, an ornament or failure of craft. From the moment he discovered his new versecraft it liberated him to express the sublime. "Divinely Superfluous Beauty," for example, draws upon and is about the sublime arbitrariness of its own artifice. In Jeffers's craft "Divinely superfluous beauty / Rules the games," and this figure of measurement includes the games of traditional metrical poetry, the work of "The poet, who wishes not to play games with words, / His affair being to awake dangerous images / And call the hawks," as he later wrote in the lyric "Triad" (*CP* 2: 309).[11]

In "Divinely Superfluous Beauty," incommensurateness among things "presides over destinies, makes trees grow / And hills tower, waves fall." The representation of that sublime superfluity draws on a versecraft that self-consciously both evokes and refuses measurement, for there is counting without modulation. Jeffers's arbitrary stress patterns are themselves best described as superfluous. This is no coincidence. Jeffers draws on a self-conscious failure to measure, the better to evoke eternity. This evocation is grounded by the craft of verse as well as an understanding of the world.[12]

I find it difficult to resist the speculation that Jeffers had the opening lines of *Endymion* echoing in his mind when he wrote his poem about "The incredible beauty of joy." Whether or not he did, Jeffers's poem provides a powerful counterpoint to Romantic notions of art:

> A thing of beauty is a joy for ever
> Its loveliness increases; it will never
> Pass into nothingness; but still will keep
> A bower quiet for us, and a sleep
> Full of sweet dreams, and health, and quiet breathing.
> Therefore, on every morrow, are we wreathing
> A flowery band to bind us to the earth,
> Spite of despondence, of the inhuman dearth
> Of noble natures, of the gloomy days
> Of all the unhealthy and o'er-darkened ways
> Made for our searching: yes, in spite of all,
> Some shape of beauty moves away the pall
> From our dark spirits. Such the sun, the moon,
> Trees old, and young. . . . (1.1–13)

Keats's heroic couplets, with their sad invocation of "health, and quiet breathing," cast a spell that Jeffers both reiterates and transcends. Jeffers also seeks to weave himself into the natural beauty he perceives. Yet his larger point is that such beauty is superfluous and incomprehensible, and *will* pass into nothingness. The end is not a sleep of sweet dreams into which beauty increases, but a measureless oblivion. For Jeffers "the inhuman dearth / Of noble natures" is not something that, although understood, he nevertheless wishes to escape by wreathing himself ever more closely to the earth with a band of flowers. Turning his attention to rock and hawk, symbols of a greater Inhumanism, he both calls out to and evokes a measureless beauty that is beyond the power of his poems to express. For Keats, "in spite of all, / Some shape of beauty moves away the pall / From our dark spirits," but in Jeffers's work, the beauty, which is really an awesome vitality, lies in that "all."

For Jeffers, the precursor who embodies the vitality of the "all" most powerfully is, of course, not Keats, but Whitman, although Jeffers rarely, if ever, refers to him. Yet Whitman's innovations in craft and representation of the sublime lurk behind much of

Jeffers's work. Ponder the figure of Barclay, the mad, violent preacher of "The Women at Point Sur." In that poem, Barclay proclaims himself a god, becomes a cult figure, and dies revising Whitman's "I contain multitudes" to "I am inexhaustible." Jeffers claimed he was not writing a fable; yet Barclay's insanity is a function of his conviction that God "has turned to love men" (*CP* 1: 323). In an authorial intrusion, Jeffers states:

> . . . I say that if the mind centers on humanity
> And is not dulled, but remains powerful enough to feel its own and the others, the mind will go mad. (*CP* 1: 308)

Barclay sounds very much like a berserk caricature of Whitman. While there are also references to Faust, Schopenhauer, and Nietzsche,[13] we should remember that this character is a Protestant American minister, not a blond beast or jaded scholar. We should be wary of allowing the German references, which are real enough along with the classical ones, to obscure the context of what is an American poem, not a philosophical tract. Barclay is speaking:

> "Don't fear. Did I forget to tell you there is nothing wicked in the world, no act is a sin?
> Nothing you can do is wicked. I have seen God. He is there in the hill, he is here in your body. My . . . daughter,"
> He said shaking, "God thinks through action, I have watched him, through the acts of men fighting and the acts of women
> As much as through the immense courses of the stars; all the acts, all the bodies; who dares to enclose him
> With *this is right* and *that's wrong*, shut his thought with scruples, blind him against discoveries, blind his eyes?" . . . (*CP* 1: 262–63)

This passage embodies Jeffers's ambivalence toward his American predecessor. At the same time as Barclay, like Whitman and Jeffers, invokes an immense power, he is nevertheless an insane, destructive force. Unenclosable and inexhaustible, he has not "fallen in love outward," away from man, like Orestes. Instead, in Jeffers's view, Barclay remains tragically and violently mired in the human world. The poem is in large part a critique of Whitman's project.

Whitman found the sublime in the multitude, as did Masters and Sandburg, who also did their best work self-consciously in the Whitmanian strain of free verse. Jeffers, like Lawrence, found it in turning away, or at least appearing to turn away, from the crowd, even from the human. Where Whitman writes "Camerado, this is no book, / Who touches this touches a man," Jeffers counters in "Post Mortem":

> Though one at the end of the age and far off from this place
> Should meet my presence in a poem,
> The ghost would not care but be here, long sunset shadow in the seams of the granite, and forgotten
> The flesh, a spirit for the stone. (*CP* 1: 205)

Or, "Who touches this touches a rock."

In concert with this revision, Jeffers also transformed Whitman's revolution in versecraft. Jeffers retained the arbitrary lineation which depends on a tension between graphic and aural organization, and does not modulate words, for Whitman's verse does not scan, and completely eschews any numerable line-to-line patterns of expectation. The only usefully countable things in Whitman are the lines, which clash with the apparent metrical disorder of the words that constitute them. In contrast to this, Jeffers forged a more regular line, but one that still functions according to arbitrarily numbered patterns of stresses. The fiction of the form is not Whitmanian organicism, but nature as a mindless, indifferent, magnificent algorithm. Jeffers used this formulation as a ground on which to turn away from the human world to which free verse opens in Whitman's work. In a sense, Jeffers redisciplined Whitman's free verse, and discovered in it a force that he intentionally defined as larger than Whitman's—the entire physical universe, in which man plays only an insignificant part.

Another important predecessor in terms of Jeffers's craft—as important to Jeffers as he was to Whitman—is Milton. Jeffers's decision to "shear the rhyme-tassels from verse" is reminiscent of Milton's decision to abandon rhyme in *Paradise Lost*, because it is a "troublesom and modern bondage" (250). Rhyme, Milton asserts, is "no necessary Adjunct or true Ornament of Poem or good Verse, in longer Works especially, but the Invention of a barbarous Age, to set off wretched matter and lame Meeter" (249). What is interesting is the fierceness of the rhetoric against ornament in both poets. Milton felt that rhyme was not appropriate in a poem that aimed to justify the ways of God to men; Jeffers has no such hope in "Mal Paso Bridge," but still aims to justify the sublime, and abandons rhyme because he is equivalently serious about that:

> This is the year when young men cannot guess
> From night to night what bed they'll sleep in.

But I in yours dark beauty of new desire,
Yours under Santa Lucian hills
Near the rough water; but beyond that nor moon
Nor guess candles the remnant nights.
Therefore I swore to drink wine while I could,
Love where I pleased, and feed my eyes
With Santa Lucian sea-beauty, and moreover
To shear the rhyme-tassels from verse.
(*Roan Stallion* 172)

In this particular stanza, the alternating 5–4 stress-counts shift in and out of a scannable iambic meter (other stanzas have different patterns), but Jeffers is declaring allegiance to his search for a mature versecraft. Indeed, that is a part of the poem's significance. Like Milton, Jeffers found a way to draw sense out variously from one verse to another that at first hardly seems like versecraft at all, rather only prose. The point is that Jeffers, the poet supposedly unconcerned with language, in his post-Romantic moment of resolution and independence, decides to feed his eyes on a wilder beauty than that which he feels the orderly sounds of rhyme can afford. In this poem he is well on the way to forging and harnessing the new versecraft that will ground his poetics of the inhuman sublime. However much turned outward, this force lies within poetry.

When, soon after, Jeffers achieved that new versecraft, he went further than merely removing rhyme from his verses. Enjambing subject and verb is usually jarring, and Jeffers marks many of his line endings in "Divinely Superfluous Beauty" with exactly such a split, as if to emphasize that this verse will not turn back on itself but continue forward like prose, flowing over arbitrarily from one line to the next. The enjambment emphasizes the graphic quality of the line breaks. The verse turns, but the syntax does not, continually forging ahead, or "outward." Even in this small, and, for Jeffers, rare joyous lyric, written several years before "The Women at Point Sur," he is drawing on his newfound craft to place the lovers in an immense, sublimely indifferent cosmos—one that contrasts with Whitman's as much as with Keats's and Milton's. In effect, Jeffers's introduction of arbitrary patterns of stress-counts allows him to abandon the figures of parallel grammar that characterize Whitman's work, and play with lineation in supple and free ways, of which this subject/verb breaking is but one.

In "The Excesses of God," the poem that Hunt has placed

directly after "Divinely Superfluous Beauty" in *The Collected Poetry*, we see the same explicit thematization of the sublime in terms of measure:

> Is it not by his high superfluousness we know
> Our God? For to equal a need
> Is natural, animal, mineral: but to fling
> Rainbows over the rain
> And beauty above the moon, and secret rainbows
> On the domes of deep sea-shells,
> And make the necessary embrace of breeding
> Beautiful also as fire,
> Not even the weeds to multiply without blossom
> Nor the birds without music:
> There is the great humaneness at the heart of things,
> The extravagant kindness, the fountain
> Humanity can understand, and would flow likewise
> If power and desire were perch-mates. (*CP* 1: 4)

The verse alternates between lines of 4 strong stresses and lines of 3. Again, the lines are not accentual-syllabic, so they present a prosodic order that is "superfluous." The lines can be counted, and the utterance has been broken into numerable segments, but in an arbitrary way whose crux is graphic order.

Like "Divinely Superfluous Beauty," "The Excesses of God" explicitly juxtaposes numerable and innumerable subjects. "To equal a need / Is natural, animal, mineral," but each thing that Jeffers names in the poem—the rain, the moon, and sea-shells—has a complement that is inhuman, beautiful, and superfluous. Unlike Keats's "flowery band," which has been wreathed into a beautiful thing by human hands, Jeffers's flowers derive their beauty from an inexplicability that no human act can rationalize. As he wrote in "The Place for No Story," a lyric in *Thurso's Landing* (1932) that describes the Carmel landscape, "No imaginable / Human presence here could do anything / But dilute the lonely self-watchful passion" (*CP* 2: 157). Again, dilution can only be understood in the context of measuring; it is even possible that all such terms, for strong poets are, among other things, tropes for the versecraft they continually practice and ponder.

In all Jeffers's inhumanist pronouncements, there is at least one human presence—Jeffers. His inevitably human art, praising the inhuman beauty, is what makes measurement possible, at the same time as it self-consciously fails to articulate the ratio evoked. He acknowledges this by using the surprising word "humaneness" (in line 11), where one might have expected "divinity." The syntax is convoluted, but in the end Jeffers is saying that "we know our God" only by acknowledging what we cannot measure, what cannot possibly be measured: "That is the great humaneness at the heart of things / The extravagant kindness." Inhumanism is still a human idea, depending for its sublimity on a juxtaposition against the limited nature of human life.

The poem is made out of verses that can be most accurately described in exactly the same terms—that in fact ground and power the interpretive terms. Just as each image in the poem describes a beauty that is a superfluous, or extravagant, gift, that can only be explained by a creator outside of, or greater than, nature, so the verses as they have been inscribed on the page are superfluously ordered. The numbering cannot be rationalized, as it is arbitrary. The beauty lies in the gap.

These observations suggest Jeffers's version of the failure or negativity that undergirds all sublime, American poetics in Whitman's wake. Jeffers says that we do not know God directly—only through the signs that exceed reason, beautiful ratios that we cannot equal, although we "would flow likewise / If power and desire were perch-mates." Jeffers cannot make a rainbow, a sea-shell, or even weeds; his power fails to equal his desire. He could make love, "the necessary embrace of breeding / Beautiful also as fire," but he has not made the physical body that creates such raw beauty from "breeding." More to the point, he *can* make a poem that thematizes sublime excess, extravagance, and superfluousness. The non-modulating and therefore arbitrary quality of Jeffers's versecraft is a fundamental basis of this art, not its ornament. The intentional failure to break numbered lines of verse into predictably numerable parts ("feet") provides a powerful tool for the evocation of that which exceeds every word. The "high superfluousness" and "extravagant kindness" of this poem draw upon its versification for their force as feelings and ideas.

This formulation is not just a reversal of the more common argument that verseform follows meaning. Rather, it gives versecraft its due, as an *a priori* source of creative power, a facet of the numerical imagination upon which each poet can draw to forge meaning in words. Whitman's praiseful representation of a sublime, human subject draws on an intentional failure of metrical verse; Jeffers turns away from man and outward to the entire physical world but does a similar thing. Far from "hysterical"

(Vendler's charge), Jeffers's craft in his best work is a well-tuned engine of sublime negativity.

III

The final theoretical question I want to explore is how Jeffers's accentual verse orders the relations among utterance, writing, and number. Readers may find my inclusion of writing and number in such a formulation odd, because most critical models of versification emphasize aural patterns as the ground of all verse making, assuming that writing in verse only orchestrates speech. In contrast, my hypothesis is that the purpose of versification is to imbue words with number. In itself this is not a new idea. "The crux of the issue is measure," as William Carlos Williams once pointed out when discussing free verse (in his definition of the term in *The Princeton Encyclopedia* of *Poetry and Poetics*), and many others have said similar things. What is unusual in my formulation is the idea that the synthesis of language with counting, no matter what form it takes in verse, is conceivable only as writing, as inscription, as a graphic technology. To put it another way: the counting that we rely on to describe versification is only possible because of writing. It is a literate, not an aural, phenomenon.

The background to this argument lies in recent speculation that writing may have evolved out of counting in the first place. Roy Harris argues in *The Origin of Writing* that the earliest writing did not grow out of attempts to represent speech, or draw pictures, but to represent number. Examining a wide range of linguistic artifacts, Harris speculates that writing emerged when people realized that the different symbols that they had developed to indicate different categories of counted things could stand for anything at all, not merely quantities. Thus they could be related to each other, not only to the things whose number they signified. The implications of such an argument for versification are profound, for it suggests that the crux of language and number in verse—an obsession of most strong poets—is writing. Indeed, verses are no more or less than written language intentionally broken up into numerable segments, and this is why even metrical verse loses its magical quality when rewritten as prose. The point is that such "rewriting" is in effect the creation of a radically different artifact. The fact that verse can be "rewritten" at all—one cannot perform a comparable function on "oral" poetry—indicates that the art of verse has always been ineluctably tied up with literacy. Indeed, the very idea of "oral" poetry cannot be conceived except by literate people.

The graphic quality of verse explains a number of things, such as the ghostly quality of meter. Because it relies on counting, meter is an abstraction that can never be fully embodied in any given performance, as Wimsatt and Beardsley realized in their crucial essay "The Concept of Meter: An Exercise in Abstraction" (in Gross, ed., 147–72). The fact that a metrical poem can be performed orally in no way weakens this argument. Such a performance is simply one enactment of the underlying abstraction out of which the verse was forged. One can never, after all, simply perform *meter;* even nonsense syllables are actual verses designed to clothe an abstract figure. One can perform only particulars, not abstractions; yet it is these abstractions that guide the making of the verse, even if they are absent, as in free verse, which retains countable lines, but intentionally frustrates the numerability of their parts. And these metrical abstractions, which are ways of counting, find their origin in the writing system.

To write verse is not to orchestrate speech, but rather to fuse speech and number together by means of inscription. The means to this end is lineation, which casts writing in numerable segments at the same time as it embodies words. There are basically two ways to do this: metrical verse, in which lines are graphically and aurally equivalent to one another (and the parts within them, feet, are equivalent); and, as I suggested, free verse, in which lines are graphically equivalent, but cannot be construed as aurally equivalent, either with one another or in their own parts. What Jeffers achieved can thus be seen as an extraordinary compromise between these two models, one which draws on an intimate understanding of the language's most profound resources.

The deepest question in this speculation is why poets do this, why they are so attracted to counting as a way of organizing art. The answer is surprisingly simple. Counting is attractive to poets not because it recapitulates breath, or the heartbeat, or the sound of beating on an anvil, or the movement of oars in oarlocks, or the cadences of music, or the meaning of the poem's words (these are only a few of the arguments that have been invoked to explain its force). Counting is not an ornament of the poem, but part of its ground, and it is attractive because, as Coleridge realized, it is exciting. Number in its simplest form, counting, is an abstraction so powerful that it verges on the supernatural. As Harris has written:

> Counting is in its very essence magical, if any human practice at all is. For numbers are things no one has ever seen or heard or touched. Yet somehow they exist, and their existence can be confirmed in quite everyday terms by all kinds of humdrum procedures which allow mere mortals to agree beyond any shadow of doubt as to "how many" eggs there are in a basket or "how many" loaves of bread on the table. (135)

Or, one might add, for how many stanzas there are in a poem, or lines in a stanza, or stresses, feet, or syllables in a line, or occurrences of particular syntactical or grammatical patterns, and so on.

Poets write in verse because it excites the numerical imagination, which is both rational and superstitious, quotidian and magical. Versification is a way of asserting the relatedness of things to one another, and it makes sense that poets, even if they define what they are doing exclusively in terms of "voice," or in resistance to "meter," also organize their writing to take advantage of the numerical possibilities of writing, the ways that counting interacts with language. They play with writing as they do with speech in order to garner and concentrate as much energy for their work as possible.

IV

Jeffers frequently troped writing, rather than speech, as the mode of his verse. Although he surely did not advance the hypotheses about its role in versification that I suggest, he frequently thematized writing as the modality of poetry, referring to his poetry as "verse" (a term that ultimately derives from the image of the turn a plow makes at the end of a furrow, from the Latin *versus*), and comparing it to inscription of one kind or another. This is not too surprising when we recall that Jeffers, like most poets before the 1950s, thought of himself as a writer, not a performer, and never gave a reading until well into middle age.

The trope of inscription undergirds a number of his poems, among them "To the Stone-Cutters," the very next poem after "The Excesses of God" in *The Collected Poetry:*

> /   /   /   /   /
> Stone-cutters fighting time with marble, you foredefeated
> /   /
> Challengers of oblivion

Eat cynical earnings, knowing rock splits, records fall down,
The square-limbed Roman letters
Scale in the thaws, wear in the rain. The poet as well
Builds his monument mockingly;
For man will be blotted out, the blithe earth die, the brave sun
Die blind and blacken to the heart:
Yet stones have stood for a thousand years, and pained thoughts
  found
The honey of peace in old poems. (*CP* 1: 5)

This poem is difficult to scan, as there are many secondary stresses, although I believe that Jeffers was counting quite carefully in this poem. We can begin by noting the preponderance of alliteration in many of the lines, and even groups of lines: rock/records; monument/mockingly; blotted/blithe—blind/blacken; stones/stood; peace/poems; and so on. I have indicated my scansion by marking syllables in the text. I think that the first pair of lines have five then two strong stresses respectively, and that the remaining four pairs are all 6,3.[14] I am not sure why Jeffers changed his scheme after the first two lines, although I can find no other way to scan the poem. It is surprising, given that the rest of the poem seems quite intentionally regular. Perhaps the best we can do is to leave these lines as examples of the "free" lines Jeffers alludes to in his correspondence with Klein.

This tease is the ground of a lyric that announces "The poet as well / Builds his monument mockingly." The poem articulates apparent cynicism about the durability of art, at the same time as it draws on a versification that intentionally eludes traditional accentual-syllabic categories of measure, and therefore scansion. Seen in this light, Jeffers's "cynical earnings" yield surprising dividends.

First, the conception of the craft of poetry in this poem is both the construction of a monument and the carving of an inscription into that monument. Note that Jeffers does not tell us what "The square-limbed Roman letters" say; what the monument says is not more significant than what it is made of, or what it says cannot be separated from the sensual material out of which it is made. In a twist on the usual sense of "writing in stone," Jeffers makes inscription a figure of evanescence, not permanence. In the long run, Jeffers tells us, writing is no more durable than speech, even writing in stone. In fact, even the stones are not durable in the long run that the poem envisions, which is eternity and "oblivion." The appropriate attitude to take toward the creation of art is therefore self-mockery, for to claim to have fought successfully against time in one's art is a delusion.

Jeffers nevertheless builds and carves a poem, albeit deprecating the force of his own verse inscription, a mere human artifact grafted onto nature, which is in turn only a spark in the void. Despite the note of solace on which the poem ends, "To the Stone-Cutters" is a poem about failure (a far different thing from being a failure as a poem). The point is that the represented failure is so ambitious that it supersedes all previous work, "The honey of peace in old poems." Pointing to the tradition, Jeffers's poem always calls itself new, or at least belated. Like the passage spoken by Orestes in "The Tower Beyond Tragedy" with which I opened this essay, "To the Stone-Cutters" cunningly denies the significance of art, and makes an ode to its own failure, in order to represent the sublime, the "outward" world and "oblivion," all the more powerfully. It is a manifesto addressed to the entire tradition, which it both masters and joins by calling all art a failure when held up to the abyss where "man will be blotted out, the blithe earth die, the brave sun / Die blind and blacken to the heart." This failure, like the Cretan paradox, can be conceived only in terms of language, specifically writing.

The poem's verse is not an ornament to this theme, or a reflection of it. Jeffers's versecraft, in which numbered lines clash with an unmeasurable (or arbitrarily numbered) arrangement of words in each line, grounds the evocation of everything that the poem is not, and cannot possibly represent: the immeasurable and sublime "oblivion" in which even all of art and nature are just a minuscule flutter. The versification is not imitating this theme; it is at its source, in much the way that the raw rock with which a sculptor or stone-cutter works must always already hold the figure to be found.

In conclusion, I return to the question of Jeffers's reputation. Jeffers's admirers have long felt, rightly, that his poetry has not received its due. This is in part because too many readers, including apologists, have taken him at his word when he dismissed craft as a game. To argue, in contrast, that Jeffers was far more concerned with craft than might at first be clear is in no way to undermine the force of the poetry, which is the only reason to study his versecraft to begin with. As Robert Bridges wrote when discussing the accentual hexameter, and considering similar arguments against the study of versecraft, "it is no honour to an art to despise its grammar" (*Accentual Verse* 111), and this has been the attitude of nearly every serious poet/scholar who has written on these questions. In his best work Jeffers was a poet of the first rank, and his hard-won innovations in versecraft inform his greater poetic project, from its center out to the margins.

Notes

1. As early as 1925 James Daly sensed the stress-based origins of Jeffers's metric, and argued that it had evolved from blank verse (in Karman, ed., 47). Herbert Klein's M.A. thesis at Occidental College, the first long critical work on the poet (1930), is "The Prosody of Robinson Jeffers." It was never published, but Lawrence Clark Powell's *Robinson Jeffers: The Man and His Work*, the first book-length study (1934), quotes Klein at length and discusses the same issues (the two men were friends). These two critics laid the groundwork for all further study of Jeffers's versification, emphasizing a stress-count model, ramified through correspondence and discussion with the poet himself. Other significant essays include: Cornelius Cunningham's "The Rhythm of Robinson Jeffers' Poetry as Revealed by Oral Reading" (1946) in which he wrongly concludes that "The beat to which Jeffers' verse tends is iambic-anapestic duple meter" (356); two essays by Edward Nickerson, one on Jeffers's use of rhyme in later poems (1974), and another that speculates on Jeffers's use of the paeon as a technique for controlling his "pace" (1975); an earlier essay by Brewster Ghiselin on the paeon in modern poetry, which briefly discusses Jeffers (1942); and Dell Hymes's recent "Jeffers' Artisty of Line" (in Zaller, ed., 226–47), which relies on Klein and Powell. Hymes, who has done groundwork in counting the stress-patterns in many poems but provides few scanned lines, argues for associations between the patterns of Jeffers's alternating stress-counts in the shorter poems, and his thematic concerns. He is writing a book on Jeffers's versecraft, whose larger concern is "to place Jeffers as a narrative poet of the West in relation to American Indian narrative poets who preceded him" (in Zaller, ed., 245). Considering Jeffers's immersion in European and American poetry, I am skeptical of sweeping claims for such a project.

2. I am grateful to Tim Hunt for providing me with much of this

material and his textual commentary on it. All unpublished texts courtesy of Tim Hunt and Stanford UP.

3. Most important among these sources is the correspondence between Jeffers and Klein, which has been published in *The Robinson Jeffers Newsletter* ("Klein-Jeffers Correspondence" 1986; hereafter "KJC").

4. Because it involves counting, Jeffers's verse is, technically, a "meter," but I am not using that term, in order to avoid unnecessary confusion with accentual-syllabic models. Jeffers did return to rhyme and traditional accentual-syllabic meters on several occasions in his later work, although these were exceptions (among them "Love the Wild Swan"). Yet despite this and other evidence that Jeffers was interested in regular versification, the vast majority of critics, sympathetic and hostile, have been content to glance at the lengthy lines in which Jeffers found his mature style, label them "free verse," and leave it at that. To get a sense of the durability of this notion, see James Rorty's praising review of *Roan Stallion, Tamar and Other Poems* in 1925 (in Karman, ed., 45), and Helen Vendler's harsh review of Robert Hass's Jeffers anthology, *Rock and Hawk*, in 1988 (16).

5. See Grudin for a discussion of the way that this paradox describes a powerful tactic for generating poetic meaning in the hands of a strong poet. As he points out, ". . . the Liar Paradox is indeed the opposite of what it seems. Rather than an assault on the bases of verbal communication, it is a manifesto of linguistic morality, an assertion of linguistic identity" (81), as it can only be articulated in language to begin with.

6. A number of Jeffers's early poems, such as this one, precede the 1920 cutoff date that Tim Hunt chose for Volume I of *CP;* this poem and several others that originally appeared in *Roan Stallion, Tamar and Other Poems* will appear in Volume IV.

7. In other places ("KJC" 22) Klein refers to the 1921 version of Bridges's book, in which an entire chapter is devoted to developing a complex theory of and scansion system for accentual verse, but in his letter he quotes the earlier version.

8. Klein's passage is drawn from Bridges's pages (73, 76, and 77), and I have reproduced the passage from there. There are some interesting changes in Klein. Some of his punctuation is inaccurate; assuming the transcription in the *Robinson Jeffers Newsletter* is correct, Klein has changed the last word in the phrase "If the number of stresses be fixed" to "mixed," which would render the statement nonsensical.

9. Jeffers does provide tantalizing clues for those who believe his work is more traditionally metrical, but I believe they issue in a cul-de-sac. Most significant is his note-sheet on "Tamar," which he included in a letter to Donald Friede on November 25, 1925 (see *SL* 52–53). At the bottom of the sheet, he had written:

5 beats to the line
  doubled in a few passages to [?] 10s
  quickened to anapests, [?] anapestic
  u u u—lyrical passages, [?]
  to 8s. (*SL* 53)

Ghiselin had not seen this note-sheet (although he had read the Alberts bibliography, from which he quotes, and probably had read Powell). At any rate, he cites Bridges on accentual verse, and argues only that Jeffers's poetry "is written in an accentual measure . . . rich in paeons" (341). The problem, of course, is that while Ghiselin's scanning of the accentual lines he looks at is convincing, foot boundaries become moot in such a scheme, because there is no syllabic norm to the line in accentual verse. Nickerson ("Robinson Jeffers" 1975) pushes Ghiselin's conclusions a bit further, concluding that Jeffers was "imaginatively experimenting with ways of measuring what has so often and mistakenly been called his free verse" (193), but realizes that this measure cannot form the basis of his verse, and that Jeffers uses a stress-count metric.

10. Helen Vendler has written that Jeffers never paid any critical attention to, among other things, "the modulation over time which is natural to a temporal art" (19), concluding that Jeffers "was not actually writing lyric. He was writing oratory—a rhythmical, emotional, sensual and imaginative public prose he had absorbed from the Greek political tradition" (19). This echoes the closer commentary of Chard Powers Smith, a critic and poet who published a massive work on versification called *Pattern and Variation in Poetry* in 1932. Smith's comments on Jeffers illustrate the aural assumptions of most verse theory. After quoting *Cawdor*, Smith comments: "There is no fixed pattern which the ear can recognize. Only the eye reader can catch the turn of one movement against the other, a provocative clash like that between line and cadence. But to the ear there is not clash. It is not inevitable that the cadences set on the page should break just where they do and nowhere else. There is no musical pattern, and it is not poetry but poetic prose" (235–36). The debate over whether *Paradise Lost* was prose or verse was intense and of long duration. See Bradford for a discussion.

11. This poem was first published in *Give Your Heart to the Hawks, and Other Poems* (1933).

12. An incomplete list of other lyrics, to look only at Jeffers's earlier work, that explicitly thematize verse and measure includes "The Treasure" (*CP* 1:102), "Post Mortem" (*CP* 1: 204–05), "Clouds at Evening" (*CP* 1: 206), "Bixby's Landing" (*CP* 1: 388), "Subjected Earth" (*CP* 2: 129), "Second-Best" (*CP* 2: 132), "Still the Mind Smiles" (*CP* 2: 310),

"Love the Wild Swan" (a metrical, rhymed poem) (*CP* 2: 410), and many others, along with countless passages in the narratives.

13. In letters Jeffers referred to the poem as a new Faust; at one point Barclay announces "I have come to establish you / Over the last deception, to make men like God / Beyond good and evil" (*CP* 1: 282).

14. Hymes gives his pattern for the poem as 6,4 7,3 6,4 7,4 6,4 (in Zaller, ed., 231). Among other things, this means that he gives the second line, "Challengers of oblivion," 4 strong stresses, which is untenable, as no word in English can bear more than one.

Works Cited

CP *The Collected Poetry of Robinson Jeffers*. Ed. Tim Hunt. 3 vols. to date, Stanford, CA: Stanford UP, 1988, 1989, 1991.

SL *The Selected Letters of Robinson Jeffers, 1897–1962*. Ed. Ann N. Ridgeway. Baltimore: Johns Hopkins UP, 1968.

Alberts, S. S. *A Bibliography of the Works of Robinson Jeffers*. New York: Random House, 1933.

Bradford, Richard. "'Verse Only to the Eye'? Line Endings in *Paradise Lost*." *Essays in Criticism* 33 (1983): 187–204.

Bridges, Robert. *Milton's Prosody and Classical Metres in English Verse by William John Stone*. Oxford: Oxford UP, 1901.

——. *Milton's Prosody, with a Chapter on Accentual Verse, and Notes*. Rev. final ed. Oxford: Oxford UP, 1921.

Cunningham, Cornelius Carman. "The Rhythm of Robinson Jeffers' Poetry as Revealed by Oral Reading." *Quarterly Journal of Speech* 32 (1946): 351–57.

Ghiselin, Brewster. "Paeonic Measures in English Verse." *Modern Language Notes* 57 (1942): 336–41.

Gross, Harvey, ed. *The Structure of Verse: Modern Essays on Prosody*. Rev. ed. New York: Ecco, 1979.

Grudin, Robert: "All Cretans Are Liars." *Hellas* 2.1 (1991): 78–82.

Harris, Roy. *The Origin of Writing*. La Salle, IL: Open Court, 1986.

Hass, Robert. Introduction. *Rock and Hawk: A Selection of the Shorter Poems by Robinson Jeffers*. Ed. Robert Hass. New York: Random House, 1987. xv–xlii.

Jeffers, Robinson. *Roan Stallion, Tamar and Other Poems*. New York: Boni & Liveright, 1925.

Karman, James. *Critical Essays on Robinson Jeffers*. Boston: Hall, 1990.

Keats, John. *The Complete Poems*. Ed. John Barnard. 2nd ed. New York: Penguin, 1973.

"Klein-Jeffers Correspondence: 1930 and 1935." *Robinson Jeffers Newsletter* 67 (July 1986): 11–27.

Nickerson, Edward. "The Return to Rhyme." *Robinson Jeffers Newsletter* 39 (1974): 12–21.

——. "Robinson Jeffers and the Paeon." *Western American Literature* 10 (1975): 189–93.

Powell, Lawrence Clark. *Robinson Jeffers: The Man and His Work*. Los Angeles: Primavera, 1934.

Smith, Chard Powers. *Pattern and Variation in Poetry*. New York: Scribner's, 1932.

Vendler, Helen. "Huge Pits of Darkness, High Peaks of Light." *Robinson Jeffers Newsletter* 77 (1990): 13–22.

William, William Carlos. "Free Verse." *Princeton Encyclopedia of Poetry and Poetics*. Ed. Alex Preminger et al. Princeton: Princeton UP, 1974. 288–90.

Zaller, Robert, ed. *Centennial Essays for Robinson Jeffers*. Newark: U of Delaware P, 1991.

7

Robinson Jeffers and the Female Archetype

THE FOLLOWING is an edited transcript of a recent American Literature Association session entitled "Robinson Jeffers and the Female Archetype." The session was organized on behalf of the Robinson Jeffers Association by Robert Zaller (Drexel University). Professor Zaller also chaired the session, which began with monologues from Robinson Jeffers's *Medea* performed by actress Lili Bita. Mark Jarman (Vanderbilt University) and Mark Mitchell (Harvard University Extension School) followed with papers, before the floor was opened to a general discussion, which included Professor Zaller and respondents in the audience, Tim Hunt (Washington State University, Vancouver), and Jacqueline Vaught Brogan (Notre Dame University). At the request of the Robinson Jeffers Association, Diane Wakoski (Michigan State University) and Betty Adcock (Meredeth College) have composed written responses to the papers and the subsequent discussion. The transcript begins after the conclusion of Lili Bita's performance.

ZALLER: I would like to introduce Professor Mark Jarman of Vanderbilt University, a well-known poet and critic, author of five books, most recently *The Black Riviera* and *Iris*, a book-length poetic narrative—much in the spirit of Robinson Jeffers himself—about a woman who becomes obsessed with Jeffers's spirit. Professor Jarman will speak to us today on one of Jeffers's most neglected poems, "The Loving Shepherdess," which contains one of Jeffers's most beautifully realized feminine figures, Clare Walker.

JARMAN: I have entitled this "Sheathed in Reality"; you may know the line from "Hurt Hawks" in which Jeffers imagines the hawk after he has killed it becoming "unsheathed from reality." My subtitle is "The Fact of Clare Walker in Robinson Jeffers's 'The Loving Shepherdess.'"

Recently I heard an exchange between a young critic and a young novelist concerning characters in the novelist's latest book, which she said dealt with gender. The critic asked the novelist how she gendered her characters. The novelist responded that she would never think of working that way. She said she began with characters who happened to be male or female; presumably gender followed from there. Though the novelist left herself open for such a question—"How do you gender your characters in a novel that deals with gender?"—I liked her answer. Of course, she would not think of gendering a character any more than she might think of portraying a character as a symbol or an archetype. I should add that this novelist works primarily in the realm of realism. If she does anything, it is to make us believe her characters conform to a world of everyday reality based on conventions of fictional representation that go back—how far? Nearly 200 years? Or all the way back to the beginning of storytelling?

My point is that Robinson Jeffers, who can hardly be called a realist, has in his poem "The Loving Shepherdess" created in his main character, Clare Walker, someone who conforms first to a world of everyday reality, even though it is the heightened reality of Jeffers's central California coast. Clare Walker may indeed be the embodiment of a female archetype or "archetypally Christian," as R. W. (Herbie) Butterfield argues, but without the reality in which Jeffers sheathes her she would embody nothing.

"The Loving Shepherdess," published in 1929 in the volume *Dear Judas*, is unlike most of Jeffers's other narrative poems, since the most dramatic action has taken place before the poem begins. Clare Walker's lover and father have had a violent confrontation, resulting in her father's death; privateers have sacked the family ranch; Clare is alone, as the poem begins, leading about ten sheep, the remnants of her family's flock. And she is pregnant with a child she knows she is physically incapable of having. The Oedipal conflict, which Robert Zaller has pointed out is the heart of many of Jeffers's narrative poems, is in the background of "The Loving Shepherdess," but it has resulted in Clare's dilemma. Clare may be a Christ-figure, a mother-figure, an ironic figure of the waning moon, the final phase of Robert Graves's White Goddess; she may even be the muse herself. First, she has to be someone we can see and believe, and there are passages in this poem where I think we do.

We see and believe Clare Walker for many reasons, but I will concentrate on four of them. First is the way other characters respond to her. Second is the way she responds to them. Third and most important is the physical fact of her body: Jeffers has spent more precise details on her than on any other character except Hoult Gore, the walking corpse in "The Love and the Hate." Fourth is her place in the landscape, that "intense realization of character rooted in place" that Zaller has said marks Jeffers's work at its best. Here she is rootless or uprooted, like Hardy's Tess or the traveling shepherdess referred to in Walter Scott's *Heart of Midlothian*, which Butterfield has noted as a possible model for Clare Walker. As she moves through the landscape, it gives her life while taking it away and finally assimilating her.

The first characters Clare Walker encounters are a group of school children who taunt her. One of them shouts, "'You killed your daddy, why don't you kill your sheep?'" Not only is this the untruth of gossip, but it has the logic or illogic of a jeer. At the end of the poem, divested of her flock and "heavily swollen / Toward child-birth," Clare camps with some outcast men. Hearing her call her absent sheep, one smiles "without mockery." That he is a "sickly, sullen boy" recalls the boys of the schoolyard, even the boy Will Brighton, a young ranch hand that she sleeps with. It is both a symmetrical moment and one that, because it has no explanation, stabs with poignancy. When the rancher Fogler aids her by giving her a pair of his wife's old shoes, then furtively kisses her knee; when Will Brighton first encounters her and says, "'Where did you drop from?'"; when Onorio Vasquez warns her that with the onset of the spring rains she ought to think of herself; when an old man who has given her shelter in his barn catches her foot in the straw and scratches her sole with his thumb nail, then declines her offer of sexual comfort; finally, whenever her sheep turn to her, follow her, even though they have an air of the fabulous about them—in all the ways other characters respond to her, she is given further depth, reality, believability.

Clare's responses to others are easier to interpret, to see as emblematic of a meaning beyond simple fact. I suppose what interests me about Clare Walker (even her name is a combination of lucidity and physicality) is the fact of her rather than her meaning. We know she loves and pities her flock, though in her current state, homeless, wandering, and due to hunger and illness not entirely sane, she leaves her flock vulnerable to disaster and one by one its members are destroyed. Still, when bathing in a pond she feels a ewe's chin on her shoulder and draws "the bony head against the soft breasts." The scene that I find most affecting and that relates most clearly to my argument occurs after Clare has spent the night with her sheep in a barn.

> . . . two coughing sheep
> Brought her to a stand then she opened their mouths and found
> Their throats full of barbed seeds from the bad hay
> Greedily eaten: and the gums about their teeth
> Were quilled with the wicked spikes which drawn, thin blood
> Dripped from the jaw. The folds of the throat her fingers
> Could not reach nor relieve; thereafter, when they coughed,
> Clare shook with pain. Her pity poisoned her strength.

I think this passage is equal to any in Jeffers. It has an exact homely sadness, especially about the unreachable folds of the sheep's throats, worthy of a stylist like Flaubert. Fact speaks for itself. Jeffers adds his note about human weakness ("Her pity poisoned her strength"), for if Clare is a Christ-figure, it behooves Jeffers's inhumanism to underline the detrimental effects of human sympathy. Yet the passage shows that Clare Walker is aware of her desires—to help her sheep—and her limits—her inability to pluck out all the barbed seeds. At the very end of the poem, when she goes into labor, knowing she will die, "she called / The sheep about her and perceived that none came." This passage, too, gives her the dignity of factuality. She may have behaved in a deluded way and have deliriously thought her dead flock had accompanied her, as the outcast men have observed, but her final response to her absent flock is awareness. Simply, they do not exist to answer her call any longer and she knows. She knows she is alone.

Clare's body as a physical fact is central to the poem and to her fate. Jeffers's very first description of her marvels how "her thin young face / Seemed joyful, and lighted from inside, and formed / Too finely to be so wind-burnt." Variations on this description continue through the poem, including comments on her chapped lips and the brownness of her skin. A few details stand out as remarkably real. At evening sitting among her flock Clare combs her hair with a "gap-toothed comb" and "the thick blond strands" hiss. When she attempts to bathe in a shallow stream, she is described as "[f]lattening herself to find the finger's depth water." Like the bodies of other Jeffers heroines, hers is lean, boyish, with "flattened flanks / Hardly a woman's." Her leanness has to do with hunger, in part, though I detect in these women of Jeffers's a certain narcissistic projection of his own body into theirs. In any event, when taking shelter in the barn where her sheep eat the bad hay, Clare smells the fried grease clinging to the old man who has given her shelter when he comes after his meal to visit her; she hungrily believes he is bringing her food. Elsewhere, describing her love affair with the man who has killed her father, she speaks of her first experience of orgasm as a "sweet fire." Jeffers gives her a body that includes appetites, even vanity—human realities. Most important is her understanding of herself as a pregnant mother. The passage which occurs in the tenth section of the twelve-part poem is, to my mind, the climax; it also contains an element that seems purely Jeffers and, therefore, disturbing. Upon learning that Clare is pregnant and doomed because of the shape of her pelvis (she has had one miscarriage already), Onorio Vasquez who has tried to help her urges her to abort the baby. She refuses to do this. She has had a mystical insight into "[t]he golden country that our souls came from." Onorio Vasquez, a visionary who appears in other Jeffers poems, knows this place as well; it is the country of his visions. But Clare, physical creature that she is, believes it is the womb. In her womb her child is experiencing that golden country. She tells Vasquez:

When I was in my worst trouble
I knew that the child was feeding on peace and happiness. I had happiness here in my body. It is not mine,
But I am its world and the sky around it, its loving God. It is having the prime and perfect of life,
The nine months that are better than the ninety years. I'd not steal one of its days to save my life.
I am like its God, how could I betray it?

Here she speaks of herself in terms that other Jeffers characters might use, characters like Barclay in "The Women at Point Sur" who denies God by taking on the responsibilities of God, Hoult Gore in "The Love and the Hate" who imagines his body is as large as the world, California in "Roan Stallion" who thinks that by killing a murderous horse she has killed God. The element these characters share is what the Greeks called *hubris*. Clare Walker's lines disturb me because they reveal the magical reasoning of someone who has included the fate of another with her fate. When Vasquez remembers or almost remembers that the Caesarean section operation would be a resolution of Clare's dilemma, it is futile. Besides, Clare, sick, starving, insane, is determined to die; many of her references include a foreknowledge of death. When she dies, all creation as she sees herself to be will expire with her. The death of the fully formed infant is still a moral dilemma, even if the child has enjoyed a few more months of the womb's golden country. Like all the admissions of Jeffers's great obsessed characters, Clare's fascinates and repels me.

In his book *Landscape into Art*, Kenneth Clark observes that "facts become art through love." If there is anything Jeffers truly loved that went into his art, it was the natural landscape where he set most of his poems: the California coast stretching from the north end of Monterey Bay as far south as Morro Rock, the coast range of mountains, and the meadows, rivers, deltas, and canyons among these features. Along with them there were the sky, sun, moon, stars, and the Pacific ocean itself. These are the most fully realized of any of the parts of his poems, be they his short lyrics or longer narratives. This seems to be so obvious that any reader of Jeffers, even one who knows the poet only from passages quoted on a Sierra Club Wilderness Calendar, would know it to be true. But as with references to Clare Walker, I want to dwell on small touches that represent her connection to this landscape and the loving transformation of it as fact. The first is the reference to Clare's walking stick, "the bent staff of rosy-barked madrone-wood / That lay in her hand." Anyone who knows the region knows the tree and its peculiar beauty. For Jeffers the phrase "rosy-barked" with respect to madrone or manzanita is almost as much a mnemonic motif as Homer's rosy-fingered dawn. The staff connects Clare to the landscape, even as she drifts through it aimlessly. The Pacific is a constant presence as well and is described at one point when the sun streams through a cloud as "the lank striped ocean," terms that almost could be applied to Clare. She makes her way through Jeffers country, and the poet refers to landmarks by the names of characters he has associated with them in earlier poems, "Cawdor's Canyon" and "Point Lobos, by a gate / Where Tamar Cauldwell used to lean from her white pony / To swing the bars." One of the last signs of Clare caught by Vasquez is "in the yellow mud / Prints of bare feet, dibbled about with many / Little crowding hoof-marks." In this regard, Clare is a visitation to the entire Jeffers landscape, like the poet's love itself walking with clarity and unusual sweetness over the places he has transformed and set down in his poems.

If Clare Walker is an embodiment of the female archetype, then I might draw strength from Robert Graves and say that not only is she Jeffers's own interpretation of Christian charity, as well as a version of human tragedy as he represented it time and again in his great landscape, but I think she represents the muse. Sadly she is doomed, like other Jeffers heroines. He has derived this convention not from Greek tragedy but from nineteenth-century narratives where female characters who step outside of social norms are also lost. That deserves a much longer treatment. My aims here are modest: to me Clare Walker is one of the most vividly imagined of Jeffers's characters, even as in some ways she is the most imaginary. He brings her to life by the ways in which he makes her a fact.

ZALLER: Our next speaker is Mark Mitchell, who has just received his ALM from Harvard University Extension School for his thesis on "Robinson Jeffers and the New Critics."

MITCHELL: Given that my particular interest in Jeffers's work lies in the lyrics of the 1921–1935 period, I am going to sidestep, for the most part, a discussion of Jeffers's female characters as they appear in the narratives, to spend my time touching on the figuration of male and female in the early mature lyrics. It is clear that there is much to say with regard to the female archetype as it is exemplified by the women in the narratives. But one finds traces of the female archetype in the lyrics without too much difficulty. In fact, there are much more than mere traces: if we look among the early lyrics of the 1920s, we find that Jeffers spends a great deal of time exploring and identifying the female and male aspects of the world that he perceives, and the advantage of looking to the early lyrics for these ideas is that Jeffers here is unburdened by demands of character and plot. In the lyrics, he can focus on the female or male aspects of the non-human, or inhuman, world without worrying about what his characters are doing.

There are, in Jeffers's early lyrics, numerous examples of unorthodox gender typing. Jeffers's "Gods," if you will, appear more often than not in female incarnations. In "Shine, Perishing Republic," life's journey is described as "out of the mother, and through the spring exultances, ripeness and decadence and home to the mother."

Similarly, in "Continent's End," we encounter an omnipresent mother-figure in the ocean to which the poet addresses his verse. He writes:

> I said: "You yoke the Aleutian seal-rocks with the lava and coral
> sowings that flower the south,
> Over your flood the life that sought the sunrise faces ours that
> has followed the evening star.
>
> The long migrations meet across you and it is nothing to you,
> you have forgotten us, mother,

You were much younger when we crawled out of the womb and
lay in the sun's eye on the tideline.

In each of these instances, the streams of existence move from a female alpha to a female omega. There appears to be nothing superior to these female elements. The dualities of this Ur-figure are almost Venusian: fertility, abundance, and creativity as well as elemental sexuality, and Jeffers admits all these characteristics in very positive ways. He is not a poet who insists upon positing the existence or "authority" of a male god.

Slightly deeper in the canon of Jeffers's work we encounter the longer lyric, "Night," which continues the female figuration I have been describing:

Over the dark mountain, over the dark pinewood,
Down the long dark valley along the shrunken river,
Returns the splendor without rays, the shining of shadow,
Peace-bringer, the matrix of all shining and quieter of shining.

The "matrix" of all shining and "quieter of all shining," that universal force from which all flows and to which all returns, is inherently female, and throughout the poem Jeffers refers to "Night" with the female pronouns "her" and "hers." "Death is no evil," the poem concludes, and we can understand that death is no evil because it entails a reunion, a reconnection, with the mother-figure from which we sprang to begin with.

If we stand back for a second and consider the implications of this female authority within the context of Jeffers's "Inhumanism," which he described as "a shifting of emphasis and significance from man to not-man" and "the rejection of human solipsism and recognition of the transhuman magnificence," then we begin to see how this female figuration of nature's fundamental energies informs virtually all of Jeffers's work.

I do not want to make too much of this point, but when Jeffers says that Inhumanism involves a "shifting of emphasis from man to not-man," I would not discount his awareness of the gender implications in that statement; for men and male energy are very frequently corrupt in Jeffers's poetry, and this shifting of emphasis to the not-man, to the over-arching female forces and natural cycles of the universe, is at some levels a valorization of these archetypal female energies.

So many of Jeffers's lyrics echo themes of humanity's dissociation from the natural world, and I think it is a fair generalization to say that he lays the blame for that dissociation upon Western culture in general and, in particular, to what he sees as an archetypally male propensity to divide, conquer, and contain. The female energy of nature is one that expands, joins, integrates, and includes—as he writes in "Continent's End,"

> "You yoke the Aleutian seal-rocks with the lava and coral sowings that flower the south."

The female force is one that binds and coheres; it is the highly valued fabric that holds things together.

If we look again to a work such as "Shine, Perishing Republic," with its linkage between a male, manufactured world of cities, on the one hand, and, on the other, its female flow of life from the mother, through the spring exultances, through the period of decadence, and back again to the mother, we see that the male energies are associated with what, in the face of the great and inevitable cycles of nature, is a very limited notion of "power." The archetypal male energy appears manifest as a hunger for power and control, whereas the archetypal female energy appears manifest as an inevitable movement toward union and reunion, a *desire for merger.*

Repeatedly, Jeffers enjoins his readers to pay more attention to these natural cycles, the energies of the female, of the not-man, and to abandon the rigid, controlling, and very limited notions of power that he associates with the male and with anthropocentric humanism in general. He repeatedly focuses on the cycles of nature and the impossibility of overcoming the demands of those cycles.

In another early lyric, "To the Stone-Cutters," he writes:

> Stone-cutters fighting time with marble, you foredefeated
> Challengers of oblivion
> Eat cynical earnings, knowing rock splits, records fall down,
> The square-limbed Roman letters
> Scale in the thaws, wear in the rain.

The stone-cutters are the "challengers of oblivion," the men who try and who fail to assert their permanence and power over nature's forces—the recurring freezes and thaws, the nourishing rains themselves. The poet, in contrast, "builds his monument mockingly" because he knows that "man will be blotted out, the blithe earth die, the brave sun / die blind and blackened to the heart." The poet accepts this vision as natural, whereas the stone-cutters—by which he is, in some ways, stretching beyond the masons constructing Tor House and incorporating all of Western civilization's attempts, characteristically male, at establishing permanence (i.e., the square-limbed Roman letters)—are always "fighting time." Theirs is a struggle, a fight, a war against the forces of nature, an assertion of that need to control—a need that the poet does not share. Jeffers sees himself living, and finding joy, within the cycle: he cherishes his place within a world more completely and inescapably bound by female forces.

If we take a look at the earliest lyrics in Volume I of *The Collected Poetry*—including "The Maid's Thought" and "To the Stone-cutters," "Divinely Superfluous Beauty," "The Excesses of God," and "To the House"—we will find that every one of them enjoins, in some capacity, these archetypal female qualities and powers.

In "The Excesses of God," to take only one of these works, we see again the reference to the authority of nature itself, and nature is feminine. Even though "god" is referred to by the masculine possessive pronoun, the attributes and manifestations of "god" are spectacularly curvaceous and sensual, and, on a syntactic level, they all lead inexorably to the necessary embrace of breeding. It is as though the rainbows, the domes of the deep sea-shells, the celestial vault hanging above the moon itself are all identified with the rounded belly of pregnancy.

The conclusion of "The Excesses of God" is also interesting in this regard, for it highlights what for Jeffers is an ongoing archetypal conflict between the male and the female imperatives: if power and desire, the male and the female, could be "perch-mates," then we would be able to perceive the great humaneness at the heart of things. Now, most people do not expect Jeffers to speak of a "great humaneness," and many readers might dismiss the poem as sentimental, or as one in which he had not formulated his more well-known "inhumanist" perspective. After all, "humaneness" is not something he seems to emphasize anywhere else.

In light of what I have said about female nature, I think such a dismissal is premature. As Jeffers sees it, the problem is that power and desire are hardly ever perch-mates; they are, in most situations in Jeffers's work, at the very core of the trouble that informs a given poetic situation. In the narratives we encounter the conflict of power and desire over and over: it is the male quest for power that tries to control the female desire; it is the female desire that tries to overcome the male need for power and control.

After these curvaceous images of domes and vaults and sea-shell walls it would be unfortunate if we arrived at the conclusion of "The Excesses of God" merely to conjure the image of a pair of lovebirds billing and cooing at each another. I would like to suggest that Jeffers may not have been intending so sentimental a picture. I think he is trying to point out the limits of the essentially male, anthropocentric view of the world. Jeffers believes, and I think quite rightly, that his contemporary readers viewed themselves as superior to the animal kingdom. If anything, they saw themselves as the stewards of nature, and nature was to be subdued and cultivated and/or destroyed as Men saw fit. Humans are not perch-mates, and his point here is that only if one is able to adapt the perspective of female nature—a perspective in which humans are no better than animals, in which humans are merely perch-mates in the hold of the cosmic ark—can the ultimate beauties of the universe be observed. Until that time, ours will be a struggle between power and desire; a unified beauty—and this female quality of unification is what I think he means by "humaneness"—will not appear.

Ultimately, in Jeffers's early lyrics these unifications and mergers are the point to which he repeatedly returns. He reiterates in a hundred different forms his sense of the interconnectedness of humanity and nature, nature and the planet, the planet and the cosmos. The male impulses in his poems—as manifest in the cities, in the vulgar mold of America—all stress independence, isolation, and unrelatedness to nature, the planet, and the cosmos. From the perspective of the male energies, these elements are subordinate to Man. Yet Jeffers repeatedly returns to his point that Man is not the measure of all things, and that the energies of the cosmic cycles, the female energies of desire, birth, death, and rebirth, will always triumph over the male energies as manifest in the quest for power, stability, and control. Ultimately Jeffers is much more sympathetic and attuned to the female energies, for these he perceives to lie at the heart of the abiding power of the universe itself.

ZALLER: I'd like to ask Tim Hunt, first, to share with the audience a little bit about what he and I were talking about earlier today. Tim has discovered a 500-line poem that sheds some light on the subject of our panel, though five hundred lines in early Jeffers is not so much as it sounds!

TIM HUNT: Well, actually the lines of this piece are pretty long. I have been working on the pre-1920 poems, and have found four that are, apparently, responses to the Russian Revolution, which in itself is surprising. In one, the original title is "The Birth of

Liberty in Russia" (he later retitled it "The Daughter of God in Russia"). In the poem, Liberty is personified as a female figure, and Jeffers sees her as justifying the war. Not quite what you would expect from the anti-political Jeffers. What took me aback—I did not expect it; the poem is kind of allegorical, not a narrative at all—is that it celebrates not only the figure of Liberty but also the revolutionary moment itself. In the middle, Jeffers breaks into a lyric interlude where he, in what seems his own voice, begs the daughter destroy him before God the father does so for his sinful relationships with other women. Then at the end of the poem, Christ (the son of God, not the daughter) is off in the margin, a figure who, like Clare, is full of pity, and impotent because of it, and therefore no longer historically relevant. The central figure is the daughter, Liberty, who will be the next coming. Throughout the poem she has been figured as both destruction and renewal. She is, of course, the precursor of Tamar, the logic behind Tamar. But she is three or four years earlier than Tamar, in the middle of the First World War, in a poem where the confluence of the political, the personal, and the religious—those three dimensions—is more explicit than Jeffers would later allow it to be. We have always thought that the eruption of Tamar was specifically connected to Jeffers's turn to narrative, but this poem shows that it was not and that it was earlier, even though this poem also shows Jeffers cannot handle it yet, and he soon veered away from it.

Is that what you wanted me to say?

ZALLER: Yes, that sounds rather like what I hoped you would say. Thank you. I think that is really an important consideration. We have always been looking for the missing link in Jeffers's development that leads to "Tamar."

JACQUELINE VAUGHT BROGAN: What Tim has discovered I think really puts into perspective a lot of the things I was asking you about last year at the ALA meeting in San Diego. As a female reader of Jeffers, I run into a real problem. For as compelling as his characters may be, I am sick to death of seeing women killed for textual narrative development, for historical development, and there is not that much difference between seeing Clare Walker die and snuff movies in New York in terms of violence against women.

I am exaggerating that on purpose, but voyeuristic watching

of female suffering—which is very much a part of Jeffers—is repugnant to actual reading women. We are sick of this. But I also make the point that what I thought he was doing was hard work, because he was taking on this sort of cultural myth that evidently kills the woman in the name of some sort of father as being something he had to get out of. Yet there was no way for him to get out of it, and so he made a text that was showing the futility of that cultural myth for both men and women.

Now, it is interesting that that text can serve as the embodiment of that whole thing and that he himself could be sympathetic—how do you write something new? Well, there you have it. He takes Christ and puts Christ out here and says the future belongs to this new woman of God. And Alicia Ostriker, who was in the audience at last year's ALA meeting, is doing this whole thing on Job in which she is taking on what Job's *wife* would have thought about having individual children killed and then having them redoubled. She figures that Job's wife is not going to experience redoubling of children as being in any way compensatory. And I was thinking that the text you had really supported my thesis that [Jeffers's] texts ultimately are not sexist but embody this whole cultural myth problematic: how do we go on and how do we write ourselves out of it? You know, given the fact that life, death, tradition are not terribly wonderful for women.

HUNT: The narrative that follows "Cawdor" somewhat reinforces your point. The working title of "Thurso's Landing" was "Helen Thurso." And it is not clear as you read the poem whether it is in fact Reave's narrative or Helen's narrative. I think Jeffers chose to call it by the place rather than after either of the characters for similar reasons. In the poem, Reave is clearly a patriarchal, rigid character who cannot respond to the energy of the landscape, the energy of a relationship, and he is finally fractured physically by this inability. When Helen runs off with her lover, Reave has no choice but to track her down and bring her back from the desert to re-establish his patriarchal dominance, even though Jeffers implies this will to dominance is seriously flawed, and this sets him off toward his destruction. In this poem you get a real sense that Jeffers cannot imagine any other alternative for his character—that is, what the male figure has to do in order maintain his power—but that he also sees this as a completely insufficient response. Since he cannot imagine another response, though, you end up with this destructive collision.

MITCHELL: This is one of the reasons the lyrics interest me in some ways, because Jeffers seems unable to reconcile his characters to bring about a change in a character like Reave Thurso. Whereas in the lyrics themselves somehow he tries to show how that change can be described and it usually has something to do with nature. But you never quite see how it has been realized in the long poems.

JARMAN: I think one of the women who comes off most strongly in his poems, though she figures in only a few, is Una Jeffers. In a poem called "All the Little Hoofprints," which is basically an anecdotal narrative of riding up into the mountains and of what is seen there, Una comes off like no other female character in Jeffers. A human being with concerns that are quite contrasting with ordinary Jeffers. So there is this woman in his poems that he is almost trying to pin down, who of course has a life of her own. I think the problem you raise about how he fixes the female characters in the poems is a real problem, and I do not think it is resolved. Except through some ingenious argument which you have sort of provided to us in the traditions of nineteenth-century narratives, novels which disposed of women time and again.

ZALLER: One can also point out that far more male characters die at the hands of women than vice versa in Jeffers's narratives. Tamar kills the male companions surrounding her; she dies at the same time, but it is a holocaust that she initiates. California kills the male stallion in "Roan Stallion." Fera Martial is responsible for the death of Hood Cawdor in "Cawdor"—and then she is responsible as well for the self-blinding of Cawdor. Fayne Fraser is responsible for the death of Lance Fraser in "Give Your Heart to the Hawks," and at the very end of the poem she is the one who is seen climbing back up the mountain to the road to resume her life after he plunges to his death. And really even more stunningly in the poem that in some ways I think is the most crucial moment in Jeffers, "Hungerfield." This is a poem about a hero who will not let a woman die; he pulls her literally back from death, and when she returns to life against her will, she says, "Why did you do this to me? Why didn't you just let me die?"

BROGAN: Well, that particular argument is not going to resolve what I am talking about, because having a woman be the guilty party, the figure who murders—it is the text of *Medea:* the victim, the woman sacrificed, who then of course has vengeance, hatred—is again an archetypal reading which is very dehumanizing to women. So that does not help me. That does not provide a genuine solution. That is just more of the same. I have been reading this since we started with the Greeks and as a woman I am tired of reading it. And I made the point last year that "Cawdor" is a very difficult text to talk about, but I have worked on it; I went through a series of possible ways of looking at it, and finally came up with what I do not think is an ingenious argument. I said I do not think that he has got out of it; that he could not find another way to write, but that "Cawdor" was a text that self-critiqued that whole tradition; that showed the problems, that was destructive to everyone, but that was not imagining a resolution yet. What is interesting is that the particular poem Tim found is imagining a resolution in which Liberty is presumably going to live, and then Jeffers obviously drops that living part.

HUNT: I would not want to argue that it is a good poem, just that it is one that challenges some accounts of Jeffers's career. There's another point that might be worth coming back to. Mark was talking about Una, and she offers another way of thinking about Jeffers's relationship to the nineteenth century. I do not think we have paid enough attention to Jeffers's relationship to the various Romantic poets that in some way enabled his project as a writer. Wordsworth, for one, is crucial. In fact, it is pretty clear now that we can document that Jeffers's reading of Wordsworth's "Preface" to the *Lyrical Ballads* in combination with moving to Big Sur helped lead him to narrative in the first place. He sees himself as regenerating Wordsworthian narrative in the twentieth century.

So think about Wordsworth's own situation in light of the questions you are raising, because Dorothy is always a figure on the margins of his texts and there is correspondence that indicates not only that Jeffers thought of Una as his Dorothy figure, but that Una thought of herself this way as well. In other words, they both used that figuration for their relationship to each other and to his poetic project. That is another way of being trapped in the same kind of thing, but he talks about her as his eyes and ears and his quickening spirit; that she is the one who has the vital relationship to the human landscape, that he steals that from her, and that he somewhat gives her voice but he does not. Lots of ambivalence there. If you put that in terms of a poem like "Point Joe," where she is in fact in the poem as the unspeaking auditor, and then think of "Point Joe" as Jeffers's version of "Tintern Abbey," there are lots of resonances.

JARMAN: When Una enters his poems she does not seem reducible to any kind of symbol or archetype. There is a little book called *Jeffers Country* in which they both provide a preface. Their prose styles are contrasting. He is rather dry, but he tells some very sharp and dramatic anecdotes. She is more lyrical; she makes love to the landscape she writes about. He has this line; I think it is from "Morro Bay," where he says, "She gave life from her eyes."

HUNT: He cannot decide if she is a sister-figure or whether she is a mother, and he uses both images. And when you look at the poems, the female figure in the lyrics is often the redemptive mother. The female figure in the narratives is more often a violational, destabalizing, even destructive younger woman who in some ways is figured as the incestuous sister. One of the first poems he ever writes about Una is a narrative in *Californians*, where the sister-brother lovers are killed by another brother in the guise of the father. And he figures her in the beginning of the poem and the end as his sister. And he casts it as a cautionary tale for himself and Una. I do not know where all this leads, but it goes back at some level to the sense that you are pointing to: that these things are highly volatile and probably never resolvable either.

ZALLER: I think we are never going to make a feminist out of Jeffers, not because he was not sympathetic to women—he was profoundly, deeply sympathetic and intuitive—but because the categories he appropriated at the time he wrote were simply not ours, and the things that were progressive then no longer seem that way. If I can try one last take on it—there was an interesting bit at the beginning about how you gender character. In thinking about that I realized, of course, that Jeffers has very sharply delineated male and female characters, but there is one character that never seems to be delineated by gender and that is God. Jeffers's vision is profoundly monistic, and he rejects dualism everywhere throughout his life. He rejects it philosophically, too. There is a key line in "Apology for Bad Dreams" where he does gender God: "He being sufficient might be still." The question in Jeffers is: why is God not still? Why is this monistic god the creator of this world? There is sometimes this living God that he cannot comprehend, and there is some kind of counter-principle. What Jeffers finds in the created world is the duality of masculine and feminine, and he somehow reimposes that fact upon his conception of God so that the female principle, the female archetype, is representing striving and life and creation. As Mark Mitchell is saying, the female is night, but the female is also blond and a harlot; the female is the sun, the moon, and the night. The female just seems to be a metaphor for the natural world. I think a lot of this sliding around back and forth represents this extreme tension in Jeffers's mind.

BROGAN: Again, though, I keep coming back to the things that trouble me, and it sounds from that description that his desire would be to be male and still double. I am talking archetypally, as when you talk about poetry and you talk about masculine and feminine endings. Females are dual, duplicitous. They cause the problems. If there is a division in God, that division means duplicity and creativity, but also destruction. It seems to be a feminine principle. When you see any created world—which makes the masculine philosophical and more unified *vs.* the fallen world—it is always feminized. So again, you cannot escape Western cultural problematics that I find deeply distressing when I read Jeffers. Again, I can be very compelled by Jeffers's poetry, but those of you saying, "Well, he sees the feminine everywhere . . ."—that does not help my problem.

At a fundamental level one can say that Jeffers has a vision as a tragic poet and that is part of what is so compelling. I do not have any problem with that. A question about whether one should valorize the tragic and dismiss the optimistic: Is that a right thing to do? Maybe not.

TWO RESPONSES TO "THE FEMALE ARCHETYPES IN ROBINSON JEFFERS"

Diane Wakoski

I believe the reason that Jeffers is such a great writer—besides all the obvious traditional beauties of his language—is that his vision of mankind is a bigger cosmic vision than most of us still can accept. What do I mean by that? I mean that he tries to step out of his human skin when he writes. The most essential part of that human skin is its sexuality, so sexual identity, either male or female, is fraught with misery, in Jeffers's vision.

Cassandra

The mad girl with the staring eyes and long white fingers
Hooked in the stones of the wall,

The storm-wracked hair and the screeching mouth: does it
matter, Cassandra,
Whether people believe
Your bitter fountain? Truly men hate the truth; they'd liefer
Meet a tiger on the road.
Therefore the poets honey their truth with lying; but religion-
Venders and political men
Pour from the barrel, new lies on the old, and are praised for
kindly
Wisdom. Poor bitch, be wise.
No: you'll still mumble in a corner a crust of truth, to men
And gods disgusting.—You and I, Cassandra.

Robinson Jeffers
ca. 1948

To focus on Jeffers's women seems beside the whole point of Jeffers's philosophy, which is that men and women alike ("You and I, Cassandra") are doomed in their human, evolutionarily misguided drive to wreak destruction through greed, avarice, desire, and power-mongering. No doubt there is a personal psyche at work in Jeffers which allows him to portray women as so much bigger, more flexible, stronger than most of his male figures. But I interpret Jeffers as caught in the paradox of trying to have an "inhuman" vision while still bound by his humanity, which includes the fact that he is a man and limited by that gender.

It is not accidental that, in this lyric poem, "Cassandra," coming after the bitter time of his *Double Axe* persecution and unofficial literary blacklisting, he makes himself equal or a twin to a woman. It is a gesture, I think, showing his stance as a poet, and one that can be found in many other of the short lyric poems. The poet is outside, an observer. "It" (the poet) can be either male, as Jeffers is, or female, as Cassandra is. The haunting lament, "You and I, Cassandra," is a statement of his equality with her, and the hopelessness of the human condition out of which, for the duration of the poem, they both remain. They both have given up their personal (i.e., gender) identities in the pursuit of truth. This lyric offers a glimpse into Jeffers's view of the godly androgyny which he wishes he could imagine in an "inhuman" world. When Mark Mitchell illustrates that Jeffers refers to God with the masculine pronoun yet implies a female identity, what I draw from that is androgyny—that god is neither male nor female, or both, in some non-sexual, non-gendered way. I think we must accept that Jeffers could himself hardly conceive of what this meant.

Yes, he is denying the civilization which he admires so much. His interest in science seems but one more aspect of his continuation of some classic ideal of civilization and human possibility. His poem "Animals" (ca. 1951) illustrates an alternative image of life-forms. First he thinks of an animal but not human species in the form of sea lions:

> It makes me wonder a little
> That life near kin to human, intelligent, hot-blooded, idle and
> singing, can float at ease
> In the ice-cold midwinter water.

Then he imagines a life which is all molecules without personalities, without all the negative traits he saw being bred into human society:

> I think about the rapid and furious
> lives in the sun:
> They have little to do with ours; they have nothing to do with
> oxygen and salted water; they would look monstrous
> If we could see them. . . .

Even in this vision of a non-human world, Jeffers has a hard time actually not conferring human passion on to his subject. This passion he seems to see as a Dionysian (sexual) manifestation, and it comes through most powerfully in all his earthy women, as the symposium critics have pointed out. But while he idealizes strong women who, as Jacque Vaught Brogan skillfully (and passionately) argues, usually have to die for their cause, or, like Medea, have to kill for their honor and survival, he seems to see both men and women equally caught in the human web of destruction. If you follow this argument, then the next step is to be outside the male-female reproductive cycle and the desperate customs which surround and preserve it.

I do not think nor am I suggesting that Jeffers had any Orlando-like sense of a two-sexed being, but I am suggesting that his image of the poet is the most traditional one in Western civilization, the image of Tiresias, who is androgynous, implying that he can see (greater seeing uncomplicated by human physicality since he is blind) with the wholeness (both sexes) of the human species. But the figure of Tiresias is more allegory than possibility. And my sense of the poet, which, like Mitchell's, comes as much from Jeffers's shorter lyrics as from his "stories," is one of a curious search throughout the universe, as humans can know it, to find a model that would omit these fierce ongoing struggles of power and desire. In "Vulture" (ca. 1963), Jeffers sums up every response in his lifetime of looking at organisms outside the human species:

To be eaten
by that beak and become part of him, to share those wings and those eyes—
What a sublime end of one's body, what an enskyment:
What a life after death.

I might be reaching far in my interpretation, but certainly everyone agrees on the strong element of Judeo-Christian myth underlying Jeffers's work; and in that myth you have to die to be born again into "the kingdom of heaven," which Jeffers might call, as he did in "Vulture," "enskyment." In an odd way, if you look at the narrative poems, all ending in some kind of human-willed death, you could allow yourself to interpret that to mean that Jeffers idealizes death in exactly the same way as the Christian religion does. Death is not just a necessity but a chance to transcend the body, to get beyond its (sexual and reproductive) limitations. I am not suggesting that entirely, but I am suggesting that he faces a paradox. In no way can Jeffers conceive of what androgyny might really be; yet without it he cannot conceive of the human race surviving.

I think Jeffers did not have a clear idea of what was possible. He saw vividly only what he thought was wrong, and his primary response was to imagine a world better than human civilization, but, of course, without people. Jeffers can give himself a kind of exemption in this world, since he takes on the role of the poet, who like Tiresias is androgynous (i.e., not human), can communicate with the dead, and prophetically speak about this. And it does seem possible for him to imagine a dead person having an existence, as we see in one of his memorable characters in "The Inhumanist," who is a dead young soldier who comes back from the war. But Jeffers does not seem to be able, ever, to bring himself to be a genuine Dionysian who can actually believe in recurring cycles as the common good. He, for all his quarrels with Christianity, remains locked in its Apollonian vision, seemingly wanting to believe in a death of the body which then returns as spirit.

The drama in his work comes from Jeffers's identification with his tragic heroes and heroines. But the power of his vision comes from his philosophy of "Inhumanism," which allows him temporarily, as a poet, to step out of his role as a man or a woman, able to commiserate with either ("You and I, Cassandra"), yet not to be specifically identified with either. One possible interpretation of that most debated stumbling block for many readers, Jeffers's self-described philosophy of "Inhumanism," is the one I am suggesting: that the only way Jeffers could conceive of a "good" world was to eliminate human sexuality and its Dionysian reproductive cycle. Probably if Jeffers had called his philosophy "ahumanism," he would have encountered less resistance. The very word "Inhumanism" implies exactly the actions Jeffers spent his life condemning—humans behaving badly toward one another. Of course, it is possible that Jeffers intended that we receive that label with the same kind of tragic irony with which he approached everything, seeing how the very pursuit of brotherly love and human compassion in the form of organized religion or governmental organizations had in fact caused more war, inquisition, oppression, suffering than if humans had actually stated their purpose to be murder, torture, deceit, and persecution.

Still, as much as he claimed not to care about human civilization destroying itself, Jeffers obviously was deeply troubled by this tragic image of civilization, which itself, like a classical hero, had to fall at the end of the drama as a result of its inherent flaw, a version of *hubris* which allows humankind to believe it can control and fix all things. I believe Jeffers sees civilization locked into this trap because greed for power and desire for possession are locked into human sexuality.

Thus, I read all his poems and dramas as illustrations of this, without any sense that his portrayal of women is qualitatively different from his portrayal of men. They are all doomed. The androgynous voice of the poet can occasionally be outside of this, but since androgyny is a fantasy or made-up condition, there is no hope in this as an alternative.

He uses his knowledge of contemporary science to imagine other worlds where other kinds of sentience could exist without this tragic flaw, could actually be androgynous in some unimaginable way, though most often he simply tries to accept the earth as it is, minus humans. That is the image he leaves us with most often in both the long and the short poems:

And when the whole human race
Has been like me rubbed out, they will still be here: storms, moon and ocean,

Dawn and the birds. And I say this: their beauty has more meaning
Than the whole human race and the race of birds. ("Their Beauty Has More Meaning," ca. 1947)

Betty Adcock

I am going to work backward with my responses, beginning with Jacqueline Vaught Brogan. I will start by standing as a witness that not all reading women find Jeffers's narratives repugnant. The assertion that reading women are (and should be) repelled by the poems seems only a new form for the tired criticism of the moralists of the 1930s and 1940s, critics unable to see the much deeper moralist in Jeffers. The argument is neither new nor made more interesting by being limited here to women, not even if one calls it by the name of the theory that wags it. Brogan ends her opening statement by declaring that "there is not that much difference between seeing Clare Walker die and snuff movies in New York in terms of violence against women." Though admitting it is an exaggeration, Brogan seems to find some validity in the analogy. I cannot imagine dignifying this with a defense. I will simply register here the strongest disagreement. And not only am I a reading woman, I am a writing woman.

It is a commonplace in academia to refer to any construction, whether or not it uses language, as a "text," and by that usage to imply that it has no author, that it is constructed entirely by the culture, and that only specialists in various disciplines can reveal its meaning or meanings. By this criterion last night's sitcom, Wordsworth, computer games, billboards, the novels of Joyce, and snuff movies are equalized as texts in the general run of cultural constructions. Taken as just another example in this kind of arrangement, poems from whatever period lose their identity and become fodder for any specialist riding his/her hobbyhorse to the rhythms of the post-postmodernist rag. I would change the terms of the discourse. Jeffers was not making a text. He was making a poem. I am quite willing to lift poetry right out of the general run of cultural constructions so that it can be treated as what it is rather than what it is not.

Ms. Brogan makes it difficult with her convenient double bind. Clare Walker is dismissed as only a victim, therefore the archetypal and dehumanized figure of degraded woman. Yet when reminded that men are killed by women as often as women are victims of men in Jeffers, Ms. Brogan replies that the Medea figure (meant to stand for all of Jeffers's active women, one supposes) is somehow the same dehumanized and archetypal figure. I would argue that these are not bedtime stories or political fables: they are tragedies. What kind of art could there be here had the stories lacked all deadly action, that which tragedy embodies by definition? "Alas . . . it is often true in life . . ." Jeffers says somewhere. Surely there is more violence in mega-urban streets than in all of Jeffers's poems. He was talking about that kind of violence, what has become the ordinary kind, as well as about something older and less easily explained. Jeffers used violence in his art as much as to understand violence, to confront it and name it rightly, as to advance narrative. His choice of tragedy was careful and deliberate. Few other poets confronted the realities of modern life as they would flower into fullness. After all, the shape of our world is not so far from tragic, and it is the poet's job to tell the truth, not to soothe the ideologically pure.

I was interested in Brogan's accurate but inaccurately framed contention that Jeffers took on something he could not get out of, in "Cawdor" and in other poems. I agree completely, but I believe he wrestled with much more than a simple cultural myth. The contradictions in his work, the poles along which the tensions that created his poetry were generated, are only partially as Ms. Brogan seems to see them. It is true, as she asserts, that resolution was impossible, at least through conventional literary or philosophical means. This is part of the greatness of his work and part of the great difficulty for his readers: a reach that attempted to include everything. And resolution was possible in the way taken by Whitman and Blake, in whose company some earlier critics placed Jeffers. I do not mind in the least being unfashionable. I can even say the word "mystic."

I also think Robert Zaller's point was a valid one: that the categories Jeffers appropriated at the time he wrote were not ours. Current critical insistence that all times are now (except when it suits the critics' occasion to notice otherwise) has a very different meaning from the same phrase in a Jeffers poem, and it reduces literature.

The panel ends with Jacqueline Brogan: "A question about whether one should valorize the tragic and dismiss the optimistic: is that a right thing to do? Maybe not." Aside from its Pollyanna tone, this statement dismays me more than any number of male or female murders for the sake of narrative advancement. Even when phrased as a question only tentatively answered, this kind of thinking looks to murder poetry itself, and I take that rather hard.

Mark Mitchell's reading of the early mature lyrics seems exactly right to me. It is more or less the reading I gave them many years ago when I discovered Jeffers's work for myself, at a time when it was impossible to discover it in any ways than on one's own. I was attracted to this work first through the lyrics, specifically through some of those cited by Mitchell. Here was a poet unlike others of his time, one who wrote with something female at the core of his work. I moved instinctively toward this, as I had moved instinctively away from Eliot, Pound, and Williams, the icons of the time. Something of my own concern for the natural world was here, and I had an incoherent, unfocused sense of the wrongness of the direction of technological society, a wrongness not addressed by the spiritual, cultural, or moral leadership, not by the artists or the philosophers. These poems touched on something deeply known, feared, and unspoken in our world: the truth that the divisive, controlling separation from nature which was our whole stock in trade as a society, and which was archetypally male, is dangerous and perhaps evil; that the greater good is in the archetypally female energies of the natural world, however hard these are, however dangerous in another way. Jeffers saw the terrible contradictions at the heart of this. He was the only writer of his time who did.

Many of Mitchell's thoughts on the lyrics would apply equally to the narratives, though the demands of character and plot make things more difficult to sort out. Certainly, we can see Jeffers's Medea as the personification of the female energies of the natural world. And if we see her in the correct context, she becomes not "woman as the guilty party, the one who murders" (as Brogan sees her) but a force in contrast to Jason. Jason is the agent of civilization, the representative of cities, money, luxury, and the power drives that build these. Medea is fierce motherhood, the feared "magic" of nature, the sexual and volatile energies that animate the archetype of the goddess, here used in more than one way. And what Medea says to Jason is something like: "If you betray me, if you send your love far from me, then I will kill your children." Whatever one may have to say about "bad woman" stereotypes and the like, the fact is that this is precisely what the planet earth has said to humankind. That voice rings true to me, though it may have little to do with actual women. We may fault Jeffers for less than well-rounded characters, but I am not so enamored of realism as Mark Jarman is. Jeffers's characters are as much forces of nature or of fate as they are people. As such, they are larger, more bitter, more awful, more powerfully compelling than ordinary people; they are the characters of ancient tragedies after all, or patterned after these.

I have said elsewhere in print that Jeffers's poetry is one reason for my having become a poet myself, though I think no direct influence is seen in my work. In the years when I was beginning to write seriously, a woman whose life was outside the academy and outside the urban meccas, especially a southern woman, had little encouragement and no incentive to write poems. Fiction, yes. Not poetry. I have not been able to understand why this was so, but it certainly was. During that time, Jeffers's work and his example served a number of purposes for me, not least in that his characters were never women who "come and go, talking of Michelangelo." Mark Mitchell points out some important strands in the complex tapestry of Jeffers's work. I am grateful for his clarity.

I read Mark Jarman's book-length poem, patterned after Jeffers and titled *Iris*, before this panel was named. On hearing that he would be part of the panel, I guessed that the focus of his paper would be "The Loving Shepherdess," though it is not a typical Jeffers narrative and Clare Walker is hardly a typical Jeffers character. The similarities between Jeffers's Clare and Jarman's Iris are interesting. The two women share an astonishing passivity, a stunned acceptance of whatever happens. Beyond this, however, the parallels are less clear. In *Iris* there is neither *chosen* sacrifice, nor the great context of a powerful landscape, nor a matching or contradicting philosophical framework. Jarman's heroine does parallel Clare in that both are realistically drawn, in their very different times and contexts.

I very much agree with Jarman that the realistic presence, the "thereness," of Clare Walker is powerful and that this realism is unusual in Jeffers. This is indeed one of Jeffers's most beautiful poems, not least because of Clare Walker's vivid placement in the California landscape, described in some of the poet's finest lines. The poem demonstrates Jeffers's control and holds a great humaneness at its core. One early critic noted that Clare is Jeffers's only completely sympathetic character. The poet's own statement defined her as ". . . one who has committed self-sacrifice, a saint I suppose, going up to a natural martyrdom. Incapable of taking thought for herself, she wanders the coast that has usually been the scene of my verses." The obvious sympathy with which Jeffers created this unusual figure in his poetic landscape is a clue to his own divided self. His statement that her martyrdom is "natural" also bears thinking about.

In that Clare Walker is mad, she can be placed with other savior-figures in the poems. She shares much with the old hermit who keeps wounds in his hands open, believing he is making antitoxin for all the people, for the ruined world—this is in a poem called "A Redeemer." The old hermit refuses comparison with Christ, saying that his sacrifice is voluntary. Clare is, of course, a Christ-figure as well, but I think with a difference meant by Jeffers to be something like that difference in the hermit. Clare makes me think too of "Fawn's Foster Mother," the woman who suckled a fawn. But most of Jeffers's true savior-figures make whatever sacrifice they make, whether of the self or of others, for the sake of power. Clare makes her sacrifice, it seems, for nothing . . . or for the small delusion that she is giving her doomed child the full nine months of heaven she imagines for it.

Lacking both desire and power, those poles delineated by Mark Mitchell, Clare Walker has no more effect than a fern shadow on a stone, though she is beautiful as such a shadow would be. I do not find this a fault in the poem, merely an interesting difference.

Clare Walker is entirely good, it seems, though hardly sane. She thinks well of every human being, identifies with any and every living thing, and would share her last food with the lowliest creature. She embodies two kinds of love it seems, both the love of man against which Jeffers warned his sons in the last stanza of "Shine, Perishing Republic," and that love cast outward to the non-human, which Jeffers counsels at every turn. In one sense she cancels herself. Such a contradiction, like the doomed child she carries, could never live. Yet I think Jeffers felt very close to Clare. I think she represented a part of the poet always present but hard to see in his works; hence, his extraordinary empathy with her.

But I have questions, too. The embodiment of love without power or desire, Clare Walker is yet the most lovingly detailed, the most realistic, perhaps the most believable (on the physical level anyway) of Jeffers's women. What are we to make of her, coming as we do into her story after the significant action, the life-changing or -destroying action that is usually the center of Jeffers's poems, has already taken place? Are we to imagine that she was different before, someone more like the larger-than-life figures of other narratives? Or was she always this futility, this failed love? And was not Jeffers's own love, that "tower beyond tragedy," without—or wishing to be without—desire or power? Is Clare this love, but with a major difference, being without vision and/or knowledge, without transcendence? Is this why she is anchored so firmly? But these are the kinds of questions and contradictions that make Jeffers's poems fascinating. If they are framed somewhat differently in this poem, that only makes it more interesting. I love this poem as Mr. Jarman does, and for many reasons, including its delicate rendering of physical detail. I do not have any neat answers to the questions the poem raises.

Had I been able to participate in the panel, I would have chosen another heroine, probably California, perhaps even Tamar. But I am very grateful to Mark Jarman for his loving and careful reading of a poem to which I had not returned for some time. I have seen Clare Walker more clearly because of it.

8

Desire, Death, and Domesticity in Jeffers's Pastorals of Apocalypse

Kirk Glaser

IN EARLY LYRICS such as "To the House," "To the Rock That Will Be a Cornerstone of the House," and "Continent's End," Robinson Jeffers builds and writes his way into the land, into a created landscape in which his home and his presence there are naturalized, as he simultaneously dreams of a pantheistic nature in which human beings are displaced from their traditional fantasies of centrality, self-importance, and permanence. His God-infused nature, though, is not an intimate place where the poet or quester meets a loving and beneficent deity. Jeffers struggles to make his vision of God conform to a nature that destroys all it creates. He imagines an elemental, often masculinized nature representing ultimate ends that subsumes a feminized, biological, and regenerative nature. At the most extreme, as in a poem such as "Post Mortem," flesh and passion, associated with feminine procreation, are set against the transcendent idea and vision of a masculine poet/prophet.

Focusing on the destructive aspects of nature and God, Jeffers repeatedly writes into the landscapes of his poems an apocalyptic vision of oblivion that serves as his source of prophetic and mystical inspiration and insight. While he turns to the processes of nature and not an explicitly Christian schema for this vision, he nonetheless presents in many poems natural forces of destruction as revelation in ways that parallel, as they revise, Christian and romantic representations of apocalypse. The pastoral landscapes that provide Jeffers with his apocalyptic vision are shaped by his powerful and at times bizarre amalgam of images of death, sexuality, gender, and domesticity. These pastorals of apocalypse provide insight into Jeffers's revisions of romantic conceptions of nature, culture, and consciousness as well as elucidate his complex and shifting relationships to and encodings of the natural world, time, and history.

Jeffers's nature (and God) works through violence as much as (or more than, he would say) it does through nurturing or love. In "Fire on the Hills," Jeffers writes,

> The deer were bounding like blown leaves
> Under the smoke in front of the roaring wave of the brushfire;
> I thought of the smaller lives that were caught.
> Beauty is not always lovely; the fire was beautiful, the terror
> Of the deer was beautiful; and when I returned
> Down the black slopes after the fire had gone by, an eagle
> Was perched on the jag of a burnt pine,
> Insolent and gorged, cloaked in the folded storms of his
> shoulders.
> He had come from far off for the good hunting
> With fire for his beater to drive the game; the sky was merciless
> Blue, and the hills merciless black,
> The sombre-feathered great bird sleepily merciless between
> them.
> I thought, painfully, but the whole mind,
> The destruction that brings an eagle from heaven is better than
> mercy. (*CP* 2: 173)

Jeffers's God, as made manifest in the natural world, is merciless. The ecology of nature provides for the continuation of life by wielding death and what seems destruction. The eagle, another version of Jeffers's hawk totem, represents the 'fierce consciousness' that Jeffers attempts to hold in mind "painfully": "The destruction that brings an eagle from heaven is better than mercy." The terror of the deer, the fire sweeping over the hillsides, and the eagle are all part of a natural order that holds a sublime beauty—a terrible beauty that inspires religious awe[1]—for the beholder who can overcome feelings of pity, a pity that holds no sway against the processes of nature. Jeffers virtually transforms the storm-shouldered, insolent eagle into an angel—"Every angel is terrifying," writes Rilke—by signifying the sky as "heaven." Also like Rilke, who writes, "For beauty is nothing but the beginning of terror," Jeffers sees terror as revelation of beauty.

Jeffers and Rilke both write out of a late romanticism, yet while Rilke's vision draws more directly on the French Symbolist tradition and his poetic landscapes reflect a mind turned inward, shaped by European landscapes long inhabited, Jeffers depicts scenes from a wilder nature to embody his sense of the annihilating power of beauty. Jeffers un-centers the speaker, thereby centralizing the landscape, prioritizing nature's processes over the thinking and feeling self. Still, he imposes his ideas—often didactically—aestheticizing and emblematizing nature to reveal a vision of sublime terror that echoes Rilke. Both poets share a vision of experiencing the sublime—coming in contact with heaven's angels, be they supernatural or utterly natural—as a trial by fire, the human being barely able to endure the vision. The awe inherent in Rilke's opening to the *Duino Elegies* feels like it could have been sparked by the same event as Jeffers's "Fire on the Hills":

> Who, if I cried out, would hear me among the angels'
> hierarchies? and even if one of them pressed me
> suddenly against his heart: I would be consumed
> in that overwhelming existence. For beauty is nothing
> but the beginning of terror, which we still are just able to
> endure,
> and we are so awed because it serenely disdains to annihilate us.
> Every angel is terrifying. (151)

And the force of "destruction" that "brings an eagle from heaven" forces the speaker of Jeffers's poem to think *painfully*, to struggle to hold the vision of the sublime, of nature's merciless processes, and not to be *consumed* by that overwhelming existence. This force of destruction becomes linked with a Shiva-like (and Zeus-like) God, associated with "the whole mind," a transcendent mind beyond mercy or apparently any emotional involvement in the conflagration. To cultivate awareness of the true nature of creation, it seems, requires cultivating what Jeffers terms an "inhuman" dispassion.

Mercy, for Jeffers, seems a human quality, not one inherent in nature, which for him is the primary source for knowing the nature of God. This poem represents one of the ways that Jeffers attempts to divorce his poetry from Christian and humanist visions that place humanity at the center of creation or that, relinquishing an anthropomorphized God, value human reason, imagination, and creativity over the processes of the natural world. Jeffers's self-proclaimed (and often misread) "Inhumanism" thus separates his poetry from the humanism of both romantic and Modernist writers, and this has been both a strength and a weakness for him as a poet. He ascribes precedence to nature over the mind and culture—even as his vision of nature reflects a romantic conception of nature as a source and spark for the creative and religious imagination. While, like Wordsworth, he perpetuates the dualities between nature and culture, he cannot find consolation in intimations of immortality inspired by nature. To the contrary, his scientific perceptions of nature (as naturalist and astronomer) force him to face his mortality and insignificance in the scheme of things—a vision that grows from an American tradition that includes the likes of Thoreau, Muir, and others. Jeffers strives to present the priority of an ideal natural world "out there" over culture or a fallen human condition (for Jeffers, fallen precisely because too great a value has been placed on humanity by the likes of dominant Christian and humanist ideologies).

The process of valorizing inhuman nature paradoxically leads Jeffers, like Thoreau, to create divisions between himself as poetic, human dreamer and the natural world in which he longs to immerse himself. Thoreau, as in the "Higher Laws" chapter of *Walden*, turns to asceticism and a longing to be free of all bodily necessities. Jeffers's response to this dilemma is in ways even more extreme. In many central poems, he turns to an apocalyptic vision by which he may fuse his imagination (and identity) with that of his God, often through his uses of the 'geologic sublime'—setting the individual and all human history in a context of geologic time.

The conflict between the observing speaker and the natural world is less pronounced, though, in "Fire on the Hills" than in other poems by Jeffers. He draws more intimately upon images from the natural world, presenting a scene more locally set in both time and space than, say, in "Continent's End," in which he abandons a feminized nature for the masculine God-vision of the "eye of fire":

> Mother, though my song's measure is like your surf-beat's
> ancient rhythm I never learned it of you.
> Before there was any water there were tides of fire, both our
> tones flow from the older fountain. (*CP* 1: 16–17)

In the latter poem, the distant gazing eye of the isolato-poet replicates his God—". . . but there is in me / Older and harder than life and more impartial, the eye that watched before there was an ocean" (*CP* 1: 16)—and this vision dominates many of Jeffers's poems.

Even in "Fire on the Hills," the gaze of the speaker who struggles for impassivity becomes associated, if painfully, with the eagle-like God who wields merciless destruction for the sake of life. The gazer remains removed from the inferno. Jeffers does not turn to his rhetoric of didacticism, abstractions, and the geologic sublime, as he often does. However, the crux of the poem remains the tension between the consciousness of the speaker who thinks and feels (or tries not to feel) and a natural world that demands of the speaker a fierce, inhuman consciousness in order to comprehend the ways of God and creation—to "remain / Part of the music, but . . . hear it as the player hears it," as he writes in "Going to Horse Flats" (*CP* 2: 543).

This dualism, this conflict he feels at the core of consciousness between the thinking/feeling self and an indifferent nature, represents Jeffers's dominant religious quest and shapes his poetic landscapes as well as his God.[2] His mysticism is rooted in a desire to worship the natural world, in and of itself, as beauty and as greater than a humanity which is one real yet inconsequential part of creation. This vision ultimately controls and shapes "Fire on the Hills." But Jeffers's vision also entails a need to pull away from the world for an idea or image of it as representation of God's inhuman beauty and as sign of the unity and source of all creation—the pattern witnessed in "Continent's End."

Jeffers thus creates varying landscapes out of his conflicting longings both to be intimately wed to the natural world, to inhabit a nature that provides meaning and haven for the human inhabitant, and to transcend nature in his mystical quest, perceiving it as so many signs of a divine intelligence. He seeks to present the absolute otherness of nature and simultaneously longs to see through it and into the "eye of fire"—to have nature both as immanent presence and as numinous sign. This leads Jeffers recurrently to create his pastorals of apocalypse—landscapes that have obliterated or 'naturalized' the accouterments of civilization. Nature both dominates as a supreme entity greater than humans and civilizations and serves as a sign of a transcendent energy, or God, that infuses all creation. Even a poem such as "Fire on the Hills" represents elements of this model, for although Jeffers focuses on a landscape without signs of human habitation, he relies upon forces of destruction as revelation.

Typically, these spaces allow Jeffers to inhabit the land as an "isolato" (to borrow Melville's term), as an isolated mystical quester as well as a modern Jeremiah who prophesies upon what he sees as the ills of modern civilization. He attains a privileged relationship to the natural world in which he describes a seemingly 'pure' nature, beyond any shapings of human imagination. And often from this location in the matrix of nature, he makes his leaps via a language that paradoxically links the vision of the poet-creator to that of the God-creator, even as it annihilates any value in this imagining, speaking self. Again, the pattern resembles that portrayed in "Continent's End." Jeffers sets history and culture in the context of his geologic sublime, so that what he sees as the narcissistic "inward" vision of humankind is obliterated, freeing the mind to perceive natural and mystical "beauty" and "truth" (two words upon which many of his poems turn).

Poems such as "Post Mortem," the final speeches of Orestes from "The Tower Beyond Tragedy," and "Bixby's Landing," poems which span his works of the late 1920s and 1930s, delineate several versions of Jeffers's apocalyptic landscapes, including his recurring desire to find peace in oblivion. Jeffers repeatedly turns the landscape into a memento mori, his thanatotic vision becoming a dominant mode in his poetry (and this represents an essential distinction between his mystical vision and that of some later poets concerned with similar themes—Mary Oliver, for instance, who seeks to inhabit the natural world through intimate, sensate immersion and a 'dying' into nature that leads to a mystical eros). Yet these poems reveal the contradictions inherent in Jeffers's longings for the peace of oblivion and his desires to inhabit the land and to create poetry. These conflicts emerge through images of gender in nature as well as the mergings and clashings of images of domestic and wild space.

Images of the house and domestic space, often associated with feminine principles and with the ills of civilization, are set against positive values located in nature. Yet even as he ascribes negative values to the domestic that become associated with destructive human passions and a misogynistic vision of women as temptresses (as in "Post Mortem"), a nurturing domesticity at times seeps into his natural world, belying yet again his need to infuse inhuman nature with emotional and moral values. Even in "Post Mortem," as well as in "Bixby's Landing," his longing to inhabit the land filters into his apocalyptic vision.

While Jeffers uses images of his house and building in the *Tamar* poems to naturalize his habitation (with the notable exception of the Usher-like house of the title poem),[3] domestic images also slip into his poems to subvert his apocalyptic vision. Jeffers's longings for a habitable world, one that offers the quester some human comfort and haven (in landscapes always sparsely settled at best), belies the visionary credo. Jeffers repeatedly represents the natural world as a place that offers enlightenment through sensate contact, yet the vision offered by this contact takes Jeffers "beyond" nature, much as the building of the house and poetry enable him to bring *inside* his life the numinous discovered in nature, even as these physical and linguistic structures also come to signify the limits of human creation and comprehension.

"Post Mortem" (published in 1927) presents Jeffers in one of his more morose moods. While the poem follows "The Tower Beyond Tragedy" (*Roan Stallion,* 1925) and several other poems in which Jeffers develops his inhumanist pantheism, it is a good place to begin discussing his conjunctions of passion and death because it is one of the first of his poems in which these contemplations lead to a fantasized apocalypse.

The poem seems generated by anxiety. At first it appears to be anxiety about the fate of the self, especially his, after death. In the first eight lines or so he ponders the ontology of ghosts:

> Happy people die whole, they are all dissolved in a moment,
>   they have had what they wanted,
> No hard gifts; the unhappy
> Linger a space, but pain is a thing that is glad to be forgotten;
>   but one who has given
> His heart to a cause or a country,
> His ghost may spaniel it a while, disconsolate to watch it. I was
>   wondering how long the spirit
> That sheds this verse will remain
> When the nostrils are nipped, when the brain rots in its vault or
>   bubbles in the violence of fire
> To be ash in metal. (*CP* 1: 204–05).

Jeffers's penchant for grisly detail again reminds one of Poe. This is only the first decomposition in the poem, the main one to be the decomposition of civilization's body.

Decomposition is set against forces of human composition, or more specifically procreation, and Jeffers's anxiety is revealed to be not so much about his personal death as about the death of the landscape that he inhabits and has helped to shape.

> . . . I was thinking
> Some stalks of the wood whose roots I married to the earth of
>   this place will stand five centuries;
> I held the roots in my hand,
> The stems of the trees between two fingers: how many remote
>   generations of women
> Will drink joy from men's loins,
> And dragged from between the thighs of what mothers will
>   giggle at my ghost when it curses the axemen,

Gray impotent voice on the sea-wind,
When the last trunk falls? The women's abundance will have
  built roofs over all this foreland;
Will have buried the rock foundations
I laid here: the women's exuberance will canker and fail in its
  time and like clouds the houses
Unframe, the granite of the prime
Stand from the heaps. . . .

Women are bizarrely and misogynously equated with procreative forces and sexual passions that are thoughtless and destructive. Women's fertility, configured as somehow independent of men here (or superior to men, completely controlling men's helpless loins), will be to blame for the violation of the coast, domesticating it beyond recognition. Male desire for possession and control of the landscape does not enter into this picture, at least not explicitly (because these desires are what brought Jeffers to the coast, and to the needs for such a poem). Even the beings who will "giggle" at his ghost are elided in the odd syntax of the sentence—"what" is "dragged from between the thighs" remains absent from the poem, perhaps because the axe*men* who alter the landscape are these obscure progeny.

One could argue that these images of women are meant to represent an abstraction, as is no doubt the case on one level, of a modern humanity that thoughtlessly overpopulates and radically alters the land. This cannot undo his rhetoric, however. He may mean to curse the "axemen" as well as the women, but repeatedly it is a feminized principle of procreation that spurs on the domestic destruction of the wilderness.

A sexual politics emerges over possession of the land. Feminine procreation (flesh and passion) is set against masculine poetic/prophetic creation (idea and vision). Jeffers's poetic energy seems to rely on a holding back of his sexual (as procreative) self. Not to hold his seed (his word)—not to hold "the stems of trees between two fingers" and plant them himself—would make him, too, a victim of the "women's exuberance" that domesticates the wild land by "build[ing] roofs over all this foreland." Surrendering to biology, in essence, would compromise his independent (geologic and cosmic) vision by which he claims connection with the primal forces that shape, by merciless destruction, the land.

Jeffers gives the impression that he wishes no one to possess the land, especially in the final lines of the poem when he beckons: "come storm and wash clean" the foreland of its human inhabitants; yet his desire for possession—to be the one envisioning and inscribing this tempest of time and storm—is exactly what controls the poem, even if he attempts to abstract it by the poem's end. Ironically (though with ecological justification), human life and abundance, unlike the rest of nature's abundance, represent a death that offers no renewal, no balance.

Jeffers's death, after all, does compose the seed of the poem's anxiety. The death of the wild land is the death of an extended self, a self projected outward into the natural world, largely by means of a (slightly) veiled masculine sexuality, a sexuality divorced from procreation or intimacy. This image of sexuality becomes a recurring trope by which he associates himself with primal, elemental forces. Yet the poem's rhetoric also belies his desire for an intimacy with the land. He wonders if his spirit may linger awhile where he "laid" the rock foundations of his home and "married to the earth" the trees which "will stand five centuries." Jeffers's language (and the actions his words represent) impregnates the land and marries him to it. The domestication of the "foreland" (a *projecting* land mass), the taming of a wild place which he scathingly attacks when carried out by the "women's" seductive "exuberance," is a valued way of inhabiting the land when tempered. It may be undertaken by the isolate, poetic gazer and maker of a single stone cottage—a home, as seen in the house-building poems of *Tamar*—that evokes the image of a hermitage and allows for the dreamer to bring the natural world *inside*, naturalizing self and house.

Independent, masculine forces, supposedly less given to exuberant procreativity, seem capable of a healthy generation. The "stems of the trees" which he has held "between two fingers" take root and grow. In Jeffers's schema, these phallic trees stand on their own, compared with the dependent, if overpowering, exuberance of "many remote generations of women" *drinking* "from men's loins." Masculine independence is configured as valuable, even associated with the geologic 'eternal.' Jeffers imagines the outcome of this particular apocalypse and sees the "granite of the prime / Stand from the heaps." The rock, which in the final lines *houses* his spirit, stands, as if rising again (like a phallus as well as a Christ reborn) to take dominion.

The lines reveal a kind of sexual anxiety as well as conflict. Women are made into succubi, draining the life force from men. Jeffers seems to fear an emasculation, the wide roofs replacing his vertical trunks. The house becomes symbol of a female, domesticated space, threatening to level and suck the life from the wild, priapic rising trunks of his trees and tower and the foreland itself.[4] What is worse, women's "exuberance" threatens *his* domain, "the rock foundations" that he "laid" on the coast cliff. For Jeffers, women as a feminine energetic principle represent a life force configured as an urge to thoughtless generation. Further, as in *Cawdor,* they drive stoic (and too proud) men to destruction. They are the temptresses, representing the reproductive forces of earth gone awry "[i]nside the four walls of humanity, passions turned inward, incestuous / desires and a fighting against ghosts," as he writes in "The Torch-Bearer's Race" (*CP* 1: 100). They confuse and allure the male hero who turns to nature not to lose himself in the cycles of life and death but to strike through these pasteboard masks, to echo Ahab, in search of a transcendent vision. For Jeffers such vision takes him into the inanimate universe and the peace of death—the point at which the poem ends, as will momentarily be seen, the point at which all language and knowing break down and the poem is left in the field of an eternal desire configured as no desire but instead "a spirit for the stone."

In a trope typifying his poems of apocalyptic landscapes, Jeffers ends "Post Mortem" by turning to the obliterating powers of his elemental God-nature for solace:

> . . . come storm and wash clean: the plaster is all run to the sea
> and the steel
> All rusted; the foreland resumes
> The form we loved when we saw it. Though one at the end of
> the age and far off from this place
> Should meet my presence in a poem,
> The ghost would not care but be here, long sunset shadow in the
> seams of the granite, and forgotten
> The flesh, a spirit for the stone.

To whom this "we" refers is not clear. On one level, it seems possibly Jeffers and his wife, Una, with whom he shared the making of this homeland. In the context of the poem, however, such domestic creativity is shut out, and the "we" seems to be Jeffers and the storm he invokes—the storm of time and nature. The land itself and nature's forces will check humanity's spread and return the "foreland" to its pristine condition. He prefers this destruction to the regenerative smothering of "women's abundance." Jeffers distinguishes this apocalyptic destruction as a purification, a release, even an end to consciousness. His ghost may rest, a spirit in the stone.

Decomposition becomes the true and final force of creation, replacing the biological "canker," the disease of unchecked human procreation. A feminized, biological, and re-generative nature exists only within the larger, controlling system of a masculine, stoic, elemental nature. The pattern of destruction inherent in this latter nature reveals to the poetic gazer (who attempts to remain *outside* the entrapping cycles of procreation) ultimate sources and truths—the sublime "beauty" that Jeffers often associates with fire/sun/stars symbolizing a transcendent God.

Death and destruction (of the human world) are reconfigured, by being aligned with natural geologic processes, as harbingers and engenderers of a new world, or rather an old world of a healthy ecosystem recovered. This is another aspect of Jeffers's God and his apocalyptic vision—the geologic forces that reduce human efforts to nothing in the flow of a cosmic time beyond historical time. As do Muir and Thoreau, Jeffers turns to the geologic sublime to praise creation, and similarly he purges his landscape of human agents (except for the poet's consciousness—and the storm's and apparently God's). Yet Jeffers focuses on the elemental, destructive forces of nature rather than the life-nurturing abundance which comprises Muir's vision. In ways this is a trope of the romantic vision that recalls Keats's "Ode to a Nightingale." Jeffers perceives the mute otherness of nature, yet instead of turning back from it and toward human consciousness and imagination (the move made by Keats as well as by Modernists such as Pound, Stevens, and others), Jeffers embraces and praises this obliterating nature as the only ultimate truth he can attain, as (supposedly) the end of all desire.

Yet the ending is more problematic than Jeffers's mere achievement of his stony, timeless consciousness. He claims to prefer his granite, unconscious immortality to that of the poet's traditional longing for immortality in verse. He knows that his poems, like the stones and trees, will not last ("the poet as well / Builds his monuments mockingly" [*CP* 1: 5]), but even imagining someone reading his poem "at the end of the age" suggests a longing for his prophecy to be read and remembered.[5]

Furthermore, his choice of the word "form" to express the foreland he longs to preserve and recover suggests a concern not just with the forms nature makes but also with poetic form and, more generally, with human consciousness creating and maintaining order. It again points to the inevitable necessity of the artist, or any human gazing upon the land, to create a landscape that cannot remain purely other. Even if the order is one that he claims predates human arrival on the land, the very act of seeing it, recording it, and his own acts of building upon it, suggest that his longing for "inhumanity," for a land freed of human desire and consciousness, is nostalgic.

Jeffers longs for an unconsciousness grasped by (his own) consciousness. He wants to impregnate the land, without acknowledging the desire, setting up the (excessive) feminine principle as the culprit. The masculine poet can gaze upon and inhabit the land while relinquishing his passion-filled flesh—"and forgotten the flesh." The body itself, then, becomes feminized, the feminine again associated with the mortal *vs.* the masculine immortal, the stony spirit. To compensate for his urges, he creates this dichotomy and imposes it upon his post-apocalyptic new world: the landscape is washed clean of all human work. Of course this, too, is subverted, for his poetic vision of the apocalypse re-impregnates the land with himself, "a shadow in the seams of the granite . . . a spirit for the stone." His ghost—he writes "*the* ghost" in an attempt to distance personal desire from the moment—"would not care but be here," in other words, *desires* to become part of the landscape.

Within the events of the poem, he wishes for a death that allows him to enter and be subsumed by the life of stone, symbol of an immortal and unchanging creation, the 'other' which Jeffers longs to unite with; it is the end of creation, the final form of his apocalypse, the return to God. The stone, though, *as* symbol and image in the poem (a stone, too, will change in geologic time, after all) of this other, is subsumed by the poet's inner dreams. Jeffers's poetic creation, driven by a desire to end desire yet formed in language and images of sexual and domestic longing, undoes the very permanence it attempts to invoke. And the anxiety of undoing death's perfect permanence figures itself even in the final lines of the poem, where Jeffers prefers to imagine his presence met in the place over the poem—a claim the reader can hardly take seriously.

In "Post Mortem" Jeffers struggles with his vision of the paradoxes of consciousness, linked to the conflicts between the mind as source of thought and poetic vision *vs.* the passions of the body. He attempts to resolve this mind/body dualism by locating the destructive nature of human passions in feminine and domestic symbols, while equating (his) disinterested mind with a God emblematized by elemental, wild nature. In "Consciousness," an earlier three-sonnet sequence from *Tamar*, a similar split occurs, though Jeffers attempts to define both 'halves' from within an almost Manichean conception of deity. This anthropomorphized God of both reason and emotion, however, represents only a stage in Jeffers's process of developing his "Inhumanism" and his particular pantheism. Yet the incomplete resolution of "Consciousness" helps to explain why Jeffers creates his gender divisions. He seeks a way out of the cycles of time and biology to attain his vision of a transcendent source and therefore needs a God separated from the passions, so he relegates human emotional nature to the feminine. This 'frees' Jeffers to create, as in "The Tower Beyond Tragedy," both his inhumanist pantheism and the stoic, ideal male hero, a Nietzschean hero, who attains the vision to reach this mystic shore opposite humanity.

In "Consciousness" Jeffers seeks to resolve the conflict he experiences between what may be termed emotional and rational consciousness. For Jeffers consciousness brings awareness of God manifest in the material world, yet both this knowledge and the very desire for unity separate him from the world and, it seems, from God. Jeffers asks in "Consciousness,"

> Then what is this unreasonable excess,
> Our needless quality, this unrequired
> Exception in the world, this consciousness? (*CP* 1: 7).

Our consciousness, like the rainbows and swirls of sea shells in an earlier poem, "The Excesses of God,"[6] is another (though excessive and differentiating) sign of God's excess. However, the answer that through consciousness we know God is no longer sufficient, as it seems to be in that poem. Even though this consciousness—"Our nerves and brain"—"springs" from and "feeds in the same pasture" as all other creation, it severs us from the world; "[i]t is something else." Nonetheless, his equating of consciousness with the things of the world breaks from the romantic and Modernist sense of consciousness as entirely other and separate from nature, even as this consciousness is the agent of our separation.

Attempting to comprehend this paradoxical consciousness that both severs us from and unites us with God, Jeffers begins to dichotomize it in the second sonnet:

> As if there were two Gods: the first had made
> All visible things, waves, mountains, stars and men,
> The sweet forms dancing on through flame and shade,
> The swift messenger nerves that sting the brain,

The brain itself and the answering strands that start
Explosion in the muscles, the indrinking eye
Of cunning crystal, the hands and feet, the heart
And feeding entrails, and the organs that tie
The generations into one wreath, one strand;
All tangible things and chemical processes
Needs only brain and patience to understand. . . .

The "understanding" consciousness, something akin to the rational mind and its organs of apprehending the material world, of which humans are a part, are created by a God who has created an orderly, seemingly mechanistic universe. Even the body is celebrated as an organism of tangible things and chemical processes: "The swift messenger nerves that sting the brain, / The brain itself and the answering strands that start / Explosion in the muscles, the indrinking eye / Of cunning crystal." Jeffers's medical training is turned to metaphysical contemplation, and what he witnesses with his scientific eye regarding nature and God is good. Even sexuality signifies order and reason (in its procreative function): "the organs that tie / The generations into one wreath, one strand. . . ." This "natural" God seems almost deistic, with the orderly processes of nature mirroring a well-designed universe and rational deity. However,

Then the other God comes suddenly and says
"I crown or damn, I have different fire to add.
These forms shall feel, ache, love, grieve and be glad."

Jeffers's Calvinist upbringing manifests itself. While his rational God creates an orderly, comprehensible world, this "other" God inscrutably bestows upon human beings the conflicts of the passions and emotions. He imagines this "uncalled for God," the source of "the rapture, the sting, the insolence," to be at war with humanity, set out "to conquer us all and capture, / Master of joy and misery, troubler of men." This God seems more like an Old Testament God, demanding mastery over humanity and an unquestioned allegiance, inscrutably meting out pleasure and pain as in the Book of Job.

This latter God is the one Jeffers writes out of his verse as he moves away from a humanist philosophy. Longing for a stoical human consciousness (so often reflected in his symbolic rock and hawk), Jeffers separates these feelings and passions from the rest of God's creation—even separating out this strand of emotional consciousness from that of the rational mind which is ruled by "brain and patience"—much as he relegates them to an unnatural "women's exuberance" in "Post Mortem." He needs to make this division, it seems, before he can imagine in later poems a speaker such as in "Fire on the Hills" who gazes upon the conflagration with god-like indifference, and who thereby sees the "terrible beauty" that is born (to echo Yeats). As Jeffers develops his apocalyptic vision and his theories of "Inhumanism," God becomes energy,[7] and the emotions are relegated to the human psyche. They are no longer located in the creative force of the universe or the poet. Even by the time he writes "Continent's End," which follows this poem by several years, he has begun to imagine God more purely as an abstract force, not an anthropomorphized figure.

Nonetheless, Jeffers admits the allure of this God—really the allure of his own consciousness to take pleasure, and consequently pain, from the "senseless beauty" of the world, as well as the role that love and desire play in moments of mystical insight:

> Still we divide allegiance: suddenly
> An August sundown on a mountain road
> The marble pomps, the primal majesty
> And senseless beauty of that austerer God
> Come to us, so we love him as men love
> A mountain, not their kind: love growing intense
> Changes to joy that we grow conscious of:
> There is the rapture, the sting, the insolence
> . . . . . Or mourn dead beauty a bird-bright-May-morning:
> The insufferable insolence, the sting.

Something happens to this God as the lines progress. What is Jeffers's divided allegiance? The "austerer" God of the purely physical, functional world presents the gazer with "senseless beauty." Jeffers's "beauty" requires no human subject to apprehend or take pleasure in it. It exists without our need to make sense (and feeling) of it.[8] Yet the God who infuses human beings with the ability to feel (and to think, though Jeffers attempts to separate these) elicits sensual response. This sensate, feeling self experiences the terrifying pleasure of natural beauty, a beauty that resembles a Kantian sublime, and through his senses and feelings comes to apprehend the numinous that infuses creation. This consciousness born of love takes Jeffers past his reasoning, scientific mind into the raptures of God, back to the moment described by Otto of awe and awareness of the *mysterium tremendum*—the rapture because he feels the presence of God at that instant of perception and apprehension; the sting and insolence because of this God's other side of pain, mourning, and death, as well as the feelings of otherness of this God who is not our "kind." His allegiance is divided, for the very senses that bring him to awe and love of both nature (the mountain) and God are the source of pain and conscious awareness of his alienation from creation and the creator. It is hard not to hear Donne, "Batter my heart three-personed God," as well as Herbert, behind these sonnets.[9]

The poem marks a point in Jeffers's development. He is divided between accepting a scientific naturalist's vision of nature and the universe, one that accounts for all creation in terms of fact, function, and mechanism, and a religious view of creation, one he is struggling to make conform to his naturalist's vision. His allegiance is divided because he still seems to need to define God as a conscious, anthropomorphized creator, a mode he will surrender, at least at times, in his poetry. This austere God who overwhelms the human animal with the abilities to feel, think, and wonder loses identity as Jeffers rejects modeling God after humankind, though the urge remains in his poetry to do so. The consciousness of God becomes located in speeches such as those of Orestes, when Jeffers invokes the geologic and cosmic sublime, giving voice to his particular creed of mystical naturalism. Orestes claims to find a world *beyond* joy and misery. Such emotions are relegated to the narcissistic world of human civilization.

All this leads to Jeffers's isolato-ism, already seen to some extent in "Post Mortem," and Orestes becomes a model hero for this romantic quest. The way for Jeffers to escape the passionate God is to transcend human need. He does this by following a *via negativa*, by turning to his mystical vision of death's peaceful unconsciousness, figured repeatedly in stones and the sea, and attained by the quest into a natural space devoid of humans—or by the imagining of such spaces in his apocalyptic landscapes. This transcendent space allows him to view the flux of time from, apparently, God's perspective (or nearly so), since for Jeffers the geologic processes of the natural world are the "fountain / Humanity can understand" (*CP* 1: 4), and through which we perceive God's will.

Orestes, as isolato quester, speaks for Jeffers's mystical naturalism in the conclusion of "The Tower Beyond Tragedy" (*CP* 1: 175–78). Through Orestes, Jeffers expresses a personal experience of mystical oneness with nature which is often more muted (or put in didactic terms rather than spoken from the first person) in his lyrics. Jeffers's identification with this Orestes is nonetheless clear: Orestes finds value in exactly those creatures and elements, and their symbolic meanings, which Jeffers admires.

Orestes has returned before dawn, after killing Clytemnestra, to say farewell to Electra and attempt to impart the knowledge of his mystical experience to her. As is typical of many of Jeffers's narrative poems, the crime, in Nietzschean fashion, opens doors of perception and new freedoms for the perpetrator. In many poems, such as "Tamar" or "Thurso's Landing," the crime is often driven by uncontrolled passions (usually initiated by the seductive and destructive powers of a woman) and leads the protagonist to madness and further destruction. In this case, however, the epiphany reveals to Orestes a way out of the destructive cycles of "incestuous" human existence. He tells Electra:

> . . . That deed is past, it is finished, things past
> Make no division afterward, they have no power, they have become nothing at all; this much
> I have learned at a crime's knees.
> ELECTRA: Yet we are divided.
> ORESTES: Because I have suddenly awakened, I will not waste inward
> Upon humanity, having found a fairer object.

Outward and inward again become embedded with qualities of good and bad, with health and sickness, with truth and illusion, sanity and madness. Orestes tells Electra: "I left the madness of the house, / to-night in the dark, with you it walks yet." The house, as in the poem *Tamar*, becomes symbol of enclosed human space, of desire and narcissism, to be escaped by the seeker of truth. It symbolizes now all the dreams that humans project of their own passionate nature upon creation. Orestes tells Electra:

> . . . Here is the last labor
> To spend on humanity. I saw a vision of us move in the dark: all that we did or dreamed of
> Regarded each other, the man pursued the woman, the woman clung to the man, warriors and kings
> Strained at each other in the darkness, all loved or fought inward, each one of the lost people
> Sought the eyes of another that another should praise him; sought never his own but another's; the net of desire
> Had every nerve drawn to the centre, so that they writhed like a full draught of fishes, all matted

In the one mesh; when they look backward they see only a man standing at the beginning,
Or forward, a man at the end; or if upward, men in the shining bitter sky striding and feasting,
Whom you call Gods . . .
It is all turned inward, all your desires incestuous, the woman the serpent, the man the rose-red cavern,
Both human, worship forever. . . .

Orestes sees, as Jeffers reiterates in many of his poems, the destructiveness of a humanity that places itself at the center of the universe, that fails to see its place in the flux of creation. Incest serves as a symbol of how humans project their lives and values and libidos upon the universe, leading to illusion, madness, and destruction. The terror, though, seems to include any human sexuality or reaching toward another person: "each one of the lost people / Sought the eyes of another that another should praise him; sought never his own but another's; the net of desire / Had every nerve drawn to the centre, so that they writhed like a full draught of fishes." Orestes laments the failures of each individual to find one's unique truth, a sense of self-worth, by a turning inward that entails a kind of Emersonian self-reliance, a turning inward that actually opens one outward. Instead, each of the "lost people" seeks the praise of another and does not explore the inner self.

Desire becomes the vehicle for this incestuous turning inward, until desire (configured, always, heterosexually) itself becomes incestuous: "It is all turned inward, all your desires incestuous." Humans 'venerating' each other, driven by sexual desire—the woman desiring the man's "serpent"; the man, the woman's "rose-red cavern"—leads to a false worship that makes humanity the center instead of a peripheral creation of the universe. Orestes preaches asceticism and chastity. In the context of the poem, this stance may have much to do with the psychology of the son who has slain his mother and now faces the temptations of his sister, but these ideas are stated throughout Jeffers's work. Electra, with a degree of truth, responds, "You have dreamed wretchedly."

Orestes's response opens into his final long speech, one that Jeffers recites in a lecture to the Library of Congress to define his pantheism. And the role of the mother in this vision of Orestes returns us to Jeffers's own ambiguous relations to the feminine and the nature with which he often associates it.

ELECTRA: You have dreamed wretchedly.
ORESTES: I have
seen the dreams of the people and not dreamed them.
As for me, I have slain my mother.
ELECTRA: No more?
ORESTES: And the gate's open, the gray
boils over the mountain, I have greater
Kindred than dwell under a roof. Didn't I say this would be dark to you? I have cut the meshes
And fly like a freed falcon. To-night, lying on the hillside, sick with those visions, I remembered
The knife in the stalk of my humanity; I drew and it broke; I entered the life of the brown forest
And the great life of the ancient peaks, the patience of stone, I felt the changes in the veins
In the throat of the mountain, a grain in many centuries, we have our own time, not yours; and I was the stream
Draining the mountain wood; and I the stag drinking; and I was the stars
Boiling with light, wandering alone, each one the lord of his own summit; and I was the darkness
Outside the stars, I included them, they were a part of me. I was mankind also, a moving lichen
On the cheek of the round stone . . . they have not made words for it, to go behind things, beyond hours and ages,
And be all things in all time, in their returns and passages, in the motionless and timeless centre,
In the white of the fire . . . how can I express the excellence I have found, that has no color but clearness;
No honey but ecstasy; nothing wrought nor remembered; no undertone nor silver second murmur
That rings in love's voice, I and my loved are one; no desire but fulfilled; no passion but peace,
The pure flame and the white, fierier than any passion; no time but spheral eternity: Electra,
Was that your name before this life dawned—
ELECTRA: Here is mere
death.

The all-encompassing "I" of Orestes makes one think of Whitman, but this "I" dwells in the inhuman universal organism where "mankind" is "a moving lichen / On the cheek of the round stone," not in the humanist universe of Whitman. And this voice tells us, "I have slain my mother. . . . And the gate's open." As in "Continent's End," Jeffers's Orestes must abandon—now even slay—the "mother" in his quest for mystical insight. In a process that echoes Freud's Oedipal model, Orestes moves into 'mother' nature only as a first stage. His experience of mystical naturalism teaches him of his connection to nature, but, as the images of this passage reveal, he moves away from a generative nature, even annihilates this natural world as he relates his experience of expanding into vaster stretches of time and the cosmos until even these starry creations vanish. He begins his flight, in typical fashion for Jeffers, as a "freed falcon," then enters the mountains and feels the "patience of stone." Yet even when immersing himself in the earth, Orestes begins to individuate himself from the 'mother,' identifying himself as isolated, like the stars, "wandering alone, each one the lord of his own summit."

Jeffers trades immersion for expansion, the two actually linked by passionless patience—of stone and cosmos. The image of the stars is contrived by Jeffers in a manner that reiterates his ideology of masculine isolatoism and links this isolate quester to a transcendent divinity. After all, why couldn't Jeffers, who avidly studied astronomy and the discovery of galaxies (his brother was a professional astronomer), have imagined the stars not as separate "lords" but as linked into a vast spiraling web by the forces that create a galaxy? Jeffers's vision requires that Orestes sever himself more and more from any web of creation, expand to become "the darkness / Outside the stars" until, finally, he again arrives at a "motionless and timeless centre," a God in the "white of the fire." He ends claiming a oneness with the universe, yet achieves this only through radical isolation not only from humanity but from nature as well.

Jeffers reveals a similar urge to break free of a feminine principle (represented through linked images of a woman's body and nature) that ensnares the (presumably male) quester into cycles of existence and desire in his description of the Buddha in "Point Pinos and Point Lobos" (*CP* 1: 92–98). Jeffers writes:

Serenely smiling
Face of the godlike man made God, who tore the web of human passions
. . . freeing himself made free
All who could follow, the tissue of new births and deaths dissolved away from him,

> He reunited with the passionless light sky, not again to suffer the shame of the low female gate, freed, never to be born again. (*CP* 1: 96)

This account again points to the hierarchy of Jeffers's cosmology. Elemental, dispassionate nature is associated with his sky and fire god, this time "the passionless light sky." And it is reached by renouncing generative, biological (and human) nature. The sky, beyond the snares of this earthly life, like the eye of fire or dispassionate rock, symbolizes passionless freedom—an escape from desires and the bonds associated with female sexuality and motherhood. The feminine as mother and temptress becomes inextricably associated with biological, generative nature. And this feminine nature, even the female body, becomes the *source* of desire, the "low female gate" through which all that Jeffers seeks to transcend comes into the world—"low" being set against a transcendent "sky." The path of the quester (and a woman, it seems, cannot take on this role) is to deny this gate of passion, as Orestes does, for an inhuman path that can only be taken in "wine-hearted solitude" (*CP* 1: 388) by the isolato journeyer.

It is worth noting that Jeffers, who goes on to question whether the Buddha's idea of freedom is "surely freedom," returns in this poem to an image of "the burnt place where that wild girl whose soul was fire died with her house." Jeffers invokes his former creation Tamar, and we see in this image the limits of his female characters. She, too, strives to break free of the cycles of birth and decay but remains caught in the web of her passions, whereas Orestes (who, to be fair, is atypical for Jeffers's male characters) slays the mother, abolishes his former dependence upon and desire for the "low female gate," "the rose-red cavern," and is able to strike out for the territories, ahead of the rest, so to speak.

Orestes's reward for slaying his mother and the dream of humanity, the two having fused into one vision of the incestuous net of the passions, is to break free from humanity, to reach the coast opposite humanity which Jeffers time and again invokes and longs for. Orestes claims an immersion in nature—"I entered the brown forest"—that opens him to a mystical vision of time and space, allowing him to perceive the interconnections of all creation. The language and rhetoric that Jeffers uses to convey Orestes's experience, though, not only reveals the difficulty of conveying such experience in the forms of language but also identifies the process by which physical, sensate immersion transforms into a transcendental vision that nonetheless remains defined by abstractions and the inextricable human values that Orestes claims to have abandoned. The passage even breaks in half when Orestes reaches the limits of language to convey his immersion experience and shifts to more abstract descriptions of his mystical awareness.

The first half of the speech records Orestes's movements outward, away from the net of humanity, a movement that takes him *into* the wide earth and heavens. He begins by claiming that he "felt" the veins of the mountains and consequently perceived the world through their geologic vision of time. Much of the speech, though, relies heavily on the verb *to be* to carry the weight of his mystical fusion, typifying the predication of mystical religious texts: "I *was* the stars . . . they *were* a part of me . . . *be* all things in all times. . . . I and my loved *are* one." The passive conveys the sense of the initiate *becoming* one with the 'other,' being taken with no effort or will of his own (with no sex or conception, freed of the cycles of birth and death) into the mystical realm.

This pattern of passive voice continues even after the shift midway through Orestes's speech, when Orestes moves away from immersion in nature and the mind-bending stretches of geologic time. Jeffers omits predicates altogether, relying for the latter part of the speech on the power of a rhetorical pattern of repetition, much as a good orator (or, as in this case, dramatist) would employ. After the initial "how can I express the excellence I have found, that has no color but clearness," Jeffers omits the passive "that has" and relies on the pattern of contrasts and comparisons to carry the energy of the lines: "No honey but ecstasy; nothing wrought nor remembered; / . . . no desire but fulfilled; no passion but peace, / The pure flame and the white, fierier than any passion; no time but spheral eternity. . . ." With the "no . . . but" pattern, Orestes attempts to define the ineffable through negations of temporal, earthly qualities that approximate and suggest eternal and mystical values.

Yet they are not exactly negations, and they can never quite escape their earth-and language-bound comparisons. To state, for instance, "no passion but peace" is not to say "*not* passion but peace." Instead, the negation calls attention to the quality of passion which Orestes experiences in this newfound mystical peace. It is fierier than any human passion, yet seemingly still invokes the quality of a passionate experience. Orestes is enraptured, like St. Theresa perhaps, but this immediately calls into question the nature of his transcendence. His rejection of all human love becomes suspect. Perhaps it is more than merely a projection of his human desires on the landscape. Yet the alternative seems to be that passion serves a function in the mystical experience, as Bataille[10] argues and the history of mysticism reveals, many mystics and religious sects claiming mystical awareness in terms that suggest a channeling of erotic energy through abstinence and asceticism. Certainly, Jeffers makes the distinction in many cases between love turned 'outward' toward God and that turned inward.

The phrases, in their telegraphing syntax, can be read in several ways. "No desire but fulfilled" could mean "no desire but [that it is] fulfilled" in his mystical experience, or "no desire but [the state of being already] fulfilled." The latter would suggest that Orestes's mystical naturalism places him in a state 'beyond' desire, whereas the former suggests a process of desire and ultimate fulfillment. The first 'reading' would seem to compromise the mystical experience, inasmuch as the desire that Orestes seeks to abolish would remain an integral part of his quest. And the language of desire recurs. Is it "*no* passion but [in its place] peace," or "no passion but [that results in] peace"? Certainly, the language of the passage suggests the ecstatic enrapture of a mystical eroticism, a lovers' union—"I and my loved are one"—that could come from a love poem, say one of Donne's *Songs and Sonnets*, as well as from a passage of St. Theresa de Avila.

Of course, the ambiguities of Orestes's speech could be accounted for by just that—speech. Orestes struggles, asking "how can I express the excellence that I have found." Language binds the mystic back in the limitations of form, a falling short of excellence. This echoes the poet's eternal dilemma—how to transform mundane language into art, to capture the numinous, or an idea, a feeling, the aliveness of a place, animal, human, in words. As is typical for Jeffers (and in the fashion of Dante and Christian mysticism), he turns to images of light to attempt to express the ineffability of the experience—no color but clearness, the white of the fire, the pure flame and the white, fierier than any passion. Clear light, white light, suggest the ultimate form of all light, containing all colors. Again, vision becomes the ultimate arbiter of knowledge, as for Jeffers in "Continent's End," as for Emerson on the bare common. White light contains the entire spectrum, and, by implication, all forms of creation are contained in this excellence. Always, though, language forces upon the utterer form and limitation.

Even time transcended results in a "*spheral* eternity." Although eternity becomes bound by the language of geometry and the limits of human conceptions, the image serves as a way outside of historical time. This idea of spheral eternity replicates passages in "Point Pinos and Point Lobos," as well as in "The Torch-Bearer's Race," of time as a wheel and the future as a more remote past. Jeffers's conception of spheral time serves as a way of transcending the pain of the present and historical time.

Orestes declares that no language has been invented to capture his experience of cosmic oneness, and Jeffers often wrestles with the limitations of human-created utterings, the form of language attempting to capture the formless essence. In this case, the falling away from sentence structure for a chant-like intonement of qualities is Orestes's/Jeffers's way of attempting to capture the ineffable. Nonetheless, the speech reiterates many standard Jeffersian ideas and images: immersion in the life of stone and mountains, the expansion to the heavens, humankind as an insignificant, yet integral, part of the vast universe, fire and light as metaphors of the unmoving mover/God.

The passage begins with the process of physical immersion in nature, with the awakening brought to Orestes through this sensate experience, but, once again, his experience moves him away from a sensed nature into a realm of ideas and abstractions, carried to this transcendent vision of pure flame and desire 'always already' fulfilled via the geologic and astronomical sublime: the grand processes of the universe carry the mystic quester to visions of the source behind and beyond creation. And while Orestes does not explicitly renounce the natural world, he has renounced humanity and the mother (by slaying her!), replicating the pattern of immersion, rejection, and transcendence in many of Jeffers's poems.[11]

Certainly, Jeffers goes to great lengths in his poetry to assert the primacy of the natural world over the human one. He time and again shows humanity to be one small element of a vast universe. In a letter discussing Orestes, he even reveals the interconnections of his mystical and ecological visions, yet even in this process he reveals a longing for this mystical nature to become a vehicle for transcendent vision:

> The conclusion of Orestes, his 'extraversion'—'I was the darkness outside the stars, I included them, they were a part of me, I was mankind also . . .', and among other instances, the thought of section IV, *Apology for Bad Dreams*, is this not something akin to a part of Buddhistic thought which says, Could we but see it rightly, we are not our *selves*, not living entities around and about which

> an alien universal life whirls in never-ending phantom-series; *we are that life*, and more than we shall ever come to know whilst we remain immersed in this all-undermining dream of Selfhood? Man should seek to free himself from self-love, self-desire ('self' meaning humanity as well) and to attain to 'the motionless and timeless centre. . . . (*SL*, 182).

Elsewhere, asserting a dependency of the human soul or spirit upon the body—"the spirit is a spark fed by the flesh and nothing without it" (*SL*, 75)—Jeffers reiterates the need of any 'transcendent' consciousness for the physical world. However, even as he denounces the illusions of the ego-self and claims an immersion in all life—"*we are that life*, and more than we shall ever come to know whilst we remain immersed in this all-undermining dream of Selfhood"—this immersion in nature serves to reveal "'the motionless and timeless center,'" a *beyond* cyclical nature that is nature's source. While Jeffers celebrates the natural world and "the beauty of things" (*CP* 1: 401) in many poems, his very use of geologic and astronomical time, coupled with his particular brand of mysticism, leads him toward a vision of creation as, if not illusion, certainly transitory, resting always on the verge of obliteration.

Nature exists as a vehicle for transcendence. Time and again—in Orestes's speech, in "Continent's End," in other poems such as "The Torch-Bearer's Race"—Jeffers works through a pattern of immersion/transcendence, often involving the rejecting or abandoning of an engendered matrix of the created world for an abstract logos. One might call this Jeffers's "high style," the poems in which he strives to attain, and to convey, the greatest mystical insight into the workings of the universe. Critics such as Everson have spent much time delineating Jeffers's notions of God in this high style, though often at the expense of understanding how this vision converges with Jeffers's vision of nature. Nor is this pattern analyzed above Jeffers's only, or even perhaps his last, word on the values and workings of nature, and our human and spiritual relationships to the natural world. In other lyrics, Jeffers turns to the natural world for visions of peace that do not entail the transcendence experienced by Orestes. However, they do still depend upon an apocalyptic vision, a nature that suggests to him peace through oblivion, an erasing of humanity from the landscape, as is the case in "Post Mortem" and as will be seen in "Bixby's Landing." These poems are enraptured with a vision of death that brings a transcendence through the peace and silence of oblivion.

Electra responds to Orestes's visionary experience by stating, "Here is mere death." This is, in many ways, a fitting critique of Jeffers's vision and poetics. Electra sees that Orestes's vision takes him out of the world (or seems to), and the only way out is through annihilation, be it annihilation of the self or the world or both. This *via negativa*, construed in its unique ways by Jeffers, lies at the heart of his apocalyptic vision. It feeds much if not all of his verse, and it shapes his visions of the natural world that he inhabits as well as his ideas and fantasies of the world that he would like to inhabit—the place and extent of humans in his ideal landscapes.

In "Bixby's Landing," Jeffers seems content to remain in the moment's unfolding of life in this particular landscape, yet this landscape seems to have an even greater value than one untouched by modern civilization precisely because it represents his pastoral of apocalypse. He can read in this landscape the end of human history, the dying back of human technology from the land which, for him, signals the rebirth of a primal nature. Jeffers invokes his geologic vision to attain this apocalyptic vision, but he does so on a less grand scale than in many of his poems, not resorting, at least not until the end, to the didactic rhetoric that erupts in, and at times disrupts, many of his poems. Most important, he does not leap to ideas of God and cosmic time. Nature is sufficient. In fact, it even becomes the locus of the "good" and the "free."

BIXBY'S LANDING

They burned lime on the hill and dropped it down here in an
iron car
On a long cable; here the ships warped in
And took their loads from the engine, the water is deep to the
cliff. The car
Hangs half way over in the gape of the gorge,
Stationed like a north star above the peaks of the redwoods, iron
perch
For the little red hawks when they cease from hovering
When they've struck prey; the spider's fling of a cable rust-glued
to the pulleys.
The laborers are gone, but what a good multitude
Is here in return: the rich-lichened rock, the rose-tipped stone-
crop, the constant

Ocean's voices, the cloud-lighted space.
The kilns are cold on the hill but here in the rust of the broken
  boiler
Quick lizards lighten, and a rattle-snake flows
Down the cracked masonry, over the crumbled fire-brick. In the
  rotting timbers
And roofless platforms all the free companies
Of windy grasses have root and make seed; wild buckwheat
  blooms in the fat
Weather-slacked lime from the bursted barrels.
Two duckhawks darting in the sky of their cliff-hung nest are the
  voice of the headland.
Wine-hearted solitude, our mother the wilderness,
Men's failures are often as beautiful as men's triumphs, but your
  returnings
Are even more precious than your first presence. (*CP* 1: 388)

While this poem is most often talked about as a source for his narrative poem "Thurso's Landing," "Bixby's Landing," despite its typical Jeffersian overstatement in the last two lines, is quite beautiful in its evocation of a place and moment. He lets the landscape and its inhabitants fill the poem with a minimum of didacticism. Nonetheless, this poetic landscape unfolds with meanings and values that reveal why, and how, Jeffers finds beauty in this particular landscape. Again, he is attracted to the edge—the border country of the continent and deep water, also the edge between human ingenuity and the land, between human history and the earth's history. Human actions leave marks on the landscape, but for Jeffers the beauty of the place rests in how our alterations of the land become naturalized and transformed by the creatures and elements who remain or return: an "iron perch / For the little red hawks," "wild buckwheat blooms in the fat / Weather-slacked lime from the bursted barrels."

It seems worth getting Jeffers's 'message' over with right away. In the last three lines, Jeffers asserts what he values most in the landscape:

Wine-hearted solitude, our mother the wilderness,
Men's failures are often as beautiful as men's triumphs, but your
  returnings
Are even more precious than your first presence.

The wilderness with its cycles and solitude, the life that existed before and that will outlast human transformations of the landscape, is for Jeffers the source of beauty. Jeffers sees the "return" of the wilderness as "even more precious" than its original existence. But this assertion does not so much resolve the poem as call into question Jeffers's values. Is he a complete misanthrope? What exactly does "wine-hearted solitude" mean? Solitude for whom? For "our mother the wilderness"? For the creatures who have come to inhabit the place? For the poetic gazer and speaker? The very images he chooses complicate his assertion and reveal, once again, how his desires and fantasies collide with his "realist's eye": the voice of isolation and "Inhumanism" that runs over the surface of many poems is undermined by a desire for a landscape that can contain human values, that becomes in a sense domesticated even as its wildness is proclaimed.

His "wine-hearted solitude" seems to be a wilderness that may contain a few humans, but only ones who do not disrupt the earth with intensive technology. All this remains vague in "Bixby's Landing." Any human inhabitants are framed out of the landscape he paints, and only their detritus remains, naturalized and taken over by the local inhabitants of birds, rocks, reptiles, and grasses. The longed-for solitude seems to be Jeffers's own. "Wine-hearted solitude" reads like a translation from an ancient Greek poem, evoking a sense of the isolated wanderer, an Odysseus severed from his people but deeply aware, because of his solitude, of his place in the universe and his relationship with the landscape.

Jeffers seldom uses the word "wild" or "wilderness" in his poetry, and this is the only place he calls nature "our mother the wilderness." He finds a contentment in this landscape. Here, the wilderness seems sufficient unto itself, an answer to Jeffers's needs, providing the balm of solitude that soothes his heart. But why does he need to feminize and domesticate the wilderness in the last moments of the poem?

In many poems, Jeffers depicts the earth or ocean as mother with a good deal of ambiguity. In "Continent's End," he reveals an urgent need to leave behind the mother (in that case, the ocean), acknowledging her as a source of life on earth but not the primal source of creation. In "To the House," the earth as mother and lover provides the stones for his creation of a haven on a coast of violent elements, and this image seems more to the point in "Bixby's Landing." Jeffers longs for the landscape to be freed of its human accouterments, yet he simultaneously needs to maintain some humanized sense of place so that he may inhabit the land. The interplay of human creation and the wilderness reclaiming it make the landscape "even more precious." "Men's failures" become "as beautiful as men's triumphs" when they are reclaimed by the mother, when they are naturalized and 'brought home,' into cycles of destruction and creation. This mother, while not Jeffers's ultimate "centre" of creation, represents the cycle of time and nature that will destroy human encroachments on the land and return nature to a supposedly pristine condition. In this poem, Jeffers's love for the natural world rather than his spiritual quest for divine truth is foregrounded.

"Bixby's Landing" seems to be a poem about decay and destruction, but it is filled with images of fertility, growth, and domesticity, and this helps to explain how he arrives at his image of "our mother the wilderness." The poem even serves as an extension of Jeffers's house into the landscape, for as he takes joy in the decay of the mine and the lime kilns, he infuses the landscape with images of a home perched on a cliff that cannot help but echo his own home. The duckhawks (peregrine falcons) and their cliff-hung nest, as "voice of the headlands," mirror Jeffers's cliff-hung nest and poetic flights. He claims himself as voice of the headland through the associations of the image.

The poem begins with a brief description of the cliff-scape's human history but quickly shifts to the predominant trope of the poem: the transformation of human artifact into natural element which reiterates Jeffers' desire for his house, and his poetry. The first image is of a smoldering landscape, a site of work that calls forth a mixed image of human destruction and production: "They burned lime on the hill and dropped it down here in an iron car / On a long cable." The reader is brought into the scene through Jeffers's angle of perspective, as if one stands "down here" below the hill with the poet pointing out the scene. Jeffers seems fascinated with the details of human work and ingenuity, even as he ultimately turns away from them for what he sees as a greater natural order.

This scene of human production and modern civilization—the burning, the iron car running along the cable, the ships warping in, the engines working—is abrogated by the next set of images. Now,

. . . The car
Hangs half way over in the gape of the gorge,
Stationed like a north star above the peaks of the redwoods, iron perch
For the little red hawks when they cease from hovering

When they've struck prey; the spider's fling of a cable rust-glued
to the pulleys.

The first simile equates the car, hanging uselessly, perilously over the cliff, with the north star. It seems an emblem of humanity, our existence perched over an abyss, our efforts to order the world always threatened by oblivion, as in "To the Stone-Cutters" and so many of Jeffers's poems. Simile, though, is quickly replaced by metamorphosis. The car may be *like* a north star, yet it has *become* a perch for hawks. The car attains a new function in nature, fittingly a perch for Jeffers's totemic hawks, emblems of "fierce consciousness" and "realist eyes," to tear at their prey. And from simile and metamorphosis, the image of the car and cable becomes a metaphor: "the spider's fling of a cable rust-glued to the pulleys." Set against the cliff and ocean landscape, fallen into disuse, the steel cable appears tenuous, no more than the strand of a spider web, easily broken and obliterated (as well as naturalized). The steel cable and car, in their time working signs of human mastery of nature, now reveal the slight control humanity may exert over the elements.

Jeffers drives home this point throughout the next nine or ten lines. Each sentence begins with an image of the lime-kilns, the structures, the workers, shifting to a description of the life that now reclaims the work-site. Several things happen in the process. The human history of the place is naturalized but in the process evaded, while the nature that returns is encoded with values that can have meaning only for a human observer. Jeffers writes, "The laborers are gone, but what a good multitude / Is here in return." Even more rapidly than in "To the Rock That Will Be a Cornerstone of the House," Jeffers passes over the history and politics of those who were there before him by naturalizing them. (One thinks of Wordsworth's similar need in "Lines Composed above Tintern Abbey" and "Home at Grasmere" to frame out of his ideal pastorals the industrial landscape or the conditions of poverty in which many laborers and farmers lived.) Jeffers is not unaware of who these "laborers" were, or their fate. In a letter, he comments on the use of Chinese laborers in the mines and that many were killed working in them (*SL*, 197). They are bone, now, returned to the earth. Their suffering and the unjust labor practices that reduced them to bone in the depths of the cliff do not figure into Jeffers's inhumanist, naturalist vision.

One could argue that such politics are not the purpose of this poem; nor are they essential to Jeffers's cosmic vision. Perhaps this is so, but the very fact that Jeffers then goes on to inscribe the landscape as now containing "a *good* multitude" of rocks, ocean voices, and "cloud-lighted space," and covered with the "*free* companies of windy grasses" that "have root and make seed" (emphasis added) reveals a politics to his poem. "Good" and "free" are values imposed on the landscape. "Good multitude" even evokes a biblical (and Puritan) typography of chosen ones arriving in a new Jerusalem.

The apocalypse is already complete for the gazer in this poem. He has arrived in the new world for which he longs in "Post Mortem." This is a typical Jeffersian trope. He often infuses what seems 'pure' description with abstract adjectives or nouns—good, free, beautiful, real, glory. His landscapes thereby take on human and religious connotations, and in some cases the poems hinge on these ambiguous words and values. In this poem, the good and the free are associated with a nature unhindered by human intrusion. The good multitude replaces the laborers and serves as emblem of a more harmonious order, one that replaces human work (incestuous and destructive, as seen in "The Tower Beyond Tragedy") with freedom and fertility—the grasses "have root and make seed" in the rotten timbers.

Jeffers remains neutral in his opinions about the lime-kilns. He does not rail against them as destructive, and he even seems fascinated with this human past. But his choices reveal that he turns to humanity only to turn away from it, toward nature for an eternal order and a locus of values with which he feels 'at home.' Ultimately, the value of this site of human endings rests in the goodness and freedom it brings to himself, the observer reveling in his "wine-hearted solitude." The place becomes his as he gazes upon it and transforms it into poetry, into his dream of home. The final image of the duckhawks reinforces this feeling of Jeffers claiming the place: "Two duckhawks darting in the sky of their cliff-hung nest are the voice of the headland." These hawks and their nest become a metaphor of Jeffers's and Una's cliff-nest, the hawks' voices speaking for the headland as surely as Jeffers feels or wishes for his voice to speak for this place. They represent a final domestication of the former work-site, a domestication that brings back "*our* mother the wilderness" to the headland, Jeffers even claiming possession of this wilderness (although he would argue that it possesses him). The voice of nature and Jeffers's poetic voice are implicitly fused.

While in "Bixby's Landing" Jeffers keeps the images and the speaker's experience largely rooted in the setting, the poem still represents a speaker who maintains a certain distance from the natural world due to his abstract ponderings, even when finding personal value and insight by being immersed in the particular landscape. In other poems, such as "Noon," "Return," "Oh Lovely Rock," and "The Beauty of Things," poems that span much of his career, Jeffers depicts more sensate, bodily experiences of the speaker in natural settings—or at least he asserts the value of experience in organic nature over any human ideas or longings for a transcendent, if nature-inspired, vision. Such poems represent a minor strain in his work, one that still often holds an apocalyptic tone, but one in which the speakers seem more willing to immerse themselves in the moment, in creation's process, in the things of the world. In many ways, this desire lies behind all his work, but only sometimes does Jeffers compose a lyric that rests in this physical immersion. In "Return," for instance, he writes,

> A little too abstract, a little too wise,
> It is time for us to kiss the earth again,
> It is time to let the leaves rain from the skies,
> Let the rich life run to the roots again.
> I will go down to the lovely Sur Rivers
> And dip my arms in them up to the shoulders.
> I will find my accounting where the alder leaf quivers
> In the ocean wind over the river boulders.
> I will touch things and things and not more thoughts,
> That breed like mouthless May-flies darkening the sky,
> The insect clouds that blind our passionate hawks
> So that they cannot strike, hardly can fly. Things are the hawk's
>   food and noble is the mountain, Oh noble
> Pico Blanco, steep sea-wave of marble. (*CP* 2: 409)

While the speaker only dreams of immersing himself, placing in the future the fulfillment of his desire to make physical contact with the rivers, alder leaves, and ocean, and while Jeffers again invokes geologic time by 'ascending' in the final image to the mountain, Pico Blanco, the dominant and desired movement of the poem remains into "things and things and not more thoughts." Jeffers seems to be responding to his own poetic tropes of abstraction as well as Western civilization's spiritual and physical uprootedness from the earth.

The apocalyptic tone remains—it is the fall of the year, "leaves rain from the skies," and Jeffers dreams of death, but this death is a return to the processes of organic nature, not a transcendent

God. The things of nature are celebrated as the source of all value. To "touch things," to touch them not only with the body but also with words that express their beingness in the poem, is to learn one's true nature, one's place in the scheme of creation.

As Jeffers states even more explicitly (though in a more abstract manner) in a late poem, "The Beauty of Things," poetry itself and "human nature" are the works of nature.

> To feel and speak the astonishing beauty of things—earth, stone
> and water,
> Beast, man and woman, sun, moon and stars—
> The blood-shot beauty of human nature, its thoughts, frenzies
> and passions,
> And unhuman nature its towering reality—
> For man's half dream; man, you might say, is nature dreaming,
> but rock
> And water and sky are constant—to feel
> Greatly, and understand greatly, and express greatly, the natural
> Beauty, is the sole business of poetry.
> The rest's diversion: those holy or noble sentiments, the intricate
> ideas,
> The love, lust, longing: reasons, but not the reason. (*CP* 3, 369)

Jeffers asserts his *ars poetica*—that poetry's only 'real' purpose is to express eternal, transhuman values and our human experiences of these eternal truths and beauties. He still conveys a sense of nature's 'otherness' from our human nature, but Jeffers imagines our human "dreams," or imagination, as nature dreaming—as nature regarding itself. Even more essentially, he breaks from the romantic paradigm of nature *vs.* human consciousness and culture. That nature provides a source for psychic recovery or inspiration for poetry is a tenet of much nineteenth- and twentieth-century American poetry. That poetry serves to express nature, that human consciousness "is nature dreaming," however, takes Jeffers's work beyond romanticism as well as distances him from Modernist traditions.

Jeffers proclaims an early ecological manifesto unknown to such philosophical forebears as Emerson and barely spoken by anyone in the United States in the 1920s and 1930s. Not only does he relocate humanity from the center of creation to an inconsequential thread in nature's vast web, but Jeffers also ultimately imagines his pantheistic God not as any entity but as energy. His God-as-energy echoes Henry Adams's dynamo as well as reveals how Jeffers attempts to integrate into his poetics the fundamental restructuring of Western cosmology brought about by modern physics and astronomy.

In this way, his poetic project reflects the desire of many modernist writers to integrate the teachings of modern science into their poetic cosmologies. The struggle to find meaning and purpose for a de-centered humanity at times leads Jeffers, like other Modernists, to his own form of alienation from nature. His apocalypse reads like a mirror image of Eliot's—both seek a transcendent vision, yet Jeffers does so by celebrating nonhuman creation while Eliot imagines an apocalypse rooted in Christian humanism. Similarly, whereas Stevens (like Keats) resolves the problem of modern alienation by valuing human imagination over nature, or H. D. by turning landscapes and images from nature into settings for exploration of the human psyche, Jeffers instead attempts to depict nature as the final reality; most of our desires and imaginings and struggles to understand our human natures distort that reality by overemphasizing the human component of creation: "Remember that the life of mankind is like the life of a man, a flutter from darkness to darkness / Across the bright hair of a fire" (*CP* 1:101).

Jeffers has thus reimagined and developed crucial elements of American nature poetry. He has helped to bring (back) into modern consciousness ideas of nature's primacy and our consciousness as an expression of nature—perceptions that such nineteenth-century writers as Muir and Thoreau began to express. His visions and ideas parallel developments in ecological and scientific theories and have provided points of departure, whether the influence be direct or indirect, for many poets and twentieth-century writers concerned with the natural world. Such perceptions are at the heart of poets like Mary Oliver and Gary Snyder. Jeffers's work also dovetails with ideas expressed by Native American poets such as Ray Youngbear, Joy Harjo, and Linda Hogan (though these poets draw images of nature from their traditional cultures rather than from a European-American lineage of writers).

Still, the images by which Jeffers represents his radical re-envisioning of nature reveal how his vision filters through his era's dominant cultural stereotypes of gender and sexuality, as well as the Calvinist and classical upbringing that feeds, and limits, his work.

The irresolvable conflict in Jeffers's work comes down to the fact that he is an essentialist poet in love with the shape-shifting natural world. Seeking pure essence, the "tides of fire" beyond nature, Jeffers often falls back on patriarchal dichotomies. He imagines nature, the field of matter in constant flux, as a feminine force of birth and death in which the passions dominate. This nature inspires the poet-seeker, but Jeffers sees cyclical nature as offering a limited field of vision—worse, it is a trap when one allows the passions of this nature, so often associated with "women's exuberance" in his poems, to dominate. The inspiration only serves as a way to 'higher' and older truths (as in Freudian theory the mother must be left for the male Logos). Again, "Continent's End" sums up this perspective:

> The tides are in our veins, we still mirror the stars, life is your child, but there is in me
> Older and harder than life and more impartial, the eye that watched before there was an ocean. . . .
> Mother, though my song's measure is like your surf-beat's ancient rhythm I never learned it of you.
> Before there was any water there were tides of fire, both our tones flow from the older fountain. (*CP* 1: 16–17)

Through his tropes of geologic and astronomical nature, he moves beyond time, out of cycles of creation, and into the eye of fire, his telos, a pure source often equated with a masculinized—abstract, logical, passionless—transcendental being, or energy, or place.

As if some part of Jeffers knows that this dialectic is not quite right, he keeps rewriting it, re-imagining nature, struggling to see and depict—"painfully" and with "the whole mind"—nature *as it is*, not as he or we would like it to be, not anthropomorphized, not as masculine or feminine, despite what the necessities of the poet, of metaphor and language, require. As he writes in "The Torch-Bearer's Race," Jeffers seeks

> . . . to drink of the fountain of the beauty of the sun of the stars, and to gaze in his face, not a father's,
> And motherless and terrible and here. (*CP* 1:101)

This struggle provides Jeffers with a fierce and controversial re-envisioning of modern humanity's relationship to the natural world that, like the flame in "Fire on the Hills," has cleared and fed the soil for new growth—hopefully before all our old habit-patterns of thinking and acting completely destroy the only world we have.

Notes

1. William Everson discusses the role of awe in the religious experience, with reference to Rudolf Otto, in *The Excesses of God: Robinson*

Jeffers as a Religious Figure. The primordial experience of the numinous, according to Otto, is what he calls the "*mysterium tremendum*," the feeling of awe and fear when approaching the unapproachable. Jeffers repeatedly falls back upon "negative concepts" and violence to describe positive feelings and awareness of the numinous, says Everson, as a means of communicating the awakening power of this awe. This results in Jeffers's excesses of language and didacticism, but it also serves him, when it works, to approach and communicate the "cosmic excess" (25, 37–38, 45).

2. The poem "Consciousness," from *Tamar*, which will be considered later, represents an early and pivotal exploration for Jeffers into the relations between human consciousness, the natural world, and the nature of God.

3. In many of Jeffers's poems, the house comes to symbolize the limits, entrapments, and enclosures of social life. One thinks of Muir abjuring Emerson's companions in the Yosemite wilderness for their limiting "house habits," refusing to sleep out under the sequoias. More to the point, Poe comes to mind, for as the incestuous House of Usher must fall, so too must the House of Cauldwell in *Tamar*. Tamar's house epitomizes Jeffers's anxieties of domesticity. The house must burn and fall, for the incest of the family symbolizes human narcissism—the destructive self-interest that obscures humanity's ability to perceive its place in the universe.

4. Nonetheless, it is depressing to visit Tor House now and see Jeffers's fears realized. Monstrous contemporary houses engulf Carmel Point and abut Jeffers's home. A few of the trees that Jeffers planted remain standing, but hardly a patch of ground remains unpaved or built upon. Joggers in designer sweats and an endless flow of tourists in cars—part of the boutiquing of California's coast, as John McKinney writes—have replaced the landscape Jeffers first settled, and helped to make famous. Of course, the blame for this rests with developers, city planners, and a capitalist system of viewing land as commodity—such political-economic concerns largely lacking from Jeffers's account.

5. Jeffers's fixation on prophets, Christ-like figures, and his jeremiads, besides the fact that he chooses to write at all, suggests a longing to remain alive in historical time.

6. This poem was not published, however, until after Jeffers's Library of Congress reading in February 1941.

7. In a letter written in 1934, responding to Sister Mary James Power's query as to his "religious attitudes," Jeffers comes to define God as the universe of "energy," drawing on modern physics, as well as an ecological model of interdependency, to define his concept of the 'inhuman' beingness of creation: "I believe that the universe is one being, all

its parts are different expressions of the same energy, and they are all in communication with each other, influencing each other, therefore parts of one organic whole. (This is physics, I believe, as well as religion.) . . . The parts change and pass, or die, people and races and rocks and stars, none of them seems to me important in itself, but only the whole. This whole is in all its parts so beautiful, and is felt by me to be so intensely in earnest, that I am compelled to love it, and to think of it as divine. It seems to me that this whole alone is worthy of the deeper sort of love; and that here is peace, freedom, I might say a kind of salvation, in turning one's affections outward toward this one God, rather than inward on one's self, or on humanity, or on human imagination and abstractions—the world of spirits" (*SL*, 221). This universe imagined as an organic whole also echoes the visions of many tribal cultures who, in their intimate contact with the earth and its beings, perceive a spiritual force that permeates creation.

In this particular quote, Jeffers does not imagine a separation of self from the source of creation. There is no fall, not even in the sense of the temporal world as fragmented sparks of the celestial, as in the Kabbalistic tradition. In his poems, though, the contradictory responses which Jeffers repeatedly experiences are not so easily resolved. He desires a unity with the land, a merging between human self and natural other, even as he witnesses the violent powers of nature that are indifferent to human interests. As in "Consciousness," Jeffers often begins or moves into a sense of distance and separation from the divine which he strives to overcome. Human consciousness, or self-consciousness, parallels the fall, even as this consciousness provides Jeffers, through creative acts, a way toward unity. Letters such as this represent an overriding belief, but the poems depict the work, conflicts, and problems inherent in arriving at and inhabiting such a vision. In poems such as "Continent's End" the outcome of such a vision borders on a negation of the world of "people and races and rocks and stars" as the only way to arrive at his brand of salvation. His salvation ironically requires a love that borders on abstraction as the only way to embrace the whole. While many of his poems depict Jeffers loving the things of the world and universe as a way to love the "organic whole," he often ends up erasing the phenomenal or imagining 'beyond' it as the only way to arrive at the comfort of 'peace and freedom.' To hold in mind the universe of energy as both a whole and a myriad of forms becomes a driving energy of Jeffers's poetic quest.

8. Jeffers states in his Library of Congress talk: "I spoke a moment ago of the beauty of the universe, that calls forth our love and reverence. Beauty, like color, is subjective. It is not in the object but in the mind that regards it. Nevertheless, I believe it corresponds to a reality, a real

excellence and nobility in the world; but as the color red corresponds to a reality: certain wave-lengths of light, a certain rhythm of vibrations. It was Plato who defined beauty as the effulgence—the shining forth of truth" (*Themes in My Poem*, 28).

In a letter to Benjamin Miller several years earlier (February 1938; *SL* 262), Jeffers further clarifies his idea of natural beauty that is also moral (earnest and noble) beauty: "When I wrote 'beauty is thy human name' I was trying to express the feeling, which still remains with me, that this human and in itself subjective sense of beauty is occasioned by some corresponding quality or temper or arrangement in the object. Why else should a quite neutral thing—a wave or the sea or a hill against the sky—be somehow lovely and loveworthy, and become more so the more it is realized by contemplation? My intelligence (such as it is) does not work here; and it is hard to express in prose even my feeling. The feeling of deep earnestness and nobility in natural objects and in the universe:—these are human qualities, not mineral or vegetable, but it seems to me I would not impute them into the objects unless there were something in not-man that corresponds to these qualities in man."

9. The music of these sonnets seems worth commenting upon. In tone and manner (as in the ideas Jeffers struggles with) they present a bridge between the poetry of the young Jeffers (in his volumes prior to *Tamar*) and his mature poetics. The language shifts between Victorian prosody—"mountain pomps" the least successful such phrase, with God's speech quoted above a beautiful example of a Victorian 'high style'—and Jeffers's unique voice, as in the last four or five lines of the sequence. In these final lines, Jeffers 'speaks' almost colloquially—"which we grow conscious of" instead of "of which we grow conscious." Or, more representative of his mature style, he speaks 'informally' within a highly stylized and rhythmic language: "There is the rapture, the sting, the insolence / Or mourn dead beauty a bird-bright-May-morning: / The insufferable insolence, the sting." The syntax seems common enough, the hyphenated phrase even having the quality of notes or the way we may try to 'telegraph' information to someone with whom we speak. Of course, the diction and subject matter, as well as the repetitions that deepen the sense of the speaker's pain and despair, take the poem out of the realm of ordinary discourse.

10. Georges Bataille's definition of the erotic, and the violence associated with it, seems particularly apt for defining much of Jeffers's work. Like Everson, Bataille focuses upon how violence disrupts mundane perceptions of experience. Bataille sees erotic energy as driven by the desire of the individual to reach beyond the discontinuity of the self (our

sense of separate existence in the world), through sexual merging with the 'other.' This merging takes one to the point of death as the sense of self is lost. But this death becomes an affirmation for "death, in that it destroys the discontinuous being, leaves intact the general continuity of existence outside ourselves. . . . Through the beloved appears . . . full and limitless being unconfined within the trammels of separate personalities" (20). This erotic death reveals a mystical vision of the continuous universe of which we are a part. The erotic, then, strikes to the core of being; it is driven by a "nostalgia" for continuity with all creation even as it is simultaneously perpetuated by the desire to hold to one's sense of immortality, to the discontinuous self "to which we cleave in terror."

11. Jeffers uses this passage in his Library of Congress speech in 1941 (his only lecture/reading tour) to define his "pantheism" and to distinguish it from what he calls "Oriental pantheism." As in "Credo," Jeffers asserts that the "outer world is real and divine" as opposed to the Hindu or Buddhist vision of the world as illusion created by mind. But Jeffers incorrectly impinges a Christian conception of a personal soul upon Buddhist belief in the process. Jeffers writes, "Another theme that has much engaged my verses is the expression of a religious feeling, that perhaps must be called pantheism, though I hate to type it with a name. It is the feeling—I will say the certainty—that the universe is one being, a single organism, one great life that includes all life and all things; and is so beautiful that it must be loved and reverenced; and in moments of mystical vision we identify ourselves with it. This is, in a way, the exact opposite of Oriental pantheism. The Hindu mystic finds God in his own soul, and all the outer world is illusion. To this other way of feeling, the outer world is real and divine; one's own soul might be called an illusion, it is so slight and so transitory. This is the experience that comes to my Orestes . . ." (*Themes in My Poetry* 23). Interestingly, Jeffers here defines the universe as a "being" and "organism," not purely energy as in his letter to Sister Mary James Power (n. 7). This truly does differentiate his vision from some schools of what he calls "Oriental pantheism" (though Jeffers's terms do call to mind Vishnu lying on the cosmic sea, from whom Brahma and the created universe arise). Nevertheless, Orestes experiences an obliteration of self in the face of vast creation, and this is closer to a Buddhist or Hindu conception than not (although to equate the myriad practices of Buddhism and Hinduism is in itself reductive). God is not found in "one's own soul" or individual mind by one practicing Buddhist or Hindu meditation. Many branches of Buddhism do not even talk of a God. The soul or self is illusory, ever changing, as much as any element of the created world. Rather, speaking

generally, the awareness of oneness with all the universe comes through the dissolving of the psychological self into mindfulness, into a Self devoid of ego-differentiation, which is exactly what Orestes experiences.

Works Cited

CP *The Collected Poetry of Robinson Jeffers*. Ed. Tim Hunt. 3 vols. to date. Stanford, CA: Stanford UP, 1988, 1989, 1991.

SL *The Selected Letters of Robinson Jeffers, 1897–1962*. Ed. Ann N. Ridgeway. Baltimore: John Hopkins UP, 1968.

Bataille, Georges. *Eroticism: Death and Sensuality* (1957). Trans. Mary Dalwood. San Francisco: City Lights, 1986.

Everson, William. *The Excesses of God: Robinson Jeffers as a Religious Figure*. Stanford, CA: Stanford UP, 1988.

Jeffers, Robinson. *Themes in My Poems*. San Francisco: Book Club of California, 1956.

9

Nature and the Symbolic Order: The Dialogue Between Czeslaw Milosz and Robinson Jeffers

Alan Soldofsky

ONE OF THE IRONIES of recent literary history is that Robinson Jeffers, the great poet of the California coast and self-described *inhumanist*, first began to be recovered for readers of mainstream American verse by the Lithuanian-born Polish poet Czeslaw Milosz. An avowed humanist who had endured Nazi occupation and Stalinist oppression and who received political asylum in France where he lived in the 1950s, Milosz started reading Jeffers shortly after he arrived in Berkeley in 1960 to teach Polish literature at the University of California. Milosz took Jeffers far more seriously than did most American poets and critics for whom at the time Jeffers was a completely marginalized figure, at best treated with scorn and at worst ignored altogether, except for a declining number of devotees—the most notable being the poet William Everson, Jeffers's only true disciple.

Milosz's interest in Jeffers was perhaps as much a geographical as an historical inevitability. For a man of letters born in a soon-to-be-annexed Baltic duchy in 1911, the year before Jeffers published his first book, *Flagons and Apples*, and three years before Jeffers came to Carmel, California in the 1960s must have seemed an exotic if not an alien place to continue his poetic practice. To get his bearings, Milosz had to reconfigure his identity once again, isolated from speakers of his native language, living almost anonymously, his European imagination unsettled by the West Coast's vast wild panoramas. Moreover, he had come to Berkeley, arguably America's most quixotic city, living through the century's most quixotic decade. He began by trying to come to terms with the place where he was. In *Visions from San Francisco Bay*, a collection of essays written in Polish and published in 1969 in France, Milosz writes:

> Berkeley clings to hills which face west, toward the Pacific, and its best hours—afternoon, dusk, the famous sunsets, evening—are unspoiled by sea fog. There are many cities and countries in my mind, but they all stand in relation to the one which surrounds me every day. The human imagination is spatial and it is constantly constructing an architectonic whole from landscapes remembered or imagined. (7)

He also read California's writers, especially Allen Ginsberg (then associated with the poets of San Francisco), Henry Miller, and Robinson Jeffers—in whom he developed an abiding interest. His encounter with Jeffers became the centerpiece of *Visions from San Francisco Bay.* The book's intended audience was European, primarily Polish émigrés and scholars who had come to the West, as well as French intellectuals. In it Milosz produces a complex discourse on topics ranging from his impressions of California's imposing physical landscape to the frailty of human life in the face of nature's indifference, from the contradictions of religion and history to the implications of the lifestyles of the student counterculture. The book was Milosz's attempt to explain the condition of his existence in California, an impossible task for him to accomplish, so he claimed, for it would require him to produce a text that simultaneously transmitted "the smell and texture of my skin, everything stored in my memory, and all I now assent to, dissent from" (3). With its publication in English in 1982, two years after Milosz received the Nobel Prize for Literature, the book also served to relegitimize Jeffers for serious American readers.

Carmel in Ulro

Leonard Nathan and Arthur Quinn in *The Poets Work: An Introduction to Czeslaw Milosz* suggest that Milosz's encounter with Jeffers is the authorizing narrative behind *Visions from San Francisco Bay:*

> The choice for Milosz is never between ideas, world views, or philosophies; it is always between persons. At the cosmic level Milosz may think the choice is between a bearded God and sophisticated demons. But in the small world of *Visions from San Francisco Bay* it is a choice between Milosz himself and the great, neglected Robinson Jeffers. (7)

Milosz and Jeffers never met. Milosz reports, however, in *Visions from San Francisco Bay* that when he first visited Carmel, a few years after Jeffers's death, he spent a long while walking around Tor House, Jeffers's handmade granite house with its squat granite tower off to one side of the garden. By then the low windswept hill on which Jeffers had once planted a eucalyptus forest for a windbreak was a neighborhood of modern, genteel homes separated from the crashing Pacific waves by an asphalt road besieged with traffic. Wandering along the beach by Tor House and watching the children and the tourists, Milosz began inexplicably to feel some link with Jeffers, something which transcended his opposition to Jeffers's philosophy and even his doubts about some of Jeffers's poetry. Milosz believed himself to be in the presence of a great poet, a spirit with whom he felt compelled to engage in dialogue. Milosz says of Jeffers: "There was something paradoxical in my fascination with him; I was surprised that I, a newcomer from lands where everyone is burdened with history, where History is written with a capital H, was conducting a dialogue with his spirit though, had we met, we would not have been able to understand one another" (93).

Undoubtedly, if they had met face to face, Milosz and Jeffers could not have understood each other. Their experience of history is too different; their differences in theology too great. In addition they would have had their cultural and linguistic disparities to negotiate. Then on what grounds could Milosz conduct his dialogue with Jeffers? No two poets of this century could hold more firmly opposed positions concerning each other's valuations, particularly about nature and divinity. Milosz—a Manichaean, Catholic Pole—found in nature's beauty nothing but a demonic indifference toward humanity, and chose to privilege divinity over nature. Jeffers—a pantheist, anti-Christian Californian—sacralized the inhuman beauty of nature's cycles of eternal recurrence, which he called God, and which he believed determined humanity's ultimate subservience to the laws of science.

The grounds on which Milosz pursues his dialogue with Jeffers, I will argue, are embedded in the "Carmel" essay and in the two poems that frame it: Jeffers's "Continent's End" and Milosz's "To Robinson Jeffers"—the only poem of his own that Milosz includes in *Visions from San Francisco Bay.* These grounds are more eschatalogical and metaphysical than simply cultural and historical:

> Did Jeffers consider consciousness only an unforgivable sin? For him the nebulae, the sun, the rocks, the sea, sharks, crabs, were

> parts of an organism without beginning or end which eternally renews itself and which he called God. For he was a religious writer, though not in the sense that his father, a Calvinist pastor, would have approved. Jeffers studied biology as a young man, and once having accepted the mathematical system of cause and effect, he dethroned the Jehovah who makes incomprehensible demands of his subjects, who appears in a burning bush and makes a covenant with one tribe. Personal relations with a deity who graciously promises people that by remaining obedient to his commands they will escape the fate of all the rest of creation were, to his mind, only proof of what lengths human insolence and arrogance could reach. (*VSF* 91)

Milosz engaged Jeffers in dialogue not merely because Jeffers writes in the language of poetry, as Nathan and Quinn suggest, or because both poets recognize the same dualities in the human experience of the universe. Milosz found in Jeffers, despite fuming at what he considered to be Jeffers's "naivete" and "errors," a peer whose poetry demanded to be granted the same intellectual weight as the writings of scientists and philosophers.[1] Moreover, Jeffers, like Milosz, is an inherently dialogic poet whose teleological position Milosz recognizes as participating in his own anthropocentric dialectic. Indeed, *Visions from San Francisco Bay* can be read as being addressed in large measure to Jeffers's position. For Milosz, Jeffers represents the continuation in California of an Arcadian vision originating with Thoreau and Whitman, a vision of an American Adam living in concord with and deriving spiritual knowledge from nature. Milosz finds such privileging of nature to be simultaneously seductive and problematic. In short, given that Milosz had come to occupy not only the same geographical but also the same textual ground as Jeffers, a dialogue between the two poets would seem inevitable.

In the "Carmel" essay Milosz authorizes his account of Jeffers by reporting: "Even during my first visit to Carmel, I asked myself if I was like him, and perhaps flattering myself, answered no. I was sufficiently like him to re-create his thoughts from within and to feel what had given rise to them" (90). The reader cannot mistake what Milosz is saying here. Milosz in this passage describes the act of re-creating his own interiorized Jeffers. Milosz goes so far in the essay as twice to describe Jeffers's position as a product of exile, a position that though imposed upon Milosz had not been on Jeffers. This dialogue, then, is being conducted with a reconstructed Jeffers—quite literally in fact, as one must recall that the essay, in its original Polish, was prefaced by Milosz's Polish translation of Jeffers's "Continent's End."

One may read *Visions from San Francisco Bay* partially as a response to "Continent's End," which is a poem about boundaries—spatial and temporal:

> I gazing at the boundaries of granite and spray, the established
> sea-marks, felt behind me
> Mountain and plain, the immense breadth of the continent,
> before me the mass and doubled stretch of water.
>
> I said: You yoke the Aleutian seal-rocks with the lava and coral
> sowings that flower the south,
> Over your flood the life that sought the sunrise faces ours that
> has followed the evening star.
>
> The long migrations meet across you and it is nothing to you,
> you have forgotten us, mother.
> You were much younger when we crawled out of the womb and
> lay in the sun's eye on the tideline.
>
> It was long and long ago; we have grown proud since then and
> you have grown bitter; life retains
> Your mobile soft unquiet strength; and envies hardness, the
> insolent quietness of stone. (*CP* 1: 16)

In *Visions from San Francisco Bay* Milosz describes the crisis in his imagination brought about by his being introduced to the vast wild stretches of America's Pacific coast, his new location. In orienting himself to his adopted region, he eventually is forced to confront nature—what he describes as "that chaos which dispenses with valuation" (10). It is through this confrontation that Milosz encounters Jeffers. Jeffers's poetry, like the very presence of the mountains and ocean, weakens Milosz's self-conscious "humanistic zeal," leaving him "with a feeling akin to nausea" as he gazes upon nature's boundless immensities (11). The problem for Milosz is that he has become decentered facing the immense breadth of the American continent, which he refers to as "a land of human aloneness" (32). He finds himself in a "here" caught at the boundaries not only of ocean and land but of America and Europe, of past and present, of the symbolic and the literal, of signifier and signified. Moreover, Milosz feels his humanistic project being undermined by his location, finding himself at the boundary of the human and the inhuman, a boundary to which Jeffers was drawn and from which Jeffers drew inspiration.

Milosz does not find solace as Jeffers did in the impartiality of nature, "the insolent quietness of stone." To Milosz, nature's impartiality feels like oppression: "Strangeness, indifference, eternal stone, stone-like eternity, and compared to it, I am a split second of tissue, nerve, pumping heart, and worst of all, I am subject to the same incomprehensible law ruling what is here before me, which I see only as self-contained and opposed to all meaning" (10). Meaning, for Milosz, is socially determined in the nexus of language, culture, technology, and art. His image for this nexus is "a cocoon of constantly renewed dependencies, which infuses time with value" (10). However, on the West Coast of North America, he finds the human cocoon ruptured by the primacy of a landscape which, from his Central European viewpoint, resists being defined "by allusions to the 'humanistically formed imagination'" (8).

For Milosz America is virgin territory, a land that has not been gradually converted into language over the centuries, inscribed with layers of signifiers like the Europe to which he was accustomed. To him California seems an uncharted region, its vast territory existing outside the symbolic order. It is as a European writing for Europeans that Milosz complains about "the oppressive virginity of this country, virgin in the sense that it seems to be waiting for its names" (8). But is the complaint simply that the continent is unwritten? Or is it that, encountering a land whose contact with Europe is relatively recent, he faces a landscape which exists outside a symbolic economy he recognizes? His earliest California poems would indicate the latter:

> I sleep a lot and read St. Thomas Aquinas
> or *The Death of God* (that's a Protestant book).
> To the right the bay as if molten tin,
> beyond the bay, city, beyond the city, ocean,
> beyond the ocean, ocean, till Japan.
> To the left dry hills with white grass,
> beyond the hills an irrigated valley where rice is grown,
> beyond the valley, mountains and ponderosa pines,
> beyond the mountains, desert and sheep.
> ("I Sleep a Lot," *MCP* 177)

Milosz's description of his location foregrounds the earth's materiality, which resists being rendered in humanistic terms. For Milosz the privileging of such materiality threatens the stability of cultural forms and practices (Christianity, for example) which he holds shield humanity against the impersonal, brutal processes of nature. The consequences of living in such an altogether material world are (to simplify Milosz's quite complex thought) both the loss of faith and the loss of the human ability to make distinctions between good and evil.

> My contemporaries (strongly effected by Manichaeanism, and like it or not, I am one of them) have moved far from any doctrines espousing harmony with nature and wise acceptance of its rhythms as a guide to behavior; paralyzed by the animal in themselves (once caged by the Soul, Reason), they have sought the Spirit passionately, but since God has been withdrawing, losing his attributes, Spirit can now be only human, the sole maker of distinctions between good and evil, set in opposition in a universe which knows neither good [n]or evil. (*VSF* 25)

Thus, according to Milosz, we in the West since the Enlightenment have come to dwell in what he calls, in his book-length essay of the same name, the Land of Ulro: "a land of the disinherited—Blake's Ulro; a land where man is reduced to a superogatory number, worse where he becomes as much for himself, in his own eyes" (*LU* 122). In Ulro, human beings inhabit a wasteland of spiritual pain, accepting the indifference of a mechanistically determinist universe, such as is imagined by Newtonian physics and the reductionism of Hegelian historicism. In his poems as well as prose, Milosz insists on being read as an exile disinherited by Europe, refashioning California into Ulro. Ulro is strongly suggested by the imagery in "I Sleep a Lot," in which Milosz, viewing the world from his home on Grizzly Peak Boulevard atop the Berkeley hills, projects himself as living somewhere cut off from the world, almost as if he were shipwrecked on some desolate island. Early in *The Land of Ulro* Milosz mentions that Sartre once wrote to Camus saying that, in view of Camus's distaste for political systems, the best place for him to reside would be the Galapagos Islands. How ironically fitting, then, that Milosz writes: "How often I have recalled those words, here, in California, which has been—for me, a Polish poet—my Galapagos" (*LU* 8). California, both as Galapagos and as Ulro, is even more strongly suggested in Milosz's long, multi–voiced poem "The Separate Notebooks":[2]

> I did not choose California. It was given to me.
> What can the wet north say to this scorched emptiness?
> Grayish clay, dried-up creek beds,
> Hills the color of straw, and the rocks assembled

Like Jurassic reptiles: for me this is
The spirit of the place.
And the fog from the ocean creeping over it all,
Incubating the green in the arroyos
And the prickly oak and the thistles.

Where is it written that we deserve the earth for a bride,
That we plunge in her deep, clear waters
And swim, carried by generous currents? (*MCP* 349–50)

The consequences of endorsing the inhuman spirit of the place, of accepting such cosmic indifference as doctrine (a product of the Land of Ulro), are for Milosz fraught with dire historical implications. By accepting the primacy of the inhuman, Milosz believes one loses the ability to respond to individual human suffering and, for that matter, to the suffering of all life. According to Milosz, Jeffers—in his desire for detachment, in privileging the inhuman—makes the error of failing to recognize the innocent suffering of individual human beings. I will come back to the political implications of Jeffers's position, as Milosz sees it, later. But one cannot help but be struck by how close Milosz seems to Jeffers's valuation when Milosz decries the diminishment of Spirit in this "neo-Manichaean" age, declaring "Spirit can now be only human." Milosz's language ironically echoes Jeffers's inhumanist position urging "the rejection of human solipsism and the recognition of the transhuman magnificence" (*DA* xxi). Jeffers, taking the same side of the material/spiritual duality as Milosz, goes so far as to say that his philosophy "provides magnificence for the religious instinct" (*DA* xxi). Jeffers sounds even more like a religious writer in an earlier draft of the Preface to *The Double Axe* when he argues that the next step in human development is "the turning outward from man to what is boundlessly greater" which he sees as "an essential condition of freedom, and of spiritual (i.e. moral and vital) sanity; clearly somewhat lacking in the present world" (*DA* 171). Jeffers would say that this turning outward is to nature—the transhuman magnificence outside the symbolic order. Milosz would say it is to a humanized God—represented through the symbolic order. In both cases the turn is toward the spiritual which both poets seek in their rebellion against an age dominated by material determinism.

Clearly, Jeffers seeks to identify himself with a materiality preexistent to human history which supersedes the symbolic order; to identify himself, in effect, with those inhuman processes that Milosz finds dreadful:

The tides are in our veins, we still mirror the stars, life is your child, but there is in me
Older and harder than life and more impartial, the eye that watched before there was an ocean.

That watched you fill your beds out of the condensation of thin vapor and watched you change them,
That saw you soft and violent wear your boundaries down, eat rock, shift places with continents.

Mother, though my song's measure is like your surf-beat's ancient rhythm I never learned it of you.
Before there was any water there were tides of fire, both our tones flow from the older fountain.

("Continent's End," *CP* 1: 16–17)

Milosz chooses not to apprehend the continent's historicity on this vast geologic scale. The reasons for his resistance to such an "impartial," scientific view of history I will come to shortly. Jeffers, on the other hand, by employing such a metahistorical scale, also can place America's pre-European history outside the symbolic economy recognized by the anthropocentric and Eurocentric Milosz, who does little to account for the trace of an indigenous presence on this continent when he describes America as virgin. For Jeffers, human history is derived from and determined by natural forces. Such forces, products of inhuman processes, resist colonization by the humanist European imagination. Milosz himself admits: "this continent possesses something like a spirit which malevolently undoes any attempt to subdue it" (*VSF* 9).

Milosz, logically, casts the Jeffers of "Continent's End" as the embodiment of that spirit. Jeffers's "eye" was present "before there was an ocean"; it watched the continents rise, shift, and be worn down. It witnessed the long migrations out of Asia through the Aleutians that brought the first inhabitants to this continent. It saw America not as virgin but as haunted country where "Dead tribes move, remembering the scent of their hills, the lost hunters / Our fathers hunted; they driven westward died the sun's death, they dread the depth and hang at the land's hem" (*CP* 1: 99).

Jeffers, too, saw America as an unwritten country, not because it lacked a history but because nature superseded its history; on its shores "the human past is dim and feeble and alien" (*CP* 1: 111). What Jeffers found when he came to Carmel in the fall of 1914 suited his poetic project: an isolated coastal village, albeit with a recent tradition of bohemianism, where human life was dominated by the craggy beauty of the landscape and the dramatic weather. The Carmel–Big Sur coast appeared Edenic to Jeffers and his wife, Una Call Kuster, who were looking to escape the social constraints of Los Angeles (their own private Ulro) which had disapproved of their unconventional love affair and marriage. Living in what he called "our inevitable place," Jeffers envisioned America as a new world piercing out of the old one, a new world which had become, because of the success of human colonization, a "land grown old, heavy and crowded" (*CP* 1: 111).

Milosz, like Jeffers, finds the human presence on the continent alien, but for Milosz that the region partially retains its wilderness character hardly makes the West Coast of North America Edenic. To his European sensibilities, the landscape's "excessive splendor"—a paradoxical inverse of Jeffers's "divinely superfluous beauty"—is menacing, and the light is lurid. Faced with the "boundless immensities" of the American West, Milosz winces. He winces because he believes such immensities invite him to exceed his human limits, to praise the inhuman beauty, to ascribe to the impersonal and demonic forces of nature those traits reserved for a humanistic deity. Milosz writes: "In the presence of nature I am not 'I'; I bear the stamp of my civilization as it does, I have a sense of dread and repugnance for the impersonal cruelty built into the structure of the universe" (*VSF* 24).

However, it is not the universe's cruelty but its beauty that Jeffers's intends to foreground. Many of Jeffers's poems praise nature, sternly insisting that we humans must come to recognize our species's place within it or face catastrophe. In an early lyric, "The Excesses of God," Jeffers claims for nature a transcendent reality which can offer humanity solace:

> There is a great humaneness at the heart of things,
> The extravagant kindness, the fountain
> Humanity can understand, and would flow likewise. (*CP* 1: 4)

At the same time, for Jeffers, nature is indifferent to human hopes and values, a material God ultimately desiring the annihilation of human consciousness which would arrogantly impose its order upon the universe. Yet Jeffers's realization of the opposition of nature to consciousness does not make nature's inhumanity any less difficult for him—or us—to accept from a human point of view. Thus, Jeffers reasons, we must uncenter ourselves from our human-centered vision of the universe. We must make our veins cold, make ourselves like the rocks—a refrain echoing through the Jeffers's canon—and see the world with inhuman eyes. At the end of his verse-drama "The Tower Beyond Tragedy," Jeffers asserts that human salvation lies not in resisting but in surrendering oneself to nature, what he elsewhere calls the "transhuman magnificence":

> I have greater
> Kindred than dwell under a roof. Didn't I say this would be dark to you? I have cut the meshes
> And fly like a freed falcon. To-night lying on the hillside, sick with those visions, I remembered
> The knife in the stalk of my humanity; I drew it and it broke; I entered the life of the brown forest
> And the great life of the ancient peaks, the patience of stone. (*CP* 1: 176–77)

Jeffers's description of nature's essential inhumanity dialectically overlaps that of Milosz, who speaks despairingly of nature's indifference. But Jeffers's error, Milosz contends, is not merely his identification with nature—whose processes end not in resurrection but in death—but his privileging nature over civilization. Still Jeffers can do no less, believing civilization's imposed symbolic order to be delusional, a product of the egoism and narcissism with which we humans deceive ourselves and with which we avoid the truth about our brief but destructive place in the cosmos that awaits our kind's ultimate destruction. Jeffers sounded this theme in "Margrave," one of his shorter narratives, which imagines human consciousness to be an infection the rest of the cosmos flees from and abhors:

> You would be wise, you far stars,
> To flee with the speed of light this infection.
> For here the good sane invulnerable material
> And nature of things more and more grows alive and cries.
> The rock and water grow human, the bitter weed
> Of consciousness catches the sun, it clings to the near stars,
> Even the nearer portion of the universal God
> Seems to become conscious, yearns and rejoices
> And suffers; I believe this hurt will be healed
> Some age of time after mankind has died,
> Then the sun will say "What ailed me a moment?" and resume
> The old soulless triumph, and the iron and stone earth
> With confident and inorganic glory obliterate
> Her ruins and fossils, like that incredible unfading rose

Of desert in Arizona glowing life to scorn,
And grind the chalky emptied seed-shells of consciousness
The bare skulls of the dead to powder; after some million
Courses around the sun her sadness may pass:
But why should you worlds of the virgin distance
Endure to survive what it were better to escape? (*CP* 2: 166)

Certainly, as Milosz reads him, Jeffers exhibits a Manichaean distaste for consciousness. "Margrave's" protagonist, sitting in jail sentenced to be hanged for kidnapping and murder, declares: "'That's the evil in the world, that letter. I—I—'" (*CP* 2: 165). That is also what Milosz finds in "The Tower Beyond Tragedy," a reading evoked in "To Robinson Jeffers": "And Agamemnon / sails the boiling deep to the steps of the palace / to have his blood gush onto marble. Till mankind passes / And the pure and stony earth is pounded by the ocean" (*VSF* 96). Though Jeffers finds consciousness the human distinction that allows us to apprehend the splendor of nature, consciousness is not an advantage: "To slaver for contemptible pleasures / And scream with pain, are hardly an advantage" (*CP* 2: 160). Yet despite this disadvantage, Jeffers still harbors hope that individual human beings can, in Nietzschean fashion, overcome their particularized consciousness by isolating themselves in nature, opening themselves up to nature's materiality, a God which defies signification. In a brief poem titled, interestingly enough, "Sign-Post," Jeffers offer us his prescription for transcendence:

Civilized, crying how to be human again: this will tell you how.
Turn outward, love things, not men, turn right away from
  humanity.
Let that doll lie. Consider if you like how the lilies grow,
Lean on the silent rock until you feel its divinity
Make your veins cold, look at the silent stars, let your eyes
Climb the great ladder out of the pit of yourself and man.
Things are so beautiful, your love will follow your eyes;
Things are the God, you will love God, and not in vain,
For that love, we grow to it, we share its nature. At length
You will look back along the stars' rays and see that even
The poor doll humanity has a place under heaven.
Its qualities repair their mosaic around you, the chips of strength
And sickness; but now you are free, even to become human,
But born of the rock and the air, not of a woman. (*CP* 2: 418)

Displacement from Nature

Milosz no doubt recognizes from his childhood fascination with the biological sciences and his own early poems his own pantheist desire for transcendence. He commemorates his youthful infatuation with nature in the essay "Remembrance of a Certain Love" in *Visions from San Francisco Bay.* In this essay Milosz reconstructs his break with his earlier pantheist idealization. The movement in Milosz toward self-consciousness is clearly opposite to that of Jeffers's pantheist project "To feel and speak the astonishing beauty of things" (*CP* 3: 369). While Jeffers insists that to represent nature's beauty as the ultimate reality "is the sole business of poetry" (*CP* 3: 369), Milosz suspects that any such representation of nature is more purely the product of language, which does not represent "the astonishing beauty of things" as much as the linguistically determined consciousness which produces the text. Milosz's position is, in short, that it is one thing to *feel* nature's astonishing beauty, quite another thing to *speak* it.

In "Remembrance of a Certain Love," Milosz recounts that what contributed most to ending his "love affair" with nature was his increased consciousness of the "intermediary" role of print. Though he felt himself to be a Romeo who fell in love outwardly with nature, he confesses that in retrospect what he had actually fallen in love with is a simulacra reproduced through the intermediary of the printed page:

> What really fascinated me were the color illustrations in nature books and atlases, not the Juliet of nature but her portrait, rendered by draftsman or photographers. I suffered no less sincerely for that, a suffering caused by the excess which could not be possessed; I was an unrequited romantic lover, until I found the way to dispel that invasion of desires, to make the desired object mine—by naming it. I made columns in thick notebooks and filled them with my pedantic categories—family, species, genus—until the names, the nouns signifying the species and the adjective the genus, became one with what they signified, so that *Emberiza citrinella* did not live in thickets but in an ideal space outside of time. (*VSF* 18)

In this passage Milosz tells us that he could best comprehend nature's materiality by means of signifiers that transcend the essential temporality of the material world. As such, nature becomes subject to representation in the symbolic order, rendered through language and the laws of logic. And as a result the wondrous materiality of the natural object—whether it be a plant, an animal, or a mountain—is supplanted by what can be only be represented in symbolic terms; by what can be named, what can be schematized.

This realization leads Milosz to discover that:

> What had been a sheaf of colors, an undifferentiated vibration of light instantly turns into a set of characteristics. . . . And so, my real birds became illustrations from an anatomical atlas covered by an illusion of lovely feathers, and the fragrance of flowers ceased to be extravagant gifts, becoming part of an impersonally calculated plan, examples of a universal law. My childhood, too, ended then. I threw my notebooks away; I demolished the paper castle where beauties had resided behind a lattice of words. (*VSF* 18–19)

Milosz's break with the intrinsic and unconscious bond he once felt with nature is described by Aleksander Fiut, whose study of Milosz's poetry has recently been translated from the Polish, as a "motif of disillusionment, loss, expulsion from a childhood paradise" (38). Fiut argues that for Milosz it is consciousness which destroys the individual's identification with all existence, thus depriving the individual of "cosmic coparticipation" (38). In this, Milosz's position seems to accord with Jeffers's. Yet for Milosz, Fiut adds, "the knowledge received in adulthood, in turn, challenges the testimony of the senses since in nature's beauty it discovers the trap of the law of preservation of the species: fascinating in its uniqueness, the individual becomes part of the paradigm" (38). His initiation into consciousness, then, is what costs Milosz his innocence, turning him away from the worship of nature which characterized such early poems as "Hymn":

> Roll on, rivers; raise your hands,
> cities! I, a faithful son of the black earth, shall return
> to the black earth.
> as if my life had not been,
> as if not my heart, nor my blood,
> not my duration
> had created words and songs
> but an unknown, impersonal voice,
> only the flapping of waves, only the choir of winds
> and the autumnal sway
> of the tall trees. (*MCP* 13)

In this poem, composed in 1935 in Paris, the young Milosz advances a pantheist vision markedly similar to Jeffers's position, privileging as eternal the material earth over the ephemeral doings of humanity:

> Before the first man
> Here were the stones, the ocean, the cypresses,

And the pallid region in the stone-rough dome of fog where the
moon
Falls on the west. Here is reality.
The other is a spectral episode; after the inquisitive animal's
Amusements are quiet; the dark glory.
("Hooded Night," *CP* 2: 3)

Thus, it is not hyperbole when Milosz contends in *Visions from San Francisco Bay* that he could re-create within himself Jeffers's pantheist thoughts. But, in contrast to Jeffers's, Milosz's pantheism is at best ambivalent and should be understood as couched within dialectical terms—what Fiut calls "a drama of knowing and naming that can be reduced to revealing the opposition between consciousness and existence and between language and object" (38). Milosz reads Jeffers as a poet who naïvely disregards such oppositions. In a 1977 essay, "A Poet Between East and West," Milosz writes,

> Reading Jeffers, I discovered that those orange-violet sunsets, those flights of pelicans, those fishing boats in the morning fog, as faithfully represented as if they were photographs—all that was for me pure fiction. I said to myself that Jeffers, who professed, as he called it "inhumanism", took refuge in an artificial world which he invented using ideas taken from biology textbooks and from the philosophy of Nietzsche. (265)

In describing Jeffers's representation of nature as "pure fiction," Milosz suggests that Jeffers makes the same error as Milosz describes himself as having made as a young man: assuming that one's representation of nature corresponds to the real thing. Significantly, Milosz does not impugn Jeffers's urge to describe from an inhuman perspective the transhuman magnificence of nature. Rather, Milosz asserts that suqh a task exceeds human strength: "I would like to trust my five senses—to encounter reality nakedly, but between me and what I see and touch there is a pane of glass—my conception of nature, imposed on me by the so-called state of knowledge, and the lessons of biology" (*VSF* 21).

Moreover, privileging the redemption of the suffering borne by individual consciousness in nature, Milosz resists all thinking that would reduce the individual to a biological paradigm. To oppose such impersonal mechanistic thinking, he allies himself with the tradition of anthropocentric thinkers that includes Emanuel Swedenborg, William Blake, and Simone Weil—especially Blake, whose position against the material determinism of Locke and Newton Milosz frequently cites, as in this passage from *The Witness of Poetry:*

> What is at stake, and Blake understood it well, was saving man from images of a totally "objective," cold, indifferent world, from which Divine Imagination has been alienated. Precisely half a century after his death, this rapid erosion of belief in any world other than one submitted to a mathematical determinism appears at the center of Dostoevsky's work and Nietzsche's work. (47)

Blake objects to the emerging positivist construct of nature on the grounds that it both denies the intervention of Divine Imagination and disregards the suffering of the world. Milosz explains in *Visions from San Francisco Bay* that "Blake disliked Nature in the same way Nature dislikes itself, as expressed in the words of St. Paul: 'For we know that the whole of creation . . . groaneth and travaileth in pain together until now' (Romans 8:22)" (160).

As if to illustrate Blake's point, Milosz in "Diary of a Naturalist" writes: "If the wax in our ears could melt, a moth on pine needles / A beetle half-eaten by a bird, a wounded lizard / Would all lie at the center of the expanding circles / Of their vibrating agony" (*MCP* 260). In this poem, Milosz narrates the loss of his own pantheist faith in the revelation that nature is the location for suffering and death. From Milosz's point of view, how could he or anyone elevate to divinity the source of such agony? How could even God be responsible for this horror and not some evil Demiurge, as the Manichaeans proclaimed? How, then, could one not fail to endorse the Christian teaching that nature is what humanity must overcome? Echoing Blake's reasoning, Milosz objects to Jeffers's pantheism, arguing that human imagination—which is Divine—was not created to submit to nature's immutable laws, her "dark glory." Rather, the imagination's purpose is to humanize nature, to domesticate it, to situate it within the symbolic order. Milosz makes this central to his argument with Jeffers in the final lines of "To Robinson Jeffers":

> Better to carve suns and moons on the joints of crosses as was done in my district. To birches and firs give feminine names. To implore protection against the mute and treacherous might than to proclaim, as you did, an inhuman thing. (*VSF* 96)

Nature's indifference to the projections of human desires and expectations, according to Aleksander Fiut, troubles Milosz through all of his *oeuvre*.[3] Fiut cites lines from "The Songs of Adrian Zielinski": "'Without end or beginning, Nature breeds /

Nothing except this: there is life, there is death'" (qtd., 41). Such lines recall Milosz's description of Jeffers's pantheism: "For him the nebulae, the sun, the rocks, the sea, sharks, crabs, were parts of an organism without beginning or end" (*VSF* 90–91).

Refiguring Apocalypse

The inhuman view of the world became expressly objectionable to Milosz after Poland's Nazi occupation. Before then in the 1930s Milosz had embraced an eschatological catastrophism, writing poems which, like many of Jeffers's, imagined the destruction of civilization and the renewal of the earth: "'a stream of boiling lava / will extinguish the cities and Noah will not escape in his ark'" (from "To Father Ch.," qtd. in Nathan and Quinn, 14). The young Milosz who wrote these lines would have likely agreed with Jeffers's vision in "Fire On the Hills" that "The destruction that brings an eagle from heaven is better than mercy" (*CP* 2: 173). Like Jeffers, the catastrophist Milosz foresaw destruction coming and thought it a tragic but necessary curative deserved by human kind.

However, with the Nazi occupation of Warsaw, Milosz was compelled by the force of history to reconsider the implications of his earlier catastrophist work. To judging from the final stanza of the World War II poem "Days of Generation," he could not avoid feeling a bitter irony:

> It is your destiny so to move your wand
> To wake up storms, to run through the heart of storms,
> To lay bare a monument like a nest in a thicket,
> Though all you wanted was to pluck a few roses. (*MCP* 32)

Given the gravity of the events Milosz witnessed in Warsaw—it would seem as if the end of the world was, indeed, already occurring. But not just materially; also ontologically.

In a radical evolution of his conception of the Apocalypse from his pre-war poetry, Milosz suggests, in "Song for the End of the World," that on the day the world ends, ordinary, daily human events will continue uninterrupted:

> On the day the world ends
> Women walk through the fields under their umbrellas
> A drunkard grows sleepy at the edge of a lawn,
> Vegetable peddlers shout in the street

And a yellow-sailed boat comes nearer the island,
The voice of the violin lasts in the air
And leads into a starry night.

And those who expected lightning and thunder
Are disappointed.
And those who expected signs and archangels' trumps
Do not believe it is happening now.
As long as the sun and the moon are above,
As long as the bumblebee visits a rose,
As long as rosy infants are born
No one believes it is happening now. (*MCP* 56)

By this account, Milosz shifts his eschatology from metaphysical to allegorical grounds, suggesting that the Apocalypse, as Fiut explains, occurs continuously in the sacral dimension, and, thus, represents not simply a change in the world's material condition but an ontological change in its reality. Therefore, being called to Judgment is an inner experience; neither the earth nor humankind would literally come to an end.[4] Yet despite the appearance of normalcy, the power of God, the regulation and protection provided humanity by the symbolic order, will have faded from the world, leaving humankind to act on its own, subject to the demonic laws of nature and history.

This is the crux of Milosz's dialogical argument with Jeffers. For Jeffers advocates that poetry should deconstruct the human cocoon—the symbolic order—through which traditional religious faith and ideology are deeply woven. Humanity's political, social, economic, and religious systems, Jeffers contends, out of which we have constructed the symbolic order, have evolved to produce a dangerous level of human interdependence and narcissism, promoting self-deception, tyranny, and violence—particularly troubling given the power of twentieth-century technology. Because our consciousness has become so enmeshed in the symbolic order, our species is losing contact with external reality, which has become at times difficult for us to distinguish from our representation of it. What poetry should offer, Jeffers suggests, is a way to explore this "virtual reality," to view nature's reality that exists beyond our narrow human boundaries. Until we look outward with "inhuman" vision, we will be unable to apprehend the immense beauty of the material universe, the living God. This is the thrust of Jeffers's apocalyptic vision in "Roan Stallion":

Humanity is the mould to break away from, the crust to break
through, the coal to break into fire,
The atom to be split.

Tragedy that breaks man's face and a white fire flies
out of it, vision that fools him
Out of his limits, desire that fools him out of his limits,
unnatural crime, inhuman science,
Slit eyes in the mask; wild loves that leap over the walls of
nature, the wild fence-vaulter science,
Useless intelligence of far stars, dim knowledge of the spinning
demons that make an atom,
These break, these pierce, these deify, praising their God shrilly
with fierce voices: not in a man's shape (*CP* 1: 189)

From Milosz's perspective, Jeffers's desire for such apocalyptic transcendence can only be disturbing, especially given Milosz's alarm over the withdrawal of divinity from the world. Milosz admits he had at one time shared, at least in part, Jeffers's secular theology—the idealization of nature as described by modern science. Such an idealization of nature he had come to consider a youthful mistake, the result of naïveté and romanticism. Yet, Milosz felt that, by continuing to believe this way, Jeffers, like all who had opposed faith with science, risked the consequences of replacing the protection of God with unchecked human arrogance. How ironic that Milosz, writing about Jeffers in *Visions from San Francisco Bay*, would sound this clarion call against the excesses of human presumption:

> Like everyone else, Jeffers longed for a hierarchically ordered space divided into a bottom, middle, and top, but an impersonal and immanent God could not serve as a keystone to a pyramid. Jeffers granted himself the superior position at the summit, he was a vulture, an eagle, the witness and judge of mortal men deserving pity. (92)

Milosz had lived through two epochs where individuals had granted themselves positions at the summit, above God, and he, like millions of his fellow citizens, had suffered. These epochs were called Fascist and Communist. The fascists attempted to apply nature's laws, vulgarized versions of the scientific determinism of Darwin, to justify their racial theories and genocidal practices.[5] The communists later practiced their own brutal forms of scientism based on Marx's theory of history and dialectical materialism. No wonder, then, Milosz would recoil from what he construes as Jeffers's need "to see himself elevated above everything alive, contemplating vain passions, vain hopes" (*VSF* 90). Milosz's central European experience had proven to him that God had indeed withdrawn His protection from the earth; therefore, poets were needed to compose ironic laments, not what Milosz takes to be hymns praising His continued indifference. To Milosz, Jeffers's God "was pure movement pursuing no direction. Universes arose and died out in Him, while He, indifferent to good and evil, maintained His round of eternal return, requiring nothing but praise for His continued existence" (*VSF* 90).

Return to Divinity

Despite his understandable pessimism, Milosz still holds out hope that human beings can find divinity in nature's innocence, sanctified through the symbolic order. Contrary to Jeffers's position, nature's divinity, Milosz argues, is contingent on divinity itself being envisioned in human terms: "The world's inhumanity, its indifference to the demands of men's hearts, is palliated when God is endowed with human features" (*LU* 215). Milosz, though hardly a primitivist, insists upon the ancient but, in a scientific age, unfashionable idea that divinity exists in a sacred realm revealed to the imagination through symbols. In the "Symbolic Mountains and Forests" essay in *Visions from San Francisco Bay*, Milosz reads landscapes as coded manifestations of a hidden Creator's intentions, be they sometimes perverse: moss-covered logs sprouting new green shoots in a redwood forest to symbolize regeneration; Crater Lake's inaccessible, excessive splendor to symbolize sterility; Death Valley as the Valley of Jehoshaphat (14–15). Accordingly, he asserts that it is left to us to redeem nature by humanizing it, a task he sets for himself in his poetic practice.

Nature itself becomes, for Milosz, a dialectic, containing simultaneously the residual, divine beauty and harmony of the original garden and a corrupted "anti-world" of horror governed by brutal laws unconscious of good and evil. To recover the world's original, divine beauty, Milosz's humanist ideology requires him to repress nature's materiality and, thus, to privilege the symbolic order. Milosz rejects—on ideological grounds—Jeffers's valorization of nature as a material God, believing Jeffers to have confused with true divinity the horrible and senseless anti-world created by a cruel Demiurge, the tyrant God of nature: "So brave, in a void, / you offered sacrifices to daemons; there were Wotan and

Thor, / the screech of Erinyes in the air" (from "To Robinson Jeffers," *VSF* 96). Yet, acceptance of the God of purposeless natural cycles, Jeffers's material God, is, for Milosz, a choice forced upon us by the scientific world view and its attendant technologies, which permeate nearly all aspects of life in the twentieth century. Nevertheless, Milosz maintains that one still has the choice to resist one's own subjection to the determinism of nature, whose end products are senseless suffering and death, by reviving in the imagination symbols of human divinity, despite the apparent increasing intangibility of the divine in the universe. In "Return," a poem from his most recent book *Provinces: Poems, 1987–1991*, Milosz confesses that he still thinks "the human soul belongs to the anti-world" (60). But, summing up his *oeuvre*'s theme of resistance, he writes: "I toiled and kept choosing the opposite: a perfect Nature lifted / above chaos and transience, a changeless garden on the other / side of time" (60).

Although reading Jeffers's from a humanist position, Milosz does not deem Jeffers's project a failure. Milosz recognizes that Jeffers is reframing as Inhumanism the dialectic of the human and inhuman attempts to resituate human salvation from chaos and transience in the radical innocence of nature, which Jeffers proclaims as the eternal Eden, as Blake had before him. What disturbs Milosz is that Jeffers depicts Eden as, though immensely beautiful, a wild and violent garden where humans have no place and where the universe, as God, is at best indifferent and in all likelihood hostile, in its unending cycles of birth and death, to the imperatives of a tragic and misdirected humanity. Moreover, Jeffers's Eden was situated in what to Milosz's mind is the anti-world, radically outside the symbolic order.

Though both poets situate human beings in the world of matter, Milosz and Jeffers find the knowledge of humanity's location problematic in differing ways. For Milosz, the highest human aspiration becomes to transcend the material realm—nature represented as blind necessity with its inviolable laws—and, thus, to overcome suffering and death. At the same time, Milosz admits to the Blakeian dualism that sets forth but does not resolve the opposition between nature as material construct of Urizen (the vision of rational science beginning with Newton) and Nature (with a capital N) as preternatural vision or representation of the divine: "Nature viewed in Urizenian terms is a dominion of death, Ulro; but Nature perceived as vision, Nature viewed as it ought to be viewed—in the Imagination, in the Holy Spirit, in Jesus—is paradise" (*LU* 218).

For Jeffers, the highest human aspiration becomes to know nature's "transhuman magnificence" directly from the position of "objective truth" and to escape the labyrinth of what he calls "human-centered illusions." Jeffers tells us in the refrain which echoes throughout his canon: "We must unhumanize our views a little, and become confident / As the rock and ocean that we are made from" (from "Carmel Point," *CP* 3: 399). Thus, he locates himself as speaking from within the divinity of nature's materiality—not human-centered consciousness—in narratives and lyrics of religious awe detached from humanistic valuations, mythologizing the doctrines of modern astronomy, biology, geology, physics, and the Spenglarian cycles of history.

Reconstructing Jeffers

Finally, I would argue that, although Milosz constructs a useful reading of Jeffers, he misreads the crux of Jeffers's epistemology. Milosz does not recognize that when Jeffers's instructs us to unhumanize our view, to "Look—and without imagination, desire nor dream—directly / At the mountains and sea" (from "De Rerum Virtute," *CP* 3: 403), he is speaking in an allegorical language. Jeffers is not suggesting that the reader become, in the Emersonian sense, a "transparent eyeball" merging with the nakedness of the elements—though Emerson's transparency and even Keats's negative capability are Jeffers's closest antecedents. Rather, Jeffers is constructing a new position that, freed from human self-consciousness, individuals will come to understand nature's beauty as signifying its essential and organic divinity and, thus, will view nature as a text that supersedes the human world: "It is in the beholder's eye, not the world? Certainly. / It is the human mind's translation of the transhuman / Intrinsic glory" (from "De Rerum Virtute," *CP* 3: 403).

For Jeffers nature becomes a material text "translated" or decoded by the mind, in accord with the precepts of science "that "gives man hope to live without lies" (from "Curb Science?" *CP* 3: 199). Jeffers admits, however, that science, though privileged, itself exists within the symbolic order and does not perfectly represent nature, which as God is ultimately unrepresentable. But he proposes that science comes closest to a true representation: "The mathematicians and physics men / Have their mythology; they work alongside the truth, / Never touching it; their equations are false / But the things *work*" (*CP* 3: 459). As a poet, Jeffers reserves for himself a "higher pleasure":

> I strain the mind to imagine distances
> That are not in man's mind: the planets, the suns, the galaxies,
> the super-galaxies, the incredible voids
> And lofts of space: our mother the ape never suckled us
> For such a forest: The vastness here, the horror, the
> mathematical unreason, the cold, awful glory,
> The inhuman face of our God. It is pleasant and beautiful.
> ("Pleasures," *CP* 3: 473)

It is this "higher pleasure" that Milosz despairingly describes in "To Robinson Jeffers": "Above your head, no face, neither the sun's nor the moon's, / only the throbbing of galaxies, the immutable / violence of new beginnings, of new destruction" (*VSF* 95). Late in the poem Milosz warns Jeffers: "No one with impunity / gives himself the eyes of a god. So brave in a void" (*VSF* 96). Jeffers, an idolater of nature, would no doubt object to Milosz's admonition on the grounds that he had given himself not the eyes of a god but the eyes to view God. Milosz's depiction of Jeffers in the poem becomes less a representation of Jeffers than an embodiment of Milosz's argument with him: "Thin-lipped, blue-eyed, without grace or hope, / before God the Terrible, body of the world. / Prayers are not heard. Basalt and granite. / Above them, a bird of prey. The only beauty" (*VSF* 96). In the poem, Milosz portrays Jeffers as a stark and hopeless figure against a background of rocky desolation and primeval violence. The lines quoted above subvert two of Jeffers's most potent emblems, the rock and the hawk, which Jeffers combines in the poem of the same title.

"Rock and Hawk," addressed to his wife, Una, is one of a very few poems where Jeffers self-consciously views the natural text as symbolic discourse. It opens with: "Here is a symbol in which / Many high tragic thoughts / Watch their own eyes" (*CP* 2: 416). The rest of the poem affirms the dialectic of brute matter and living consciousness: how consciousness, by vesting beauty in material things, authorizes matter's insensate beauty—a dialectic central to Jeffers's lyric production:

> This gray rock, standing tall
> On the headland, where the sea-wind
> Lets no tree grow,

Earthquake-proved, and signatured
By ages of storms: on its peak
A falcon has perched.

I think, here is your emblem
To hang in the future sky;
Not the cross, not the hive,

But this; bright power, dark peace;
Fierce consciousness joined with final
Disinterestedness;

Life with calm death; the falcon's
Realist eyes and act
Married to the massive

Mysticism of stone
Which failure cannot cast down
Nor success make proud. (*CP* 2: 416)

In his gloss of Jeffers's emblems, Milosz collapses the rock's vested nobility into "basalt and granite," base, unarticulated stone; he collapses the falcon's fierce consciousness into a "bird of prey," a carnivorous, demonic bird. Thus, Milosz refigures as symbols of a blind determinism that which Jeffers has figured as symbols of unending material consciousness.

"To Robinson Jeffers," read as the product of Milosz's ideological position, denies to the material universe the potentiality of consciousness unless first vested with human, i.e., divine, likeness: "For them [the Slavic poets], the sun / was a farmer's ruddy face, the moon peeped through a cloud, / and the Milky Way gladdened them like a birch-lined road. / They longed for the kingdom which is always near, always right at hand" (*VSF* 95). Moreover, in his poem Milosz claims a privileged knowledge contrasted to, as Milosz constructs it, Jeffers's material determinism—a position which Milosz cannot fully represent and to which Milosz denies the potentiality of divinity: "And yet you did not know what I know. The earth teaches / more than the nakedness of the elements" (*VSF* 95).

What is Milosz's privileged knowledge? In his "Essay in Which the Author Confesses He Is on the Side of Man, for Lack of Anything Better" in *Visions from San Francisco Bay*, Milosz writes:

> We are unable to live nakedly. We must constantly wrap ourselves in a cocoon of mental constructs, our changing styles of philosophy, poetry, art. We invest meaning in that which is opposed to

> meaning; that ceaseless labor, that spinning, is the most purely human of our activities. For the threads spun by our ancestors do not perish, they are preserved; we alone among living creatures have a history, we move in a gigantic labyrinth where the present and the past are interwoven. The labyrinth protects and consoles us, for it is anti-nature. Death is a humiliation because it tears us away from words, the sounds of music, configurations of line and color, away from all the manifestations of our anti-natural freedom, and puts us under the sway of necessity, relegates us to the kingdom of inertia, senseless birth, and senseless decay. (176)

What Milosz discloses in this passage is that his doctrine that our "anti-natural freedom" allows us to live outside the sway of necessity is based upon privileging the labyrinth of mental constructs which relegates nature to be represented as "the kingdom of inertia." For Milosz, meaning (human divinity) is opposed to nature (senseless birth and decay), which he resists as the ultimate subjection to necessity. To assert nature for the term of divinity, and *history* (culture) for the cycles of senseless birth and decay, would contradict his epistemology. Jeffers's epistemology, on the other hand, does exactly that.

Situating the Symbolic: A House of Stone

Jeffers would have us shift our view to what lies outside the human labyrinth, to valorize the nonhuman world upon which the human labyrinth is constructed. The problem for Jeffers is how to represent the nonhuman world in its own terms, "without imagination, desire nor dream." The only possibilities would be to find language that is itself of the nonhuman world or, short of that, to posit that the nonhuman world interpenetrates the site of language, the symbolic order. Credit Milosz for understanding that at least part of Jeffers's solution was formal; that Jeffers's long, free-verse line came from "listening to the ocean breathe, trying in his own words to be true to that single, age-old rhythm" (*VSF* 89). But Milosz's formal solution does not fully account for how Jeffers rationalized his dependence on the symbolic order to represent unhuman nature's "towering reality."

To attempt to understand this paradox, one must look more closely at where Jeffers situates himself. The critic David Wyatt has observed that Jeffers in his early Tor House poems "domesticates some of the forces of the nonhuman world as allies while warding off some of the others as threats," positioning himself "within a stable human space and against the mutability of an outer one" (178).[6] That stable human space is the site of language, which becomes Jeffers's instrument of domestication and visionary possession of the nonhuman. Certainly, Tor House itself is, literally and figuratively, a representation of the protected position from within which Jeffers wrote his poems. But what Tor House symbolizes is not only Jeffers's enclosure within a human space—and symbolic order—but also, through its stones, that human space's origin in the nonhuman world of material nature. Thus, Tor House demonstrates how, in the formation of the symbolic order, the nonhuman world interpenetrates the human—a process which Jeffers recognizes as operating in the building of Tor House as well as in the making of poems:

> I did not dream the taste of wine could bind with granite,
> Nor honey and milk please you; but sweetly
> They mingle down the storm-worn cracks among the mosses,
> Interpenetrating the silent
> Wing-prints of ancient weathers long at peace, and the older
> Scars of primal fire, and the stone
> Endurance that is waiting millions of years to carry
> A corner of the house, this also destined.
> Lend me the stone strength of the past and I will lend you
> The wings of the future, for I have them.
> How dear you will be to me when I too grow old, old comrade.
> (from "To the Rock That Will Be a Cornerstone of the
> House," *CP* 1: 11)

Jeffers might well have rationalized that language's origin—and the origin of poetry—are similarly situated, products of inhuman nature but domesticated over hundreds of millennia by human usage.

Notes

1. Milosz writes: "'Jeffers, his forerunner Whitman, and Cavafy are tangible proof for me that the poet not yield to the scientist and the philosopher, on the condition, however, that his language, in which thought and image are fused in the high temperature of the emotions, retains something of intellectual communicativeness'" ("Proba ujawnienia," *Kultura* (Paris) 182.12 [1962], qtd. in Fuit 191).

2. It is also Aleksander Fiut's view that Milosz's description of the dryness and desolation of the California landscape implies an allusion to the Land of Ulro. See Fuit 57.

3. In *The Eternal Moment*, Fiut argues that, to oppose nature's inhuman indifference, Milosz in his poems gives nature a more accessible and familiar appearance, filling its oppressive infiniteness with consolingly humane figures from folk and religious imagination. See Fiut 41.

4. For a full discussion of the allegorical dimension of this poem as well as a treatment of Swedenborg's allegorical interpretation of the apocalypse, see Fiut 78–79.

5. Fiut offers a clear explanation of how Fascism utilizes vulgarized versions of scientific theories to justify brutal social control. See Fuit 43.

6. I disagree with Wyatt's contention that Jeffers only rarely locates himself in this position. Whenever Jeffers assumes the authority of science, he locates himself in a human space.

Works Cited

CP Jeffers, Robinson. *The Collected Poems of Robinson Jeffers*. 3 vols. to date. Ed. Tim Hunt. Stanford: Stanford UP, 1988, 1989, 1991.

DA Jeffers, Robinson. *The Double Axe and Other Poems*. New York: Liveright, 1977.

LU Milosz, Czeslaw. *In the Land of Ulro*. Trans. Louis Iribarne. New York: Farrar, 1984.

MCP Milosz, Czeslaw. *The Collected Poems, 1931–1987*. New York: Ecco, 1988.

VSF Milosz, Czeslaw. *Visions from San Francisco Bay*. Trans. Richard Lourie. New York: Farrar, 1982.

WP Milosz, Czeslaw. *The Witness of Poetry*. Cambridge: Harvard UP, 1983.

Fiut, Aleksander. *The Eternal Moment: The Poetry* of *Czeslaw Milosz*. Trans. Theodosia S. Robertson. Berkeley: U of California P, 1990.

Milosz, Czeslaw. "A Poet Between East and West." *The Michigan Quarterly Review* 16.3 (1977): 265.

——. *Provinces: Poems, 1987–1991*. Trans. Czeslaw Milosz and Robert Hass. New York: Ecco, 1991.

Nathan, Leonard, and Arthur Quinn. *The Poet's Work: An Introduction to Czeslaw Milosz*. Cambridge: Harvard UP, 1991.

Wyatt, David. *Fall into Eden: Landscape and Imagination in California*. New York: Cambridge UP, 1986.

10

All Flesh Is Grass

William Everson

> The voice said, Cry.
> And he said, What shall I cry?
> All flesh is grass,
> And all the goodliness thereof
> Is as the flower of the fields: . . .
> Surely the people is grass.
> The grass withereth, the flower fadeth:
> But the word of our God shall stand forever.
>
> Isaiah 40:6–8

Creature-Consciousness

"The satisfaction that men take in evidences of the life of nature and its power, and above all in surpassing manifestations of that power, is one of the perennial roots of religion" (Wilder 141). With these words Amos Wilder opens his chapter on "The Nihilism of Mr. Robinson Jeffers" in *The Spiritual Aspects of the New Poetry.*

If Jeffers ever read this book, it could not have pleased him, for he knew himself to be no nihilist, or one only in a very highly qualified and extended sense. But one part of the chapter must have given him delight. Wilder quotes from a scientist's report, *The Vesuvius Eruption of 1906: Study of a Volcanic Cycle*, written by a student of volcanic phenomena, Dr. Frank A. Perret. As Wilder presents the text in his extended quote, it is a fitting introduction to the central feature of our study:

> Strongest of all impressions received in the course of these remarkable events, greatest of all surprises . . . was, for the writer, that of an infinite dignity in every manifestation of this stupendous releasing of energy. No words can describe the majesty of its un-

> folding, the utter absence of anything resembling effort, and the all-sufficient power to perform the allotted task and to do it majestically. Each rapid impulse was the crest of something deep and powerful and uniform which bore it, and the unhurried modulation of its rhythmic beats sets this eruption in the rank of things which are mighty, grave and great.
>
> There was present also the element of awe, in all its fullness. The phenomena entered, through their intensity, that sphere where the normal conditions of Nature are overpassed, and one stands in the presence of greater and more elemental forces than any he has known hitherto. This tends to induce a state of mind which hardly recognizes as entirely natural this transformation of the visible universe, and with difficulty one accepts the dictum of reason, that all will pass and the normal return as before; and so, for the many, the events of this and the succeeding days of ashy darkness seemed to show that—even as the younger Pliny wrote of similar conditions in this same region nearly two thousand years ago—"the last eternal night of story has settled on the world."
>
> But it is precisely this projection beyond the borderland of the obvious which gives to such events their majesty—the dignity which, allied with the mysterious, is thereby perfected. The sense-walls of the Universe are shattered by these higher values of power, and Deity is indirectly more in evidence than in the case of the lesser things. A blade of grass as surely, but far less forcibly, reveals the truth that That which manifests cannot be seen, nor heard, nor felt, except through and because of the manifestation. (Wilder 141)

This passage could have been written by Jeffers himself, though the deity is but mentioned. The poet would have *invoked* him.

It is a commonplace of philosophical psychology that there can be no conception in the mind which has not been based upon a prior sense impression in the body. From this it follows that the priority of the image, the image which precedes mentality, endows the religious spirit with the plenitude of its material forms. The ordinary man sees God in Nature or he sees Him not at all. By extension, the God-thirsting man sees Him everywhere, for Nature is omnipresent. Moreover, Nature's manifold forms shimmer and glow with an intense vibration, the rudimentary abstract that gives them the universal character of existence. Both sides tend to endow the substance of tangible things—against which the claims of pure transcendence are always shattering—with the ineradicable impress of divinity. Thus even the system of Plotinus, "than which," in the words of the *Encyclopedia Americana*, "nothing is more opposed to pantheism," collapses into absorption, making as it does of God "so pure an abstraction that even thought, without being separated from individuality, cannot attain to it." For "even from the bosom of this school a prolific source of pantheism was born" (21: 249).

The poet exults. Stunned by the impact of spontaneous wholeness revealed everywhere about him, he manifests the words that will clue its essence, not at all intimidated by Eliade's dictum that "language, being analogical, is obliged to suggest whatever surpasses natural experience in terms that are borrowed from that experience." Born of the experience rather than borrowed from it, his speech bears the impress of the same vibration, achieves consonance with the sum of things, registers wholeness through the relevance of utterance. What is uttered is established, exists of the phenomenon that evoked it. Emerson said that nature is the language of God. It is fittingly spoken, for "in the beginning was the Word." And in that beginning is its end. The Word, then, is all.

For Nature itself holds the clue to the divine. In its myriad forms, the great plenitude of being is poured out, streaming from the womb of potentiality, exploding into act. A kind of metaphysical combustion seems smoldering in the fabric of things, a surge of incipient energy, breaking out of the bounds of its nuclear forms, and disappearing into the beyond. It is this transformation the poet celebrates.

Gazing about him with an enravished eye, he becomes the menstruum through which the presence of things achieves participation in the world of the abstract, the dimension of mind. The word sings. Stimulus and response are one; they are the quintessential divinities sealed in the multiplicity of shapes: "The signature of all things." In the web of transcendent words, the poet fuses potency and act. For the poet, potentiality is the domain of his sovereignty, not as between cause and effect, but as between corresponding identities. But it is from act to potentiality that he emerges as the preceptor of unity—the pure pantheist.

For wherever he looks, the scale and vastness present to the poet simply the correspondences of what he is, plunging back from act to potentiality, to realize the mystery of inchoation. His sovereign authority is this investiture in the common substance of coexistence. His mind dazzles with mutuality, but his spirit is cool with a searching recognition, knowledge gazing at its own preknowledge, the four eyes of comprehension absorbed in the synthesis where nothing divides. The hierarchies of being fade before the universality of the contingent, the degree that subsumes in his expression. His godlike thirst is sourced in his propensity, the sovereign seizure of the Word. Language for him is the divine abyss. Out of it float and emerge the shapes of unconceived essences. What he utters is greater than what he intuits, and this is his sinecure within the criteria of value. He gives back to the world, to the common mind, the coeval images of its own existence. His declaration "I speak truth" is no lie.

Then where resides his humility? What becomes of his creaturehood? His creaturehood is the marginal condition lurking at the corners of his failure. Unable to sustain manifestation, he slumps back into the contingent. Correspondences elude him. He mumbles the formulae of sentient approximation. The mundane substance of measurable observance, the scrutinies of observed distinction, clot his lips. And in the trap of the contingent, he merely babbles. "The poets lie too much." Gazing through the lens of the learned astronomer, he exclaims like any journalist, marveling at the distances that separate mote from mote. From the pure pantheist of ineluctable transcendence, he becomes the philosophical pantheist of empirical immanence. His tongue is shut. He has reentered history, and he has become no more than its most imaginative expresser. When he fails his vocation, he becomes its slave.

In the cultural dethronement, following Galileo, of what Eliade termed "the supreme hierophany, the incarnation of God in Jesus Christ" (124), it inevitably came about that the cosmos itself assumed the aspects of the divine, but not in the sense of mere comparison. In that crisis of intellectual consciousness which we call the Copernican revolution, the substitutive natural hierophany that supplanted Christ could be nothing less than the Immensity itself. Philosophical pantheism—the substitutive religion that prevailed between Copernicus, who rendered incarnation obsolete, and Einstein, who restored it to feasibility—has somehow always been associated with the development of astronomy.

For if it is physics which analyzes the substance of the cosmos, it is astronomy which measures its scale. More than any other science, it is astronomy which presents to the intellect the configuration of the cosmos itself. And it is in the configuration, the image, that man's intellect, in the deeps of its residual cognition, discerns its God.

Thus, at the decline of Rome, it was the development of Syrian astrology that gave the mystery cults invading the empire on every side the force to produce the intellectual climate in which Neoplatonism was transmuted from gnosticism to pantheism. Again it was the development of astronomy following Galileo that gave the pantheistic insights of Bruno and Spinoza their force in men's thought. For as the skeptical spirit, in its conquest of space and time, canceled out the efflux of the divine by reducing the numinous, or awesome, to the principle of mere material cause-and-effect, that spirit nevertheless could not refrain from stretching upward and outward in search of the source of awe in the terminal limits that define each dimension: the place Mystery lurks. And when, with the advance of cognizance in the wake of the advance of astronomy, it expands with the illimitable cosmos, the mind itself tingles on inchoation, and the numinous awe it was busily canceling out in the search for pure objectivity—devouring all hierophanies up from sacred stone and sacred tree to the divine Jesus Himself—when that awe overwhelms the mind with sheer vastness, and its concomitant, sheer duration, then a greater awe returns upon it than any particular hierophany could wring from its depth. Although the mind could nowhere bow to the individual symptom, the particular hierophany, it suddenly finds itself on its knees before the archetype of every hierophany, namely the All. Thus a perennial contradiction is reborn.

For, as the *Catholic Encyclopedia* puts it, "to a thoroughgoing pantheist there can be no creaturehood. All is all. This contradiction falls into place because even philosophically pantheism is not so much a doctrine as it is an attitude, the implication of views expressed in terms of the world, God, the Absolute, or Infinity. What it does is to emphasize the immanence of God in the world and de-emphasize or ignore His transcendence over the world" (10: 947–50).

Thus Jeffers can say:

> Another theme that has engaged my verses is the expression of a religious feeling, that perhaps must be called pantheism, though I hate to type it with a name. It is the feeling—I will say the certainty—that the universe is one being, a single organism, one great life that includes all life and all things; and is so beautiful that it must be loved and reverenced; and in moments of mystical vision we identify ourselves with it.[1]

So said the poet, with his philosophical back to the wall, when compelled to defend his position.

If he is not absolutely consistent in the various attestations to be found in his verse, it is no wonder. "For since," continues the

Catholic Encyclopedia, "no philosopher has as yet failed to make some distinction between the transcendent and immanent aspects of divine being, there never has been a complete and utter pantheism" (10:947–50).

This is unequivocally stated, but returning to the *Encyclopedia Americana* we find the same tone, if not the same words. The historians of ideas, regardless of dogmatic adherence, boil down their subjects into the most terse formulae. Here it says of pantheism: "The doctrine stands midway between atheism and dogmatic theism" and goes on to observe:

> The origin of the idea of a God with the theist and the pantheist is the same. It is by reasoning upon ourselves and the surrounding objects of which we are cognizant that we come to infer the existence of some Superior Being upon whom they all depend, from whom they proceed or in whom they subsist. Pantheism assumed the identity of cause and effect, and the consequent adequacy of each effect, rightly interpreted, to indicate its cause. (21: 249)

It is for this reason that I called the poet, in the throes of his creative vision, the pure pantheist—because in the deeps of the creative intuition, that is the way he sees reality. But the vision is unsustainable, and when he slumps back into creaturehood, his tongue falters.

Now the poetic vision, although an illuminative state, does not exist in isolation because, invested in language, it proceeds by two channels, the channels of thought and feeling. The poet can only ascend to vision by virtue of them, and when he descends from vision, these remain, like filaments in a light bulb, not incandescent but nevertheless there. It is thus no accident that our study is not destined to treat of Jeffers the poet *per se*; it will not be a selection and analysis of his best passages. Nor will it, as we have said, treat of his thought, which has already found so much attention. Rather, it will focus upon his feelings, and it defines him as a religious poet by virtue of their predominantly religious character. But we have only to glance at his verse to be aware at the outset that this feeling-content projects us into a contradiction with his thought, a contradiction which he resolved in what we can only call his cosmic vision.

To a degree this is, of course, true of every poet: once we have retired from the domain of the unifying vision, the upper register that transcends distinctions, we are back in the inferior categories of thought and feeling. And when it comes to Jeffers, we encounter as radical a difference between them as we expect to find in someone of complex and agonized sensibility. The son of a clergyman, he naturally began as a theist, and it was here that all his feeling-responses took shape. His thought came later, much later. An intensive scientific training must have confronted him with the atheistic premises, the dominant alternative to the theistic impress of his formation, so that between them his pantheism emerged to provide a resolution for the intellectual split common to his time and culture. Although his scientific education led him to *think* in terms of a God of immanence, his deep religious sensibility could only decree that he *feel* in terms of a God of transcendence. It is this latter voice that we are exploring in our study, and it is everywhere evident. Time and again in his poetry he is brought to his knees, as it were, before the recognition of a God so vast, so overwhelming, so infinitely beyond all the discernible manifestations of the concrete, that every syllable he utters suggests, above the voice by which he speaks them, the implications of his awe: "I am nothing." It is with this cry that we can begin our investigation of the work of Jeffers as it applies to Rudolf Otto and the Idea of the Holy.

Otto posits as the very basis of that idea a state of being which he can only categorize "creature-consciousness," or "creature-feeling"—the emotion, he says, of a creature submerged and overwhelmed by its own nothingness, a nullity of self realized in contrast to that which is infinitely beyond it, to a being inexpressibly supreme above all creatures. Furthermore, he rejects any attempt to conceptualize it. All that his term creature-feeling can express, he insists, is the note of a submergence into nothingness before an overpowering, absolute might, a total, annihilative force. "Everything turns upon the *character* of this overpowering might, a character which cannot be expressed verbally, and can only be suggested indirectly through the tone and content of a man's feeling-response to it. And this response must be directly experienced in oneself to be understood" (10). As an instance he notes Abraham's self-abnegating cry after pleading on behalf of the men of Sodom: "Behold now, I have taken upon me to speak unto the Lord, which am but dust and ashes" (9). And in correspondence to this, one remembers Job's effacement of all he is before the Lord's absoluteness: "Behold, I am vile. What shall I answer thee? I will lay mine hand upon my mouth" (Job 40:4).

But Otto takes care to insist that this feeling, for all its depth of interiority, is no mere subjective state. Rather, the creature-feeling is itself a manifestation of quite another psychic component, an element which, he says, by its nature is denotative of something beyond, an objective recognition of the existence of what is radically other than, and infinitely superior to, the experiencing self. No mere subjective state can engender self-inferiority. The self cannot feel inferior to itself. What it can feel is its vulnerability before that which it recognizes as imponderably greater than it, that which can overwhelm and annihilate it. Out of this recognition religion itself is born. And because of it religion can be affirmed as a true, rather than an evasive response to the self's travail in its ordeal of existence.

However, this objective recognition of cosmic inferiority stands as polar opposite to the self's counter-knowledge, its corresponding intuition of superiority upon which secularism, as distinct from the religious attitude, is founded. For such is the superiority of the human intellect to the material categories of being around us that we not unnaturally relate from a position of advantage, eschewing the disadvantage of a self-effacing inferiority to that which transcends us. What is natural and easy becomes habitual and reflexive, and as success follows success in its conquest of the phenomenal world, the self, turning inward, becomes preoccupied with its own discriminations and in time exalts itself by diverting all its energies to its byplay of instigation and control.

Following this, civilization and then culture erect a context of interreactive congratulatory ritualism, a preoccupation which thoroughly indoctrinates every nascent generation until, in time, a veritable haze of deceptive self-consciousness hangs over all man's activity. Religion itself partakes of it, and though indispensable, the weakness or defective side of that very indispensability is precisely its tendency to augment, by repetition and custom, the glare of self-preoccupation, of self-absorption, which covers all man's thought. Although theology can conceptualize human inferiority to God, conceptualization cannot produce the creature-feeling, the shuddering realization of self-effacement and nullity in which that recognition must achieve finality. When religion shirks or flees from this painful necessity, it becomes (by a kind of hideous reversal of functions) itself the primary vehicle of human pride. Our corruption is complete.

It is specifically against this deceptive complacency, this blind presumption of collective human sufficiency, that Jeffers directs the holy violence of his utterance. And he does it not by reference to higher and higher categories of psychic and spiritual perception, which is the gnostic's feature, but by a brusque shift of emphasis back toward "inferior" categories, the world of material phenomena and processes. For he intuits that it is precisely in these categories and objects that the numinous now obtains: it is precisely by considering humanity from a point of view *below* these categories that the all-important creature-feeling may be restored to him, that he can at last see himself as he is, as his basic situation in existence proclaims him to be.

Jeffers's most obvious technique in securing this fundamental transferral of attitude, this shift from deceptive superiority to realistic inferiority, is that of reduction. Although his work continually implies such devaluation by its tone, often enough he breaks out in direct statement, inverting the vaunted domain of man to minuscule proportions. For instance, in "Apology for Bad Dreams," he depicts an outrageous act, a woman and her son torturing a horse, which is itself, by definition, subhuman. Then, drawing perspective above it with increasing elevation, he secures, through an inexorable reduction, this processive devaluation of man within the grandeur of the cosmos he inhabits:

Seen from this height they are shrunk to insect size.
Out of all human relation. You cannot distinguish
The blood dripping from where the chain is fastened,
The beast shuddering; but the thrust neck and the legs
Far apart. You can see the whip fall on the flanks . . .
The gesture of the arm. You cannot see the face of the woman.
The enormous light beats up out of the west across the cloud-
bars of the trade-wind. The ocean
Darkens, the high clouds brighten, the hills darken together.
Unbridled and unbelievable beauty
Covers the evening world . . . not covers, grows apparent out of
it . . . (*CP* 1: 208–09)

Sometimes the reduction is not the sustained diminution of receding vision and heightening consciousness, but rather is fleetingly glimpsed, a glance in passing, one momentary insight into the essential transience of earth's most permanent fixtures, its most basic proportional diminutions, as in this passage from "Mara":

He found himself for a lightning moment
Outside the flux and whirl of things, observing the world
From a fixed point. He saw the small spinning planet,
Spotted with white at the poles and dull red wars
Branding both cheeks, and the sun and the other stars like a herd
of wild horses
On the vast field, but all vanished with the lightning (*CP* 3: 56)

And sometimes the uses of reduction are applied not only to size and quantity but to life-processes themselves. These are telescoped together, as in the vision of the archetypal eagle in *Cawdor*. The great captive bird, dispatched out of mercy, strips bondage in a mighty leap of death and soars:

> This rose,
> Possessing the air over its emptied prison,
> The eager powers at its shoulders waving shadowless
> Unwound the ever widened spirals of flight
> As a star light, it spins the night-stabbing threads
> From its own strength and substance: so the aquiline desire
> Burned itself into meteor freedom and spired
> Higher still, and saw the mountain-dividing
> Canyon of its captivity (that was to Cawdor
> Almost his world) like an old crack in a wall,
> Violet-shadowed and gold-lighted; the little stain
> Spilt on the floor of the crack was the strong forest;
> The grain of sand was the Rock. A speck, an atomic
> Center of power clouded in its own smoke
> Ran and cried in the crack; it was Cawdor; the other
> Points of humanity had neither weight nor shining
> To prick the eyes of even an eagle's passion. (*CP* 1: 511)

Man is infinitesimally reduced, but Jeffers cannot abide at this level. The reduction continues in the eagle's inexorable ascent:

> This burned and soared. The shining ocean below lay on the shore
> Like the great shield of the moon come down, rolling bright rim to rim with the earth. Against it the multiform
> And many-canyoned coast-range hills were gathered into one carven mountain, one modulated
> Eagle's cry made stone, stopping the strength of the sea. The beaked and winged effluence
> Felt the air foam under its throat and saw
> The mountain sun-cup Tassajara, where fawns
> Dance in the steam of the hot fountains at dawn,
> Smoothed out, and the high strained ridges beyond Cachagua,
> Where the rivers are born and the last condor is dead,
> Flatten, and a hundred miles toward morning the Sierras
> Dawn with their peaks of snow, and dwindle and smooth down
> On the globed earth. (*CP* 1: 511–12)

The imagery has become at once more symbolic and more rarefied, as the height increases, but the moral is not lessened, the application remains human:

> It saw from the height and desert space of unbreathable air
> Where meteors make green fire and die, the oceans dropping westward to the girdle of the pearls of dawn
> And the hinder edge of the night sliding toward Asia; it saw far under eastward the April-delighted
> Continent; and time relaxing about it now, abstracted from being, it saw the eagles destroyed,
> Mean generations of gulls and crows taking their world: turn for turn in the air, as on earth
> The white faces drove out the brown. It saw the white decayed and the brown from Asia returning;
> It saw men learn to outfly the hawk's brood and forget it again; it saw men cover the earth and again
> Devour each other and hide in caverns, be scarce as wolves. It neither wondered nor cared, and it saw
> Growth and decay alternate forever, and the tides returning. (*CP* 1: 512)

Sometimes the reductive device is positioned from a terminal stasis, the very fixity adding, in contrast to the momentary glimpse, or the telescoped process, an almost pitilessly unwavering finality of judgment, as in this passage from "The Broken Balance":

> I remember the farther
> Future, and the last man dying
> Without succession under the confident eyes of the stars.
> It was only a moment's accident,
> The race that plagued us; the world resumes the old lonely immortal
> Splendor; from here I can even
> Perceive that that snuffed candle had something . . . a fantastic virtue,
> A faint and unshapely pathos . . .
> So death will flatter them at last: what, even the bald ape's by-shot
> Was moderately admirable? (CP 1: 375)

But the registration of creature-feeling, while it may employ them, is never dependent upon such objective devices for its presence in the poem. More often it manifests itself in the deeper sense that Otto means, a profound affective condition of awed awareness. It is as if Jeffers's imagination is in a perpetual state of tenuousness before the vastness of things, and it is this acute apprehension which must account for his obsession with permanence, and the valuation of phenomena that are less changeful than flesh. Secular mentalities, irked by what seems almost a perverseness, seek out flaws in the logic, or resort to semantic quarreling, to indict his trend. But the religious mind understands well enough that these permanences which obsess him are operating as symbols, abiding points on which to found the deeper consciousness, and are clues to the dark core of the creature-feeling that shapes the human undercast of anxiety.

For the reductive devices we have instanced here have, as such, their obvious limitations. Though dramatic, and convenient to categorize, they cannot of necessity occur with any very great frequency; otherwise, like all devices, they become increasingly tedious and cancel themselves out. The greater thing, the unconscious bodying-forth of the feeling-response, occurs more pervasively and more subtly in the palpable lyrics. These epiphanies of religious awareness would be more fruitful to explore, but the larger prospect must here occupy us, involving though it does an inevitable simplification. But before going on to specific details, it must be emphasized that everything Jeffers wrote was touched by his acute awareness of this underlying disparity between the human ego and the greater reality it fails to contemplate, an awareness that constitutes the principal factor by which we recognize him as an essentially religious poet.

"Autumn Evening," taken almost at random from among dozens of poems, must serve for example. Here the creature-feeling colors but does not obtrude. Explicitly attested in no more than the turning of a phrase, it nonetheless suffuses the whole before the poem closes and is let go by. Note how the so-called pathetic fallacy, largely deemed a liability by critical opinion, is here potent, powerfully evoking the felt experience:

Though the little clouds ran southward still, the quiet autumnal
Cool of the late September evening
Seemed promising rain, rain, the change of the year, the angel
Of the sad forest. A heron flew over
With that remote ridiculous cry, "Quawk," the cry
That seems to make silence more silent. A dozen
Flops of the wing, a drooping glide, at the end of the glide
The cry, and a dozen flops of the wing.
I watched him pass on the autumn-colored sky; beyond him

> Jupiter shone for evening star.
> The sea's voice worked into my mood, I thought "No matter
> What happens to men . . . the world's well made though." (*CP* 1: 117)

The choice idiomatic pungency suddenly reveals the underlying irreconcilability between the human and the divine in the religious heart of the poet. Man is restored to his creaturehood: he looks again upon his world with awe.

Mysterium Tremendum

Of all man's experiences, the awareness of God is his most fundamental and, by a kind of maddening contradiction, his most intangible and incommunicable. Back at the beginning, it must have been this first awareness that brought home to him the disquieting isolateness that set him off from the brutes. For what natural propensity does he possess but some animal he knows of excels him in its exercise? Not sexual transport, certainly. There are in his range of experience several species that he cannot hope to equal in the physical ecstasy with which they couple. Not in parental devotion. The sow grizzly displays an unfailing capacity for self-sacrifice on behalf of her young that no woman can equal. Not in nuptial fidelity. Canada geese mate once and, if death severs the union, remain single to the end. Not in hunger for home. The pigeon returns unerringly to its nest, and the salmon seeks the headwaters of its spawn in order to reproduce itself in the matrix of its origins.

And so it goes. Wherever we look, some animal (as by a special faculty) exceeds us in an exercise of virtue we unreflecting regarded as our own. We tacitly acknowledge this by symbolizing our most esteemed propensities under specific forms of animal life: the lion for courage, the dog for devotion, the serpent for cunning. Civilized man, reaching higher, places that superiority in his capacity to entertain abstractions, his gift for abstract thought, and this is correct. But long before he could promulgate elementary equations, he must have been aware of this intuitional distinction as an experience of the reality of God, a special faculty placing him outside the pale of sentient life. Knowing God, man stood apart from all creation—and felt himself alone.

And yet, once experienced, this uniqueness remained inexpressible. It still does. How many adequate accounts of it survive in the history of thought? How many descriptions of it exist that really convey to us, to any human being at all, the truth that everyone, whether a great mystic or simple dolt, intuits but cannot express? Does there actually exist a man who does not know what is meant when the word "God" is uttered? Does there actually exist an animal who does? Yet when it comes to the expression of it, there is hardly a poem in the whole of literature that gives any sufficient impression. Here all is analogical, representative but not actual; everything said is "in a manner of speaking." And when by accident or grace a poet emerges who succeeds ever so slightly in giving back some impression of the reality all men experience, we honor him above every other, placing him in a category apart. All poets declare how they feel about God and count on being understood; but how many of them can give back to us our own awareness of the existence of God, make us reexperience what we all know by intuition, make apparent to us *what God is?*

Now, this "what God is," or, more properly, this "as God is," becomes the second step in Otto's analysis of the Idea of the Holy. After establishing the fundamental situation of the numinous as something manifesting itself in a general condition of creature feeling, he goes on to specify the object of this numinous consciousness, knowing full well, however, that only in terms of feeling can it be reflected positively in his mind. "Its nature is such that it grips or stirs the human with this and that determinative state" (12). Seeking to isolate the deepest and most fundamental element in all strongly felt religious emotion, he goes at once to that which lies outside the characteristics we usually attribute to it—such things as trust, or love, or faith unto salvation. All these things, of course, may be involved, but they do not comprise the essence of the numinous feeling. Above them and beyond them exists an element which may, quite apart from them, affect us profoundly and occupy our minds with a most bewildering strength:

> Let us follow it up with every effort of sympathy and imaginative intuition wherever it is to be found, in the lives of those around us, in sudden, strong ebullitions of personal piety and the frames of mind such ebullitions evince, in the fixed and ordered solemnities of rites and liturgies, and again in the atmosphere that clings to old religious monuments and buildings—to temples and to churches. (12)

If we do so follow it, he assures us, we shall realize "that we are dealing with something for which there is only one appropriate expression, *mysterium tremendum.*" Once again, as with the specification of the numinous, he has reached back into the Latin to designate more precisely the components of what he seeks, and having done so presents us with what we intuit as the straight force of an archetype:

> The feeling of it may at times come sweeping like a gentle tide, pervading the mind with a tranquil mood of deepest worship. It may pass over into a more set and lasting attribute of the soul, continuing as it were, thrillingly vibrant and resonant, until at last it dies away and the soul resumes its "profane" non-religious mood of everyday experience. It may burst in sudden eruption up from the depths of the soul with spasms and convulsions, or lead to the strongest excitements, to intoxicated frenzy, to transport, and to ecstasy. It has its wild and demonic forms and can sink to an almost grisly horror and shuddering. It has its crude, barbaric antecedents and early manifestations, and again it may be developed into something beautiful and pure and glorious. It may become the hushed, trembling, and speechless humility of the creature in the presence of—whom or what? In the presence of that which is a *mystery* inexpressible and above all creatures. (12)

Otto is not unaware that, in calling the object of this numinous consciousness the *mysterium tremendum*, his conceptualization can only proceed negatively. As a concept, *mysterium* denotes merely what is concealed, what cannot be grasped, that which is beyond specification. But, he insists, "though what is enunciated in the word is negative, what is *meant* is something absolutely and intensely positive" (13)

This extreme disparity between positive feeling and negative concept is at the root of our inability to express the universal comprehension of "what God is." It is responsible for this astounding paradox that the most emphatic affirmation known to man can only be expressed conceptually in negative terms. But, wonder of wonders, this "pure positive" can be *experienced* in the perplexing ambivalence of our feelings, "feelings which our discussion can help make clear to us, insofar as it arouses them actually in our hearts" (13).

Before going on to a deeper analysis of what Otto means by the component elements in the numinous, it is well to state that so far as concerns Jeffers, the poet never seeks to deal with the *mysterium tremendum* as the pure "inexpressible" in the way traditional with mystical poets. That he is indeed aware of it, his work everywhere makes clear: it is the primary fact of his life; it stands before all his reflection, all his labor, all his creativity. It is for him the very charge, force, and meaning of reality. That he does not attempt to register it in its intrinsic presence is due rather to the type of religious poet he is than to any inadequacy of feeling. That is to say, as *poet* he is more the prophet than the contemplative. As such, he is concerned, once he has acknowledged its omnipresence, to adumbrate the impact of the *mysterium tremendum* upon the life of man, its social, moral, and political dimension, than to register it in its utter ineffability.

This distinction between the poet as contemplative and the poet as prophet is important, for by means of it we are able to orient the position of the artist in the broad field of religious experience. Writers on mysticism are wont to analyze it in terms of its grades, the levels of ascent from mundane reflection to infused contemplation, and they naturally see the aesthetic as an experience that one transcends as one approaches in vision the intrinsic reality of the Unapproachable. Sometimes they see art as a mere making, a virtue of the practical intellect, and hence in this way also relegate it to an inferior place in the mystical ascent. Now since many religious poets are primarily mystics—as was, for instance, St. John of the Cross—their poems do fall within this mystical context, and their voices often sound like the last murmur before the vast speechlessness possesses them, and they are indeed alone with the Alone.

However, this prevalence of the mystical element in great religious verse is deceptive. What the theoreticians fail to recognize is another kind of charismatic activity, itself directly involved with the numinous, and this, as noted above, is prophecy. Prophecy might be called the overflow of contemplation; it begins where mysticism leaves off. Whereas mysticism ascends, prophecy descends. From the psychological point of view, the contemplative experiences his abysmal inferiority to that which he approaches, and his voice dies in speechlessness. The prophet, however, experiences the divine superiority to the underextending mundane reality he confronts. It is this situation of a transcendent point of view which the *mysterium tremendum* has given him that endows the prophet with the force of authority, the almost reckless propensity for extreme declaration, and out of it the voice speaks explicitly and emphatically.

Now it is apparent that, charismatically, poetry is closer to prophecy than it is to mystical contemplation. Even in the psychological order, poetry follows inspiration rather than precedes it. Therefore it is unwise to restrict the aesthetic to its passive dimension, as an intermediary step to the divine, something to be transcended. In poetry the aesthetic becomes the *vehicle* of the divine. It is divinity plus the human tongue giving it utterance, and so crucial is its function that the tongue becomes as important as the message. Thus when it comes to specifying the grades of religious feeling, we find that Jeffers, contemplative though he be, always speaks with the authority of positive indication. He speaks as one who has experienced the *mysterium tremendum*, knows what it means, and is telling the world what he knows.

This is why when pursuing the analysis that follows throughout the course of Otto's book, we find many examples from Jeffers illustrative of these attributes, but none relating to the mystery *per se*. There is nothing of the transparent visionary condition we see in, say, the Sufi mystic: "I went from God to God, until they cried from me in me, 'O thou I.'"[2] Jeffers does not speak from the point of view of one who annuls the self as he approaches the divine—this he keeps to himself—but he does emphatically speak from the point of view of one who comes back, of divinity's specific application to the human condition, and this he shouts to the world.

However, before going on, there is a factor relevant to the *mysterium tremendum* in its infused transcendence for which Jeffers does show great concern, and that is the question of how men interpret it, the attribution made of it by those who have known it. And we may as well discuss it here before we go on to more specific effects, for by doing so we prepare ourselves to understand a good deal of what is to come in regard to the way the poet expresses himself. For every man defines himself, positively or negatively, over against the practice and the opinions of those around him.

As a religious psychologist, Jeffers is acutely aware of the impact of the *mysterium tremendum* on the individual psyche, and in his rendition of religious character among the figures of his narratives, he has depicted, at one time or another, several of the affective states we encounter in our analysis. While he himself is never in doubt about the reality of the *mysterium tremendum*, from the point of view of objective delineation, he is not uncritical. Rather, for him nothing is more revelatory of man's endemic blindness than the appalling way in which our omnivorous eccentricity misappropriates the most transcendent charismatic perception. Thus the whole of *The Women at Point Sur* is the portrayal of a man progressively destroyed by his misconception of the incredible shift in consciousness that he is undergoing, a shift entered through violation, misapplied through an obsessively fixed formula (*God thinks through action*), and jettisoned through the lust for disciples. The whole nexus of the poem is built upon the paradox of the incredible reality experienced through direct perception, progressively nullified by a malfunction of attribution.

However, setting aside for now the problem of *The Women at Point Sur*, let us consider a vignette of obvious misattribution at its crudest. Old Fraser in *Give Your Heart to the Hawks* patently simulates the *mysterium tremendum* out of emotional need and nothing else, attributing divine ordination to meteorological fact:

> The rain held off; for two hundred and forty days there had been
>   no rain
> But one sun-drunken shower. The creek was dry rock and
>   weary gray roots; the skin of the mountain crumbled
> Under starved feet; the five carcasses of hawks that Lance had
>   hung on the fence-wire dried without odor
> In the north wind and rages of the sun.
>   Old Fraser walked under
>   the moon along the farm-drive beside them,
> Saying, "Lord if thou art minded to burn the whole earth
> And spat off the dust from thy hands, it is well done,
> The glory and the vengeance: but if anywhere
> Rain falls on hills, remember I beseech thee thy servant's place,
> Or the beasts die in the field." While he was praying
> The moon dimmed; he felt a flutelike exultance
> Flow up from the V of his ribs to his wrinkled throat:
> He was not abandoned: and looked aloft and saw
> A little many-colored man's-palm-size cloud
> Coasting the moon from the southeast, the storm-side.
> The old man exalted himself; he had power upon God; and
>   anxiously
> Repressing his joy for fear it waste the event
> Beforehand, compelled his heart to remember bitterness,
> His two sons lost, one dead, the other in rebellion,
> And poverty and scorn and the starved cattle. "Oh Lord God,
> As in old time thou didst choose one little people for thine out
>   of all the earth,
> So now thou hast chosen one man, one old man, foolish and
>   poor: but if thy will was made up

To punish the earth, then heed not my voice but arise and
punish. It is rank with defilement and infidelity
And the music of the evil churches." He saw a shining white
form at the garden-gate, and for a high moment
Believed that some angel, as unto Abraham . . . It was Lance
(*CP* 2: 367–68)

This concern regarding the attribution of the *mysterium tremendum*, the misconception of its nature and function by those who experience it, finds its most salient expression in a soliloquy of Jesus in the play *Dear Judas*. Written after *The Women at Point Sur*, his peak work, this play appears as a kind of afterthought and is his most unsatisfactory work. But I think this particular soliloquy is crucial because in it Jeffers most completely expresses what he regarded as Christ's misconception of the *mysterium tremendum* that had been vouchsafed him. And because Christ has been the key figure of the great epoch of man that is now closing, Jeffers purports to expose his misconception as fatal to the entire epoch, a poisonous seed staining its entire course, precipitating the fatal torque that would in the end sever it within itself and splinter it into a thousand painful fragments. Jesus speaks:

Three . . . four times in my life I have been one with
our Father,
The night and the day, the dark seas and the little fountains, the
sown and the desert, the morning star
And the mountains against morning and the mountain cedars,
the sheep and the wolves, the Hebrews and the free nomads
That eat camels and worship a stone, and the sun cures them like
salt into the marrow in the bones;
All, all, the times future and past
The hanging leaves on one tree: there is not a word nor a dream
nor any way to declare his loveliness
Except to have felt and known, to have *been* the beauty. Even the
cruelties and agonies that my poor Judas
Chokes on: were there in the net, shining. The hawk shone like
the dove. Why, there it is! Exultation,
You stripped dupe? I have gathered my ruins. (*CP* 2: 27–28)

Thus far the *mysterium tremendum* is remembered as the inclusive vision charged with wonder and the synthesis of revelation. But now comes the attribution: out of the mouth of Jesus, the orthodox theological doctrine of the mystical body of Christ is indicted as an unsound ego-need, a kind of lust for love as ultimate self-congratulation:

Life after life, at the bottom of the pit comes exultation. I seem to remember so many nights?
In the smell of old cypresses in the garden darkness. And the means of power,
All clear and formed, like tangible symbols laid in my mind. Two thousand years are laid in my hands
Like grains of corn. Not for the power: Oh, more than power, actual possession. To be with my people,
In their very hearts, a part of their being, inseparable from those that love me, more closely touching them
Than the cloth of the inner garment touches the flesh. That this is tyrannous
I know, that it is love run to lust: but I will possess them. The hawk shines like the dove. Oh, power
Bought at the price these hands and feet and all this body perishing in torture will pay is holy
Their minds love terror, their souls cry to be sacrificed for: pain's almost the God
Of doubtful men, who tremble expecting to endure it. Their cruelty sublimed. And I think the brute cross itself,
Hewn down to a gibbet now, has been worshiped; it stands yet for an idol of life and power in the dreaming
Soul of the world and the waters under humanity, whence floating again
It will fly up heaven, and heavy with triumphant blood and renewal, the very nails and the beams alive.
I saw my future when I was with God; but now at length in a flashing moment the means: I frightfully
Lifted up drawing all men to my feet: I go a stranger passage to a greater dominion,
More tyrannous, more terrible, more true, than Caesar or any subduer of the earth before him has dared to dream of
In a dream on his bed, over the prostrate city, before the pale weary dawn
Creeps through his palace, through the purple fringes, between the polished agate pillars, to steal it away. (*CP* 2: 28–29)

However, though Jeffers himself rejects the attribution of Christ as to the meaning of the *mysterium tremendum* vouchsafed him, he does not in every instance show himself contemptuous of it, as in the case of Old Fraser. Rather, if the attitude of the believer is palpably simple and without spiritual ambition, he accords it a sympathy of treatment that is close to credence. The

Christian ingredients in the experience of Onorio Vasquez (such as his touching plea to take the place of the crucified hawk in the Prelude to *The Women at Point Sur*) he retains with sympathetic expression, but the best instance is that of the Indian woman named California in *Roan Stallion*. Abused by her drunken husband on the day before Christmas, she yet is determined that her little girl will have something for the feast, and, late as Johnny's callousness in bed has detained her, she hitches the mare Dora to the buckboard and drives to Monterey. Coming back in the dark, she runs into trouble at the ford. Try as she might, she cannot make her horse go through:

THE MARE

Stopped, her two forefeet in the water. She touched with the
whip. The mare plodded ahead and halted.
Then California thought of prayer: "Dear little Jesus,
Dear baby Jesus born to-night, your head was shining
Like silver candles. I've got a baby too, only a girl. You had
light wherever you walked.
Dear baby Jesus give me light." Light streamed: rose, gold, rich
purple, hiding the ford like a curtain.
The gentle thunder of water was a noise of wing-feathers, the
fans of paradise lifting softly.
The child afloat on radiance had a baby face, but the angels had
birds' heads, hawks' heads,
Bending over the baby, weaving a web of wings about him. He
held in the small fat hand
A little snake with golden eyes, and California could see clearly
on the under radiance
The mare's pricked ears, a sharp black fork against the shining
light-fall. But it dropped; the light of heaven
Frightened poor Dora. She backed; swung up the water,
And nearly oversetting the buggy turned and scrambled
backward; the iron wheel-tires rang on boulders. (*CP* 2: 185)

Jeffers accepts this incident as something ostensibly true and makes no attempt to undermine its veracity, as he does in *Dear Judas*, when the miracles of Christ are presented as trumped-up instances in a case of programmatically contrived spiritual ambition.

As a final example, the poem "A Redeemer" might be instanced, for the Christian element is here, and denigrated, but the attribution is otherwise. Here the man has obviously experienced the *mysterium tremendum*, and he responds to it in an extreme way, taking upon himself a kind of Christ-appropriation. But the values he expresses, as attribution, are Jeffers's own. The poet would seem, by this device, to risk jeopardizing his philosophy by putting it in the mouth of a person of questionable mentality, but he obviously does not fear this, moving through the thread of discourse without undue self-consciousness—in fact, with complete ease. This ease of handling, whether treating the miracle of the ford in *Roan Stallion* or the placing of his own values in the mouth of a questionable mind, shows, I believe, the primacy of Jeffers as dramatic artist to any of the philosophical tenets he holds so passionately. Give him a dramatic situation, and he treats it with authority, no matter how much he seems to have jeopardized it with philosophical tendentiousness:

> The road had steepened and the sun sharpened on the high
>   ridges; the stream probably was dry,
> Certainly not to be come to down the pit of the canyon. We
>   stopped for water at the one farm
> In all that mountain. The trough was cracked with drought, the
>   moss on the boards dead, but an old dog
> Rose like a wooden toy at the house-door silently. I said "There
>   will be water somewhere about,"
> And when I knocked a man showed us a spring of water.
>   Though his hair was nearly white I judged him
> Forty years old at most. His eyes and voice were muted. It is
>   likely he kept his hands hidden,
> I failed to see them until we had dipped the spring. He stood
>   then on the lip of the great slope
> And looked westward over an incredible country to the far hills
>   that dammed the sea-fog: it billowed
> Above them, cascaded over them, it never crossed them, gray
>   standing flood. He stood gazing, his hands
> Were clasped behind him; I caught a glimpse of serous red under
>   the fingers, and looking sharply
> When they drew apart saw that both hands were wounded. I said
>   "Your hands are hurt." He twitched them from sight,
> But after a moment having earnestly eyed me displayed them.
>   The wounds were in the hearts of the palms,
> Pierced to the backs like stigmata of crucifixion. The horrible
>   raw flesh protruded, glistening
> And granular, not scabbed, nor a sign of infection. "These are
>   old wounds." He answered, "Yes, they don't heal." He stood

Moving his lips in silence, his back against that fabulous basin of mountains, fold beyond fold,
Patches of forest and scarps of rock, high domes of dead gray pasture and gray beds of dry rivers,
Clear and particular in the burning air, too bright to appear real, to the last range
The fog from the ocean like a stretched compacted thunderstorm overhung; and he said gravely:
"I pick them open. I made them long ago with a clean steel. It is only a little to pay—"
He stretched and flexed the fingers, I saw his sunburnt lips whiten in a line compressed together,
"If only it proves enough for a time—to save so many." I searched his face for madness but that
Is often invisible, a subtle spirit. "There never," he said, "was any people earned so much ruin.
I love them, I am trying to suffer for them. It would be bad if I should die, I am careful
Against excess." "You think of the wounds," I said, "of Jesus?" He laughed angrily and frowned, stroking
The fingers of one hand with the other. "Religion is the people's opium. Your little Jew-God?
My pain," he said with pride, "is voluntary.
They have done what never was done before. Not as a people takes a land to love it and be fed,
A little, according to need and love, and again a little; sparing the country tribes, mixing
Their blood with theirs, their minds with all the rocks and rivers, their flesh with the soil: no, without hunger
Wasting the world and your own labor, without love possessing, not even your hands to the dirt but plows
Like blades of knives; heartless machines; houses of steel: using and despising the patient earth . . .
Oh, as a rich man eats a forest for profit and a field for vanity, so you came west and raped
The continent and brushed its people to death. Without need, the weak skirmishing hunters, and without mercy.
Well, God's a scare-crow; no vengeance out of old rags. But there are acts breeding their own reversals
In their own bellies from the first day. I am here" he said—and broke off suddenly and said "They take horses
And give them sickness through hollow needles, their blood saves babies: I am here on the mountain making

Antitoxin for all the happy towns and farms, the lovely
blameless children, the terrible
Arrogant cities. I used to think them terrible: their gray
prosperity, their pride: from up here
Specks of mildew.

But when I am dead and all you with whole hands
think of nothing but happiness,
Will you go mad and kill each other? Or horror come over the
ocean on wings and cover your sun?
I wish," he said trembling, "I had never been born."

His wife came from the door while he was talking. Mine asked
her quietly, "Do you live all alone here,
Are you not afraid?" "Certainly not," she answered, "he is
always gentle and loving. I have no complaint
Except his groans in the night keep me awake often. But when I
think of other women's
Troubles: my own daughter's: I'm older than my husband, I have
been married before: deep is my peace." (*CP* 1: 405–06)

But when the question arises as to the *correct* attribution of the power experienced in the *mysterium tremendum*, Jeffers, in a thousand instances studded throughout his verse, declares that attribution must be foregone, that the experience is its own reward, that for the truly self-possessed to be God-possessed ought to suffice, that the fundamental error lies in the temptation to help others through the attribution of its energies. In his "Meditation on Saviors," written at the same time as "A Redeemer" and appearing in the same volume, he examines the problem with great closeness—and incidentally achieves one of his best examples of expository verse. Attribution, he declares, is the temptation of the would-be savior rather than an authentic solution, because death is, actually, its own deliverer:

a huge gift reserved quite overwhelms them at the end; they
are able then to be still and not cry.

And having touched a little of the beauty and seen a little of the
beauty of things, magically grow
Across the funeral fire or the hidden stench of burial themselves
into the beauty they admired,

Themselves into the God, themselves into the sacred steep
unconsciousness

. . .

they need no savior, salvation
comes and takes them by force,
It gathers them into the great kingdom of dust and stone, the
blown storms, the stream's-end ocean. (*CP* 1: 401)

And he concludes with the only acknowledgment as to the value of consciousness he ever concedes:

With this advantage over their granite grave-marks, of having
realized the petulant human consciousness
Before, and then the greatness, the peace: drunk from both
pitchers (*CP* 1: 401)

And finishes with his only concession to the powers of love, but sheerly qualified by the necessity of turning love from itself to its absolute, and so be freed of its obsessiveness:

But while he lives let each man make his health in his mind, to
love the coast opposite humanity,
And so be freed of love, laying it like bread on the waters, it is
worst turned inward, it is best shot farthest.

Love, the mad wine of good and evil, the saint's and murderer's,
the mote in the eye that makes its object
Shine the sun black; the trap in which it is better to catch the
inhuman God than the hunter's own image. (*CP* 1: 401)

There seems to be an implicit acknowledgment here that love is the aftereffect, not the consequence, of the *mysterium tremendum*. The central problem of life remains the problem of attribution: what one does with one's power, to whom or upon what does one lavish one's love? But mostly Jeffers fears love as the trap that sucks the savior to its service. By qualifying its imperatives, he hopes to place himself in a relationship which will free him to consummate its inception without succumbing to its force.

Demonic Dread

During World War II there was a popular saying to the effect that "There are no atheists in the foxholes." It served well as a religious slogan for the general public when so many lives were in jeopardy, but it never convinced any atheists, at least none I knew.

My best friends, or those who happened to be safely out of the foxholes, disgustedly demurred: "Put a man under insuperable strain for days and weeks, threaten his rationality through a crescendo of terrific assaults on his sensibility, reduce him to a quivering jelly of benumbed consciousness, drive him back upon the most elemental, the most unreflective neural reactions, afflict him until the very substratum of his being is induced to clamor out a name implanted in his infancy—'God!'—and then gloat triumphantly, 'There are no atheists in the foxholes!' This is detestable. It is religion's last ditch resort to a formula more pathetic than the unfortunate victim in the foxholes. But as for a thinking man's solution to the problem of God, it is absurd."

Neither Christian nor atheist at that time, this disclaimer never really convinced me. I had experienced religious awe enough times not to require foxhole experience to verify my sense of the absolute. I knew that awe is the product of vulnerability, and to the reflective man it does not take conditions of extremity to bring home to him how vulnerable he actually is. We do not experience the change in attitude from agnosticism to religious belief by virtue of rational reflection. Rather, we are brought to our knees by an experience of such profundity, of such import, of such awe, that we are unable any longer to sustain detachment. Awe seizes us like a fist, asserts itself into the field of our emotional comprehension, and renders us incapable of defiance. Like atheists who lose their objectivity in the foxhole, we learn the cry of the heart that brooks no denial, and never, when it at last occurs, begrudge the extremities that life had to exact of us by way of our assaulted sensibility in order to render us palpable to everything that this awe now offers. If we are confronted instantly with the problem of attribution, neither do we begrudge all the soul-searching it will exact of us, for the decision we arrive at will be by virtue of the peace it yields us. Our wrestling has just begun, but at least it has begun.

For though attribution may be the central problem of life (how we employ the surging energies released by our experience of the divine, the *mysterium tremendum*), before the problem of its use can be solved, it is necessary to know what it is. Only those who have experienced it have been tempted by it. Only those who have tasted power have craved to employ power. Existing before love, that "mad wine of good and evil, the saint's and murderer's," awe itself awaits as the primary experience that preestablishes action and constitutes the datum out of which all salvific attempts, be they good or bad, will pour. Jeffers may be a prophet by virtue of his attempt to rectify the course of human action, but he is intensely preprophetic in his power to understand, to grasp the shuddering immediacy of the superior reality that constitutes the essence of the religious experience.

It is for this reason that, when Otto begins to analyze the elements of the *mysterium tremendum* itself, we feel we are in a position to move up with Jeffers beyond detached objectification to experience his own direct involvement. The first of these is what Otto calls "the Element of Awefulness" and which he finds designated not so much by concepts as by what he calls "ideograms," in this case the ideogram of "absolute unapproachability" (19). Having observed, as we saw, that conceptually *mysterium* denotes what is hidden and esoteric, what is beyond conception or understanding, and that the term does *not* define the object more positively in its qualitative character, a matter to be experienced only in our feelings, so too, he goes on to say, with the *tremendum*, where *tremor* is in itself merely the perfectly familiar and "natural" emotion of *fear*. Here, also, the term is taken, aptly enough but still only by analogy, to denote a quite specific kind of emotional response, a response wholly distinct from the feeling of being afraid, and it goes back to the most primitive roots of religion. "Let us give a little further consideration to the first crude, primitive forms in which this 'numinous dread' or *awe* shows itself. It is the mark which really characterizes the so-called 'religion of primitive man,' and there it appears as 'demonic dread'" (15). We begin, therefore, this probe into the complex field of the element of awefulness by a search to establish the presence of demonic dread in the work of Jeffers.

It is Otto's contention that this absolutely basic and seemingly atavistic emotion constitutes the fundamental element in religious experience—and that however much a higher development seems to supersede and outstrip it, something of its underlying intensity must be, and in fact is, retained:

> This crudely naive and primordial emotional disturbance, and the fantastic images to which it gives rise, are later overborn and ousted by more highly developed forms of the numinous emotion, with all its mysterious impelling power. But even when this has long attained its higher and purer mode of expression it is possible for the primitive types of excitation that were formerly a part of it to break out in the soul in all their original naivete and so to be experienced afresh. (16)

Jeffers is well aware of this "crudely naive and primordial emotional disturbance" and often depicts those fantastic images to which it gives rise. His narratives are rich with incidents of the preternatural, manifestations of the occult, and strange epiphanies. That such manifestations of the preternatural are truly relevant, constituting authentic adjuncts of religious experience, Otto makes clear and is especially concerned to dissociate them from any kind of assimilation to a purely natural fear:

> That this is so is shown by the potent attraction again and again exercised by the element of horror and "shudder" in ghost stories, even among persons of high all-around education. It is a remarkable fact that the physical reaction to which this unique "dread" of the uncanny gives rise is also unique, and is not found in the case of any "natural" fear or terror. We say "my blood ran icy cold," and "my flesh crept." The "cold blood" feeling may be a symptom of ordinary, natural fear, but there is something non-natural or supernatural about the symptom of "creeping flesh." (16)

Otto is careful, too, to skirt the natural tendency to assume this shudder is a matter of simple intensity, fear compounded by fear until it touches a degree that threatens the ego:

> And any one who is capable of more precise introspection must recognize that the distinction between such a "dread" and natural fear is not simply one of degree and intensity. The awe or "dread" *may* indeed be so overwhelmingly great that it seems to penetrate to the very marrow, making the man's hair bristle and his limbs quake. But it may also steal upon him almost unobserved as the gentlest of agitations, a mere fleeting shadow passing across his mood. It has therefore nothing to do with intensity, and no natural fear passes over into it merely by being intensified. I may be beyond all measure afraid and terrified without there being even a trace of the feeling of uncanniness in my emotion. (16)

Considered under such a light, most of the difficulties which Carpenter wrestles with, for instance, in his chapter on "Philosophy and Religion," wherein the inconsistencies of Jeffers's attitude to supernaturalism are noted, fall into perspective. "How can he justify," Carpenter asks, "the use of supernatural beings in his own poetry, when he attacks the supernatural pretensions of orthodox religions?" (112).

Actually, what Jeffers attacks in orthodoxy is, as we saw, the attribution made of the presence of supernatural phenomena, not the existence of such phenomena, which of course he freely employs. Of these instances, the short poem "Local Legend" from the *Hungerfield* volume will serve.

Two Spanish cowhands from Monterey
Riding, a moonless midnight, to their beds on the coast
Heard a child crying in the pinewood
On the ridge of the Carmel hill; they beat the bushes and found
A naked babe laid on the needle-floor
In the dark screaming. They picked it up, how could they leave
  it there?
One of them huddled it under his coat;
They had not ridden a hundred yards when a fountain of fire
Spouted from the babe's mouth: the man
Shrieked, and flung his foundling into the bushes; they never
  stopped galloping
Until they'd forded the Carmel River
And let the blown horses breathe.—That is all. The story,
Senseless as other supernaturalisms
Might even be true, for who would take the trouble to invent it?
But most of us, one time or another,
Have taken unhappy causes or hopes to heart, and gotten well
  burnt. (*CP* 3:398)

Other instances that might be mentioned are the Christ-child vision in *Roan Stallion*, the shore-line ghosts and other preternatural powers in *Tamar*, the calling up of his father's ghost in "Come, Little Birds," and the talking stones in *The Tower Beyond Tragedy*. Rather than attempting to localize these examples in terms of Jeffers's philosophy, we can see their place in his work more consistently when we regard them as instances of the closeness of his religious feeling to its primordial sources, authentic elements of universal religious experience.

Thus in "Mara," when the man Ferguson encounters the personification of his split mind and engages it in dialogue, most contemporary poets would be content to let the incident stand as a purely psychic encounter; but Jeffers, with his telling and instinctive naiveté, suddenly concretizes the episode into the category of "demonic dread" by sending the man's dog, hackles raised, out of his presence. "Mara," written at a time of great weariness for the poet, is not a great poem, but at several points in it Jeffers reveals his instantaneous capacity to go the limit, letting us understand his radical closeness to the primitive religious spirit.

But this astonishing accessibility to movements of primordial feeling is perhaps most powerfully demonstrated in the narrative poem *Hungerfield*, when the protagonist fights Death in physical combat. In this last of his narratives, the poet is obviously weary of life, terribly longing for finality, and patently disinclined to maintain the maximum psychic intensity that pervades his best narratives. But suddenly in Hungerfield's encounter with Death, something in the poet, despite his weariness, lets go. One feels he is speaking directly out of himself, out of his own unconscious heart, when he says of the man that "While his mind lied his blood and body believed." The generalized narrative mentality is secular and sophisticated, but the feeling-sources of demonic dread are as primitive as Beowulf. Listen to the long development of mood that readies all for the moment of decisiveness. Hungerfield's mother Alcmena is failing, and Hungerfield tells her she will not die:

> It is a common lie to the dying, and I too have told it; but Hungerfield—
> While his mind lied his blood and body believed. He had seen Death and he would see him again.
> He was waiting for his enemy.
> Night deepened around the house; the sea-waves came up into the stream,
> And the stream fought them; the cliffs and standing rocks black and bone-still
> Stood in the dark. There were no stars, there were some little sparkles of glowworms on the wet ground,
> If you looked closely, and shapes of things, and the shifting foam-line. The vast phantasmagoria of night
> Proceeded around that central throat begging for breath, and Hungerfield
> Sat beside it, rigid and motionless as the rocks but his fingers twitching, hunched like a cat
> To spring and tear. (*CP* 3: 382)

Thus the scene is delineated, suspenseful, bated, a mood of contained consequence, of impending urgency:

> Then the throat clicked and ceased. Hungerfield looked at it; when he looked back
> The monster was in the room. It was a column of heavy darkness in the dim lamplight, but the arrogant head
> Was clear to see. That damned sneer on his face. Hungerfield felt his hair rise like a dog's

And heard Death say scornfully: "Quiet yourself, poor man, make no disturbance; it is not for you.
I have come for the old woman Alcmena Hungerfield, to whom death
Will be more kind than life." Hungerfield saw his throat and sprang at it. But he was like a man swimming
A lake of corpses, the newly harvested souls from all earth's fields, faint shrieks and whispers, Death's company.
He smote their dim heads with his hands and their bowels with his feet
And swam on them. He reached Death's monstrous flesh and they cleared away. It had looked like a shadow,
It was harder than iron. The throat was missed, they stood and hugged each other like lovers; Hungerfield
Drove his knee to the groin. Death laughed and said,
"I am not a man," and the awful embrace tightened
On the man's loins; he began to be bent backward, writhing and sobbing; he felt the years of his age
Bite at his heart like rats: he was not yet fifty: but it is known that little by little God abandons men
When thirty's past. Experience and cunning may perhaps increase
But power departs. He struck short at the throat and was bent further backward, and suddenly
Flung himself back and fell, dragging Death down with him, twisting in the fall, and weasel-quick on the floor
Tore at the throat: then the horrible stench and hopelessness of dead bodies filled the dim air; he thought
He had wounded Death. What? The iron force and frame of nature with his naked hands? It bubbled and gasped,
"You fool—what have you done!" The iron flesh in his grip melted like a summer corpse, and turning liquid
Slid from his hands. He stood up foaming and groped for it; there was nothing. He saw in the stair-door
Arab, and Ross his brother, and the hired cattle-hand
Staring with eyes like moons. They had heard a chair crash and seen the fury; Arab had screamed like a hawk,
But no one heard her; now she stood moaning, gazing at him. But Ross entered the room and walked
Carefully wide around him to their mother's bed. The old woman was sitting up and breathed easily, saying
"I saw it all. Listen: they are taking him away." A strain of mournful music was heard, from the house

Flitting up the black night. This was the time—it was near
midnight here—for a quarter of an hour
Nobody died. Disease went on, and the little peripheral
prophetic wars, the famines and betrayals,
Neither man nor beast died, though they might cry for him.
Death, whom we hate and love, had met a worse monster
And could not come. (*CP* 3: 383–84)

The almost unbelievable poetic audacity of a writer who can assume the risks of such narration is only to be accounted for by reference to the concept of authority—a poet's incalculable sense of the authority of his craft and his vocation.

We have shown Jeffers's proclivity for demonic dread in the full potential of its uncanny and terrifying horror, but Otto has noted that it may also steal upon a man almost unobserved, arising as the gentlest of agitations, a mere fleeting shape passing across his mood. Jeffers too knows this. In "Haunted Country," written during the period of his choicest lyrics, the poem touches such an element in a beautifully modulated aesthetic experience. Demonic dread flickers like foxfire in and about the evocative imagery, the morose concepts, fitfully illuminating the specifications of detail:

Here the human past is dim and feeble and alien to us
Our ghosts draw from the crowded future,
Fixed as the past how could it fail to drop weird shadows
And make strange murmurs about twilight?
In the dawn twilight metal falcons flew over the mountain,
Multitudes, and faded in the air; at moonrise
The farmer's girl by the still river is afraid of phantoms,
Hearing the pulse of a great city
Move on the water-meadow and stream off south; the country's
Children for all their innocent minds
Hide dry and bitter lights in the eye, they dream without
knowing it
The inhuman years to be accomplished,
The inhuman powers, the servile cunning under pressure,
In a land grown old, heavy and crowded.
There are happy places that fate skips; here is not one of them;
The tides of the brute womb, the excess
And weight of life spilled out like water, the last migration
Gathering against this holier valley-mouth
That knows its fate beforehand, the flow of the womb, banked
back
By the older flood of the ocean, to swallow it. (*CP* 1: 111)

Excess is the prolonged and abiding fault of Robinson Jeffers, in art if not in life, but how beautiful are the forms with which he endows it, and how close his excesses cleave to that cosmic Excess before which the soul of man must cower. In its grip, demonic dread becomes for him a kind of appetite by which he savors the divine.

Jeffers, then, is well aware not only of the dread but its transmutation into higher forms of awareness. In this he accommodates himself within the main current of religious consciousness, and no one among contemporary religious writers more fittingly illustrates a certain retention, the value of which Otto insists upon, in the appropriation of primitive within sophisticated religious states:

> Though the numinous emotion in its completest development shows a world of difference from the mere "demonic dread," yet not even at the highest level does it belie its pedigree of kindred. Even when the worship of the "demons" has long since reached the higher level of worship of "gods," these gods still retain as *numina* something of the "ghost" in the impress they make on the feelings of the worshipper, viz., the peculiar quality of the uncanny, and "aweful" which survives with the quality of exaltedness and sublimity or is symbolized by means of it. And this softened though it is, does not disappear even on the highest level of all, where the worship of God is at its purest. Its disappearance would be indeed an essential loss. The "shudder" reappears in a form ennobled beyond measure where the soul, held speechless, trembles inwardly to the farthest fibre of its being. (17)

"O passionately at peace," cries Jeffers, speaking of Night in his magnificent poem of that name, "you being secure will pardon / The blasphemies of glowworms, the lamp in my tower, the fretfulness / Of cities, the cressets of the planets, the pride of the stars" (*CP* 1: 115). And he goes on to scale out the dimension that dwarfs the mind into its underrealms of instinctive awe:

> This August night in a rift of cloud Antares reddens,
> The great one, the ancient torch, a lord among lost children,
> The earth's orbit doubled would not girdle his greatness, one fire
> Globed, out of grasp of the mind enormous; but to you, O
> Night
> What? Not a spark? What flicker of a spark in the faint far
> glimmer
> Of a lost fire dying in the desert, dim coals of a sand-spit the
> Bedouins

Wandered from at dawn . . . Ah singing prayer to what gulfs tempted
Suddenly are you more lost? To us the near-hand mountain
Be a measure of height, the tide-worn cliff at the sea-gate a measure of continuance. (*CP* 1: 115)

Or suddenly he can take the veritable shudder itself and affirm it directly, as it comes into him, registering it with the shock of direct impact, powerful and intense, yet partaking of the heights rather than the crudity of the experience:

I am past childhood, I look at this ocean and the fishing birds, the streaming skerries, the shining water,
The foam-heads, the exultant dawn-light going west, the pelicans, their huge wings half folded, plunging like stones.

Whatever it is catches my heart in its hands, whatever it is makes me shudder with love
And painful joy and the tears prickle . . . the Greeks were not its inventors. (*CP* 2: 526)

No better instance can be found of the combination of creature feeling and its quality of the soul submerged in a power greater than itself, together with that other feeling of absolute unapproachability and its accent of almost revulsion from and terror before a majesty greater than one is worthy to contemplate, than the episode in *Roan Stallion* when the woman California breaks free and rides to the hill summit to immolate herself before the vastness of the world below and the numinous power localized in the presence of the stallion.

She stood then,
Shaking. Enormous films of moonlight
Trailed down from the height. Space, anxious whiteness, vastness. Distant beyond conception the shining ocean
Lay light like a haze along the ledge and doubtful world's end. Little vapors gleaming, and little
Darknesses on the far chart underfoot symbolized wood and valley; but the air was the element, the moon-
Saturate arcs and spires of the air.
Here is solitude, here on the calvary, nothing conscious
But the possible God and the cropped grass, no witness, no eye but that misformed one, the moon's past fullness.
Two figures on the shining hill, woman and stallion, she kneeling to him, brokenly adoring.

He cropping the grass, shifting his hooves, or lifting the long
head to gaze over the world,
Tranquil and powerful. She prayed aloud, "O God, I am not
good enough, O fear, O strength, I am draggled.
Johnny and other men have had me, and O clean power! Here
am I," she said, falling before him,
And crawled to his hooves. (*CP* 1: 193)

Quite enough has been instanced to establish the centrality to Jeffers's power of this underlying attitude. If he has been called overwhelming, it is because his heart is founded on an awareness of power that outreaches any dimension of the mind, is actually the source of reality itself, the power that, in keeping all in being, sustains the poet in his incorrigibly innocent heart.

Notes

1. Robinson Jeffers's "The Poet in Democracy," published as *Themes in My Poems*, is cited here from Melba Berry Bennett, who works from Jeffers's original manuscript rather than from the revised published version.
2. Unfortunately, I have been unable to locate my source for this quotation.

Works Cited

CP *The Collected Poetry of Robinson Jeffers*. Ed. Tim Hunt. 3 vols. to date. Stanford, CA: Stanford UP, 1988, 1989, 1991.

Bennett, Melma Berry. *The Stone Mason of Tor House*. Los Angeles: Ward Ritchie, 1966.
Carpenter, Frederic. *Robinson Jeffers*. New York: Twayne, 1962.
Catholic Encyclopedia. New York, 1967.
Eliade, Mircea. *Myths, Dreams, and Mysteries*. New York: Harper, 1957.
Jeffers, Robinson. *Themes in My Poems*. San Francisco: Book Club of California, 1956.
Otto, Rudolph. *The Idea of the Holy*. London: Oxford UP, 1923.
Wilder, Amos. *The Spiritual Aspects of the New Poetry*. New York: Harper, 1940.

A REVIEW OF JEFFERS SCHOLARSHIP

Critical Studies

Most serious scholarship on Jeffers began appearing in the 1960s, very shortly after the poet's death. Radcliffe Squires's seminal *The Loyalties of Robinson Jeffers* (U of Michigan P) had been published in 1956, examining the poet's philosophical concerns and predecessors, Nietzsche and Schopenhauer, Lucretius and Spengler, and reviewing contemporary criticism with a search through Jeffers's poems for principal themes. This work was extended in Mercedes Monjian's monograph *Robinson Jeffers: A Study in Inhumanism* (U of Pittsburgh P, 1958), and was completed in Arthur Coffin's key *Robinson Jeffers: Poet of Inhumanism* (U of Wisconsin P, 1971).

Previously, Lawrence Clark Powell's general overview, *Robinson Jeffers: The Man and His Work* (Los Angeles: Primavera P, 1934) and Rudolph Gilbert's somewhat uncritical but appreciative *Shine, Perishing Republic: Robinson Jeffers and the Tragic Sense in Modern Poetry* (Boston: Bruce Humphries, 1936) had been the only references available. Powell's provided an overview of biography, themes, poetics, and philosophical base; Gilbert's attempted to place Jeffers in the Western literary tradition.

In 1962, the year of the poet's death, Frederic Carpenter's *Robinson Jeffers* (New York: Twayne) expanded on and updated Powell. This work was followed shortly by Brother Antoninus/William Everson's *Robinson Jeffers: Fragments of an Older Fury* (Berkeley: Oyez P, 1973), which brought both Jungian and Freudian insights to the poet. Everson's clarifying essay, "Archetype West," in *Regional Perspectives* (American Library Association) followed in 1973. In the same year, Robert Brophy's *Robinson Jeffers: Myth, Ritual, and Symbol in His Narrative Poems* (Cleveland: Case Western Reserve UP) probed Jeffers's use of biblical, Greek, Roman, and Mediterranean fertility-god myths in his narrative poems.

Shortly thereafter, Bill Hotchkiss published his *Jeffers: The Sivaistic Vision* (Auburn, CA:: Blue Oak P, 1975), a re-examination of Jeffers's critics and a close reading of a substantial number of poems, along with a reconsideration of Jeffersian tragedy. William Nolte's *Rock and Hawk: Robinson Jeffers and the Romantic Agony* (Athens: U of Georgia P, 1978) was a searching rehearsal of Jeffers's romanticism, while Kenneth White's *The Coast Opposite Humanity* (Llanfynydd, Carmarthen, Wales: Unicorn, 1975) provided an insightful essay on Jeffers's philosophy and poetics by an English poet.

In 1977 Marlan Beilke released, at his own press in Amador City, California, the exhaustive *Shining Clarity: God and Man in the Works of Robinson Jeffers* (Quintessence Publications), dwelling on the poet's religious themes and philosophy/theology. In 1983, Robert Zaller's *The Cliffs of Solitude: A Reading of Robinson Jeffers* (Cambridge: Cambridge UP) provided an admirably thorough review of Jeffers's plot devices of incest, castration, and parricide in their Freudian context, relating them to Jeffers's own psychological struggles, which forced him to redefine his relationship to nature, to women, and to God. In 1987 *The Enduring Voice: A Tor House Journal* (St. Paul: Mariposa P) yielded yet another, somewhat lyrical interpretation of Jeffers by John Dotson, the outcome of his year as poet-in-residence. In the same year, James Karman's *Robinson Jeffers: Poet of California* (San Francisco: Chronicle) provided an overview with new insights into the poet's life and poetic works. Then, in 1988, William Everson published the capstone to his Jeffers insights (a wide range of books, essays, lectures, and special editions of the poet) with *The Excesses of God: Robinson Jeffers as a Religious Figure* (Stanford, CA: Stanford UP), in which he argued convincingly, using Rudolph Otto's *The Idea of the Holy* (London: Oxford UP, 1923) for specialized vocabulary and resonances, that Jeffers should be approached not as a philosopher but as a mystic, that his themes are witnesses to God and not arguments on the divine nature of the world.

Two recent collections of Jeffers criticism are James Karman's *Critical Essays on Robinson Jeffers* (Boston: Hall, 1990) and Robert Zaller's *Centennial Essays for Robinson Jeffers* (Newark: U of Delaware P, 1991). Karman provides a representative spectrum of Jeffers criticism from the beginning: several typical reviews for each volume of the Jeffers canon and a final selection of thirteen overarching essays. Zaller's representative essays are, on the whole, more recent and were specially written for the volume.

Finally, it should be noted that some very important critical and textual commentary is to be found in the form of introductions, forewords, and afterwords to critical editions of Jeffers's work, especially in the 1970s and 1980s.

Biographical Studies

A definitive Jeffers biography is yet to be written. Early biographical sketches were provided by George Sterling's *Robinson Jeffers: The Man and the Artist* (New York: Boni & Liveright, 1926) and Louis Adamic's *Robinson Jeffers: A Portrait* (Olympia: U of Washington Chapbook, 1933). Mabel Dodge Luhan's *Una and Robin* (Friends of the Bancroft Library) came from the same era though it was not published until 1976 because of Una Jeffers's lifetime unwillingness to allow it in print. Melba Bennett came close to biography in her 1936 monograph, *Robinson Jeffers and the Sea* (San Francisco: Gelber, Lilienthal), probing, under the guise of water and coastal imagery, the poet's psychic wellsprings. Una Jeffers's first husband's second wife, Edith Greenan, produced an enthusiastic vignette of the Jeffers household of the 1930s in her *Of Una Jeffers* (Los Angeles: Ward Ritchie, 1939).

Throughout the many years of their acquaintanceship, Melba Bennett patiently collected materials for her masterwork on the poet. Jeffers collaborated by providing information and answering queries under what seems to have been an agreement that nothing be published until after his death. Ultimately, *The Stone Mason of Tor House: The Life and Works of Robinson Jeffers* (Los Angeles: Ward Ritchie) was published in 1966, just two years before Bennett's death. It provides very useful information, especially on Jeffers's early years; but, not having access to what has proved to be voluminous Jeffers correspondence, the biographer seems to have been stymied regarding the mid-1920s onward and consequently resorted to merely recording Jeffers's yearly publications and their critical reception. At least three times since Bennett's effort, biographies have been launched, but so far none has been brought to publication. In some ways James Karman's *Robinson Jeffers: Poet of California* (San Francisco: Chronicle, 1987), though ostensibly a general introduction to the poet, currently gives the most accurate and revealing glimpses of Jeffers's life and work. Much biographical information can be culled from Ann Ridgeway's *The Selected Letters of Robinson Jeffers* (Baltimore: Johns

Hopkins UP, 1968) and from various series of Una Jeffers's letters appearing in the *Robinson Jeffers Newsletter.*

Bibliographical Studies

The definitive Jeffers bibliography came just eight years after the poet's first critical reception, in Sydney S. Alberts's *A Bibliography of the Works of Robinson Jeffers* (New York: Random, 1933). The perennially promised second edition never appeared, but the remaining bibliographic information can be pieced together from Covington Rodgers's "Robinson Jeffers" in Matthew Bruccoli's *First Printings of American Authors* (Detroit: Gale Research, 1978) and from checklists of Jeffers's separately published poetry and prose by Robert Kafka and Robert Brophy in the *Robinson Jeffers Newsletter.*

Bibliography covering secondary sources (criticism on Jeffers) can be found principally in Alex A. Vardamis's chronological *The Critical Reputation of Robinson Jeffers* (Hamden, CT: Archon, 1972) and Jeanetta Boswell's alphabetically organized *Robinson Jeffers and the Critics, 1912–1983* (Metuchen, NJ: Scarecrow P, 1986).

The *Robinson Jeffers Newsletter* (Occidental College and California University, Long Beach), which was launched in the year of Jeffers's death (1962), has been a vehicle for short articles, memoirs, bibliographical studies, and a series of Una Jeffers letters. The best and most typical publications of its first twenty-five years was collected in *The Robinson Jeffers Newsletter: A Jubilee Gathering* (Occidental) in 1988. The newsletter has issued two supplements: *An Index to the First Lines of Robinson Jeffers' Poems* (1984) and *An Index to Robinson Jeffers' Published Poems, Their First Appearances, and a Directory to Their Manuscripts* (1988).

WORKS BY ROBINSON JEFFERS: A Chronological Listing

Flagons and Apples. Los Angeles: Grafton, 1912. A slim booklet of early love lyrics, imitative of the English Romantic poets. Reissued by Cayucos Books, 1970.

Californians. New York: Macmillan, 1916. Lyrics and narratives, still imitative, reflecting the Big Sur country and anticipating later themes. See reissue by Cayucos Books, 1971.

Tamar and Other Poems. New York: Peter Boyle, 1924. Dramatically different poetry: free verse, long line, themes of incest, biblical and mythical allusion.

Roan Stallion, Tamar and Other Poems. New York: Boni & Liveright, 1925. *Tamar* volume expanded with a new narrative and a drama, "The Tower Beyond Tragedy." First major publisher.

The Women at Point Sur. New York: Liveright, 1927. 175-page narrative about a renegade minister grotesquely seeking God. Sexual themes and violence. Turned away many critics. See reissues in 1975 and 1977 (including five poems originally intended for this volume).

Cawdor and Other Poems. New York: Liveright, 1928. Adaptation of the Hippolytus-Phaedra theme to the Big Sur coast. See reprinting of the narrative poem by New Directions in 1970.

Dear Judas and Other Poems. New York: Liveright, 1929. Jesus's passion story as a Noh play. Second tale: a female Christ-figure, "The Loving Shepherdess," on the Sur coast, pursuing a pilgrimage to death in childbirth. See reissue in 1977.

Descent to the Dead: Poems Written in Ireland and Great Britain. New York: Random House, 1931. Poems on the occasion of the 1929 family stay on the northeast Irish coast and travel through Ireland, Scotland, and England.

Thurso's Landing and Other Poems. New York: Liveright, 1932. Tragic hubris and heroic triumph-through-pain on a coastal ranch.

Give Your Heart to the Hawks and Other Poems. New York: Random House, 1933. A Cain and Abel story urging transvaluation of values on a ranch above Pfeiffer Beach.

Solstice and Other Poems. New York: Random House, 1935. An adaptation of the Medea myth to the California Coast.

Roan Stallion, Tamar and Other Poems. New York: Random House/ Modern Library, 1935. This volume re-popularized Jeffers. Additional poems from the 1927 *A Miscellany of American Poetry.* New introduction by Jeffers.

Such Counsels You Gave to Me and Other Poems. New York: Random House, 1937. Scottish ballad motif as vehicle for Oedipal conflict.

The Selected Poetry of Robinson Jeffers. New York: Random House, 1938. Comprehensive collection. Important introduction.

Be Angry with the Sun and Other Poems. New York: Random House, 1941. Strong response to World War II.

Medea. New York: Random House, 1946. Adaptation from Euripides. Triumphant New York theater production in 1947 with Judith Anderson. See reissue with "Cawdor" in 1970.

The Double Axe and Other Poems. New York: Random House, 1948. Turbulent political poems against World War II and all wars. Received with almost universally hostile criticism. See reissue in 1977 with eleven "suppressed poems." Also *In This Wild Water,* 1976.

Poetry, Gongorism and a Thousand Years. Los Angeles: Ward Ritchie, 1949. *New York Times* article, defining the "great poet" as one who avoids trends and writes to be understood in the far future.

Hungerfield and Other Poems. New York: Random House, 1954. Powerful tale with lyric frame reconciling Jeffers with his wife's death.

Visits to Ireland. Los Angeles: Ward Ritchie, 1954. Excerpts from Una Jeffers's diaries edited by Jeffers and containing entries by him.

Themes in My Poems. San Francisco: Book Club of California, 1956. Principal text and readings of Jeffers's 1941 lecture at the Library of Congress. Themes of death, war, culture cycles, pantheism, the self-torturing god, hawks, and poetry as discovery.

The Beginning and the End and Other Poems. New York: Random House, 1963. Posthumous collection. Uneven with inauthentic editing by Melba Bennett. Final statements on mankind in the shadow of nuclear war. Title poem recapitulates evolution.

Robinson Jeffers: Selected Poems. New York: Vintage Books, 1965. Slim paperback, mostly lyrics, from his long career.

Not Man Apart: Lines from Robinson Jeffers/Photographs of the Big Sur Coast. Edited by David Brower. San Francisco: Sierra Club,

1965. Seascapes, promontories, canyons, beaches by famous photographers of the region alongside Jeffers poems. Foreword by Loren Eiseley.

The Selected Letters of Robinson Jeffers. Edited by Ann Ridgeway. Baltimore: Johns Hopkins UP, 1968. Revealing correspondence, illustrated by striking Leigh Wiener photographs.

Robinson Jeffers: A Long Poem, Cawdor, Medea by Euripides. New York: New Directions, 1970. Introduction and notes by William Everson. Reissue of narrative and drama from the 1928 and 1946 volumes.

The Alpine Christ and Other Poems. N.p.: Cayucos Books, 1974. Edited with preface, introduction, and afterword by William Everson. Early lyrics mostly unpublished, with a fragment from an unpublished drama of World War I.

Brides of the South Wind: Poems, 1917–1922. N.p.: Cayucos Books, 1974. Edited with preface, introduction, and afterword by William Everson. Early published and unpublished poems.

The Women at Point Sur. Auburn, CA: Blue Oak, 1975. Reissue with afterword by Bill Hotchkiss.

In This Wild Water. Los Angeles: Ward Ritchie, 1976. Edited by James Shebl. Poems "suppressed" by the editors of Random House from *The Double Axe* manuscripts, with correspondence from publishers. Preface by Robert Brophy.

The Women at Point Sur and Other Poems. New York: Norton-Liveright, 1977. With textual note and afterword by Tim Hunt. Printing five poems originally intended for the 1927 volume.

The Double Axe and Other Poems. New York: Norton-Liveright, 1977. Foreword by William Everson. Eleven "suppressed poems" added. Afterword by Bill Hotchkiss.

Dear Judas and Other Poems. New York: Norton-Liveright, 1977. Afterword and textual note by Robert Brophy.

What Odd Expedients and Other Poems. Edited by Robert Ian Scott. Hamden, CT: Shoestring, 1981. Twenty-five mostly unpublished poems written about World War II, compiled from manuscripts at the Humanities Research Center, University of Texas.

Rock and Hawk: A Selection of Shorter Poems by Robinson Jeffers. Ed. Robert Hass. New York: Random House, 1987. Important introduction. 161 poems, of which six are short narratives or narrative excerpts. Includes "Roan Stallion."

Robinson Jeffers: Selected Poems. The Centenary Edition. Edited by Colin Falck. Manchester: Carcanet, 1987. Appreciative introduction: "Robinson Jeffers: American Romantic." Sixty lyrics, three short narratives, and "Medea" excerpt.

Where Shall I Take You To: The Love Letters of Una and Robinson Jeffers. Edited by Robert Kafka. N.p.: Yolla Bolly P, 1987. Foreword by Garth Jeffers. Fifty-seven letters written between 1910 and 1913. From papers at the University of Texas, Austin.

Songs and Heroes. Los Angeles: Arundel, 1988. Edited by Robert Brophy. Thirty-three early unpublished poems, written about the time of *Flagons and Apples.*

The Collected Poetry of Robinson Jeffers. Edited by Tim Hunt. Stanford: Stanford UP. Vols. 1–3, 1988, 1989, 1991. Vol. 4: notes and apparatus forthcoming.

The Collected Letters of Robinson Jeffers. Edited by James Karman, Robert Kafka, and Robert Brophy. Stanford: Stanford UP. Work in progress. Letters of Una Jeffers to be included.

A concordance to Jeffers's poems is being prepared by William Miles, based on the four volumes of *The Collected Poetry.*

Major Jeffers manuscripts can be located at the Beinecke Library of Yale University, at the Humanities Research Center, University of Texas, Austin, and at Occidental College, Jeffers's alma mater.

CONTRIBUTORS

TERRY BEERS is Assistant Professor of English at Santa Clara University. He has published in *American Poetry*, *Diacritics*, *Reading Research Quarterly*, and *Quarry West*. He is currently executive director of the newly formed Robinson Jeffers Association.

ROBERT BROPHY is Professor of English at California State University, Long Beach. He is the author of *Robinson Jeffers: Myth, Ritual, and Symbol in His Narrative Poems* (Case Western Reserve UP, 1973), *Robinson Jeffers* (Western Writers, 1975), and editor of Jeffers's *Dear Judas and Other Poems* (Norton-Liveright, 1977), *Whom Shall I Write For?* (Laguna Verde, 1979), and *Songs and Heroes* (Arundel, 1988). Since 1968 he has been the editor of the *Robinson Jeffers Newsletter*.

WILLIAM EVERSON/BROTHER ANTONINUS, poet of the San Francisco Renaissance, master printer, is the author of *Robinson Jeffers: Fragments of an Older Fury* (Oyez, 1968) and *The Excesses of God: Robinson Jeffers as a Religious Figure* (Stanford UP, 1988). He edited Jeffers's *Cawdor/Medea* (New Directions, 1970), *Californians* (Cayucos, 1971), *The Alpine Christ* (Cayucos, 1974), *Brides of the South Wind* (Cayucos, 1974), and *Dear Judas and Other Poems* (Norton-Liveright, 1975). As master printer he designed an edition of Jeffers Tor House poems, *Granite and Cypress* (Lime Kiln, 1975). He is the author of a justly famous threnody for Jeffers, "The Poet is Dead."

KIRK GLASER has finished a dissertation at the University of California, Berkeley: "Journeys into the Border Country: The Making of Nature and Home in the Poetry of Robinson Jeffers and Mary Oliver," 1993. Currently working on a young adult fantasy novel, he has published poems and translations from the Spanish in *The Threepenny Review*, *Berkeley Poetry Review*, and other magazines, including several bilingual publications in Mexico.

TIM HUNT is Professor of English at Washington State University, Vancouver. He is author of *Kerouac's Crooked Road: Development of a Fiction* (1981) and editor of *The Collected Poetry of Robinson Jeffers* (Stanford UP, 1988–91). His essays on Jeffers have appeared in *American Literature*, and *Centennial Essays for Robinson Jeffers* (U of Delaware P, 1991) among others.

DAVID ROTHMAN received his Ph.D. from New York University in 1992 with a dissertation: "The Whitmanian Poets and the Origin of Open Form." He is a contributing editor at *Hellas* and has served as editor of *PSA News: The Newsletter of the Poetry Society of America*. His essays have appeared in *The Eighteenth Century: Theory and Interpretation and Restoration*. His poems have appeared in *Appalachia*, *The Gettysburg Review*, *Harvard Magazine*, *The Kenyon Review*, and *The Atlantic*.

ALAN SOLDOFSKY is Associate Professor of English at San Jose State University. In 1987 he hosted a major Jeffers centennial conference in San Jose. In 1990 he guest-edited a significant Jeffers symposium for the University of California, Santa Cruz, journal, *Quarry West*. He has published two volumes of poems, *Kenora Station* and *Staying Home*.

ALEX VARDAMIS teaches American and Comparative Literature at the University of Vermont. He is author of *The Critical Reputation of Robinson Jeffers* (Archon, 1972), which will soon appear in a second edition, and essays in the *Robinson Jeffers Newsletter* and in *Centennial Essays for Robinson Jeffers* (U of Delaware P, 1991) among others.

ROBERT ZALLER is Professor of History at Drexel University. He is the author of *The Cliffs of Solitude: A Reading of Robinson Jeffers* (Cambridge UP, 1983), and the editor of *The Tribute of His Peers: Elegies for Robinson Jeffers* (Tor House Press, 1989) and of *Centennial Essays for Robinson Jeffers* (University of Delaware P, 1991). His essays on Jeffers have appeared in *Agenda*, the *Robinson Jeffers Newsletter*, *Western American Literature*, in James Karman, ed., *Critical Essays on Robinson Jeffers* (G. K. Hall, 1990) and James B. Hall et al., eds., *Perspectives on William Everson* (Castle Peak Editions, 1992).